BRIDGES IN CHINA
2013—2023

人民交通出版社股份有限公司
北 京

## 编辑委员会

**主任委员** 项海帆

**副主任委员** 邓文中　凤懋润

**委员**
郑皆连　林元培　王景全　秦顺全　杨永斌
陈政清　张喜刚　包琦玮　邵长宇　徐恭义
韩振勇　顾安邦　韩　敏　刘正光　牛　斌
肖汝诚　周世忠　葛耀君

## 编写组

**主编** 项海帆

**副主编** 葛耀君　肖汝诚　孙利民　杨志刚

**分篇负责人**

长大桥梁　葛耀君　杨詠昕
悬索桥　肖汝诚　田仲初　贾丽君
斜拉桥　孙利民　邵长宇　崔　冰　夏　烨　阮　欣
拱式桥　李国平　沈　殷
梁式桥　徐　栋　刘　超　王昌将
城市桥梁　徐利平　朱乐东　操金鑫
中国参建的国外桥梁　孙　斌　杨志刚　廖　玲

**特邀翻译** Paul Gauvreau

**其他参编人**
陈业恺　王　硕　方根深　宋超林　芦旭朝
檀忠旭　罗　锐

## 编辑统筹

**策划编辑** 孙　玺　卢俊丽

**责任编辑** 卢俊丽　李　晴　李　瑞　陈虹宇

**美术编辑** 周逸斐

## Editorial Committee

| | |
|---|---|
| **Chairman** | Xiang Haifan |
| **Vice-chairman** | Deng Wenzhong, Feng Maorun |
| **Members** | Zheng Jielian, Lin Yuanpei, Wang Jingquan, Qin Shunquan, Yang Yongbin |
| | Chen Zhengqing, Zhang Xigang, Bao Qiwei, Shao Changyu, Xu Gongyi |
| | Han Zhenyong, Gu Anbang, Han Min, Liu Zhengguang, Niu Bin |
| | Xiao Rucheng, Zhou Shizhong, Ge Yaojun |

## Compilation Board

| | |
|---|---|
| **Compiler-in-chief** | Xiang Haifan |
| **Deputy Compiler-in-chief** | Ge Yaojun, Xiao Rucheng, Sun Limin, Yang Zhigang |
| **Compilers** | |
| *Long Major Bridges* | Ge Yaojun, Yang Yongxin |
| *Suspension Bridges* | Xiao Rucheng, Tian Zhongchu, Jia Lijun |
| *Cable-stayed Bridges* | Sun Limin, Shao Changyu, Cui Bing, Xia Ye, Ruan Xin |
| *Arch Bridges* | Li Guoping, Shen Yin |
| *Girder Bridges* | Xu Dong, Liu Chao, Wang Changjiang |
| *Urban Bridges* | Xu Liping, Zhu Ledong, Cao Jinxin |
| *Overseas Bridges Built by China* | Sun Bin, Yang Zhigang, Liao Ling |
| **Contributing Translator** | Paul Gauvreau |
| **Other Contributors** | Chen Yekai, Wang Shuo, Fang Genshen, Song Chaolin, Lu Xuzhao |
| | Tan Zhongxu, Luo Rui |

## Managing Editor

| | |
|---|---|
| **Sponsoring Editor** | Sun Xi, Lu Junli |
| **Editor in Charge** | Lu Junli, Li Qing, Li Rui, Chen Hongyu |
| **Art Editor** | Zhou Yifei |

李国豪（1913—2005）

十年前，为纪念我们敬爱的李国豪老师的百岁诞辰，我们出版了《中国桥梁 2003—2013》大型画册，以记录21世纪以来中国桥梁工程所取得的卓越成就。由于此书采用中英文对照的方式，而且印刷和装帧十分精美，被中华人民共和国交通运输部选作礼品书，赠送给世界各国政要，让他们了解中国在自主建设桥梁的过程中所取得的辉煌成就，为中国"一带一路"合作计划发挥了良好的宣传和示范作用。

2023年我们迎来李国豪老师的一百一十周年诞辰，十年间，中国桥梁界继续奋进，又建成了一大批技术更先进的桥梁工程，尤其是在东南沿海和西部山区的公路和铁路建造中，面对江河湖海和崇山峻岭，中国桥梁界不畏艰难险阻，建成了许多跨越海湾、大河和深谷的大跨度桥梁，把工业化和绿色桥梁建造技术发挥到极致，也把中国桥梁的技术水平往前推进了一大步。为此，我们决定继续出版《中国桥梁 2013—2023》，以纪念十年间中国桥梁工程师们勇于创新、砥砺前行的光辉历程，用按照时间顺序排列的110座桥梁铭记李国豪老师和其他桥梁前辈为开辟中国桥梁自主建设道路所做出的重大贡献。

十年间，中国桥梁界还走出国门，为其他国家修建了不少重要桥梁，得到了各国的好评，这一举措不但增进了中国与其他国家的友谊，也进一步丰富了经验，提高了建桥水平。我们要牢记李国豪老师"理论联系实际，发展桥梁科技"的教导，勇于创新，用创新的成果提高国际竞争力，克服不足，为尽早实现从桥梁大国走向桥梁强国而继续努力。

项海帆

2023年4月

# 序言

# PREFACE

Ten years ago, to commemorate the 100th birthday of our beloved teacher, Professor Guohao Li, we published a large photo album entitled *Bridges in China* (2003-2013) to record the remarkable achievements of Chinese bridge engineering since the turn of the 21st century. Because it was written in both Chinese and English, as well as the high quality of its printing and binding, the book was selected by the Ministry of Transport of the People's Republic of China for political figures around the world. The book showcases the brilliant achievements of China in the entire process of building bridges independently and for this reason it has played an important role in promoting the "Belt and Road Initiative" cooperation plan.

This year marks the 110th birthday of Professor Li. During the past decade, China's bridge industry has continued to forge ahead, as demonstrated by the large number of more advanced bridges have been built. Especially in the construction of highways and railways along its southeast coast and western mountainous area, China has overcome difficulties in crossing obstacles of all kinds, including rivers, lakes, seas, mountains and ridges, to build many long-span bridges across wide gulfs, large rivers and deep valleys. It has pushed industrialized and green construction technology to the limit, and in so doing has greatly advanced the technical level of the Chinese bridge industry.To commemorate the glorious journey of Chinese bridge engineers who have been brave to innovate and forge ahead over the past 10 years, we are publishing this new photo album entitled *Bridges in China* (2013-2023). This book also includes 110 bridges in chronological order that commemorate the primary contributions made by Professor Guohao Li and other pioneers who opened up the road of independent bridge construction in China.

In the past decade, the bridge industry of China has also gone abroad and built many important bridges that have earned praise from many countries. This initiative has not only enhanced China's friendship with other countries, but also has further improved the level of bridge construction and enriched the experience of China's engineers. Keeping Professor Li's instruction— "Combine theory with practice to develop bridge science and technology" — in mind, we should be brave in innovation, use innovative achievements to improve international competitiveness, overcome deficiencies, and continue to make great efforts to transform China from a large bridge-building country into a bridge-building powerhouse as early as possible.

*Haifan Xiang*
April 2023

# 目录 / Contents

## Chapter 1  Long Major Bridges — 001 / 第一篇 长大桥梁

|  |  |  |
|---|---|---|
| Introduction | 002 | 引言 |
| Danyang-Kunshan Grand Bridge | 004 | 丹昆特大桥 |
| Shanxi-Shaanxi Bridge over Yellow River | 008 | 晋陕黄河特大桥 |
| Hangzhou-Ruili Dongting Bridge | 010 | 杭瑞洞庭大桥 |
| Yueqing Bay Bridge | 012 | 乐清湾大桥 |
| Hong Kong-Zhuhai-Macao Bridge | 014 | 港珠澳大桥 |
| Jinan Highway and Railway Bridge over Yellow River on Shijiazhuang-Jinan Railway Passenger Dedicated Line | 018 | 石济铁路客运专线济南黄河公铁两用桥 |
| Pingtan Strait Highway and Railway Bridge | 020 | 平潭海峡公铁两用大桥 |
| Zhoushan-Daishan Bridge | 024 | 舟岱大桥 |
| Quanzhou Bay Sea-crossing Bridge | 026 | 泉州湾跨海大桥 |
| Kinmen Bridge | 028 | 金门大桥 |

## Chapter 2  Suspension Bridges — 031 / 第二篇 悬索桥

|  |  |  |
|---|---|---|
| Introduction | 032 | 引言 |
| Yingwuzhou Bridge over Yangtze River | 034 | 鹦鹉洲长江大桥 |
| Guiyang-Weng'an Expressway Bridge over Qingshui River | 038 | 贵瓮高速公路清水河大桥 |
| Baoshan-Tengchong Expressway Bridge over Long River | 040 | 保腾高速公路龙江大桥 |
| Jijiang Bridge over Yangtze River | 042 | 几江长江大桥 |
| Fuma Bridge over Yangtze River | 044 | 驸马长江大桥 |
| Xingkang Bridge | 046 | 兴康大桥 |
| Nansha Bridge | 048 | 南沙大桥 |
| Yangsigang Bridge over Yangtze River | 052 | 杨泗港长江大桥 |
| Egongyan Rail Transit Bridge | 056 | 鹅公岩轨道大桥 |
| Hongjun Bridge over Chishui River | 058 | 赤水河红军大桥 |
| Wufengshan Bridge over Yangtze River | 060 | 五峰山长江大桥 |
| Jin'an Bridge over Jinsha River | 064 | 金安金沙江大桥 |
| Tiger Leaping Gorge Bridge over Jinsha River | 066 | 虎跳峡金沙江大桥 |
| Wujiagang Bridge over Yangtze River | 068 | 伍家岗长江大桥 |
| Weng'an-Kaiyang Expressway Bridge over Kaizhou Lake | 070 | 瓮开高速公路开州湖大桥 |
| Fenghuang Bridge over Yellow River | 072 | 凤凰黄河大桥 |
| Beikou Bridge over Ou River | 074 | 瓯江北口大桥 |
| Xianxin Road Bridge over Yangtze River | 078 | 仙新路长江大桥 |
| Qinzhou Longmen Bridge | 080 | 钦州龙门大桥 |

| | | | |
|---|---|---|---|
| Chapter 3 Cable-stayed Bridges | 083 | 第三篇 / 斜拉桥 | |

| | | | |
|---|---|---|---|
| Introduction | 084 | 引言 |
| Changsha Northwest Uplink Connecting Line Bridge | 086 | 长沙西北上行联络线特大桥 |
| Langqi Bridge over Min River | 088 | 琅岐闽江大桥 |
| Huanggang Bridge over Yangtze River | 090 | 黄冈长江大桥 |
| Jiangshun Bridge | 092 | 江顺大桥 |
| Tongling Highway and Railway Bridge over Yangtze River | 094 | 铜陵长江公铁大桥 |
| Polonggou Bridge | 096 | 迫龙沟特大桥 |
| Guiyang-Qianxi Expressway Bridge over Yachi River | 098 | 贵黔高速鸭池河大桥 |
| First Beipan River Bridge | 100 | 北盘江第一桥 |
| Wangdong Highway Bridge over Yangtze River | 104 | 望东长江公路大桥 |
| Second Wuhu Highway Bridge over Yangtze River | 106 | 芜湖长江公路二桥 |
| Zhuankou Bridge over Yangtze River | 108 | 沌口长江大桥 |
| Second Fengdu Bridge over Yangtze River | 110 | 丰都长江二桥 |
| Baishatuo Bridge over Yangtze River | 112 | 白沙沱长江大桥 |
| Jiayu Bridge over Yangtze River | 114 | 嘉鱼长江大桥 |
| Baoding South Station Cable-stayed Bridge of South Extension Project of Lekai Street | 116 | 保定乐凯大街南延工程保定南站斜拉桥 |
| Chizhou Bridge over Yangtze River | 118 | 池州长江大桥 |
| Shishou Bridge over Yangtze River | 120 | 石首长江大桥 |
| Pailou Bridge over Yangtze River | 122 | 牌楼长江大桥 |
| Pingtang Bridge | 124 | 平塘大桥 |
| Shanghai-Suzhou-Nantong Highway and Railway Bridge over Yangtze River | 126 | 沪苏通长江公铁大桥 |
| Nanjing Jiangxinzhou Bridge over Yangtze River | 130 | 南京江心洲长江大桥 |
| Third Wuhu Bridge over Yangtze River | 134 | 芜湖长江三桥 |
| Qingshan Bridge over Yangtze River | 136 | 青山长江大桥 |
| Wuxue Bridge over Yangtze River | 138 | 武穴长江大桥 |
| Chibi Highway Bridge over Yangtze River | 140 | 赤壁长江公路大桥 |
| Bianyu Island Bridge over Yangtze River on Beijing-Hong Kong High-speed Railway | 142 | 京港高铁鳊鱼洲长江大桥 |
| Baijusi Bridge over Yangtze River | 144 | 白居寺长江大桥 |

| Chapter 4   Arch Bridges | 147 | 第四篇 / 拱式桥 |

| | | |
|---|---|---|
| Introduction | 148 | 引言 |
| Yunnan-Guangxi Railway Bridge over Nanpan River | 150 | 云桂铁路南盘江特大桥 |
| Shanghai-Kunming High-speed Railway Bridge over Beipan River | 154 | 沪昆高铁北盘江特大桥 |
| Meishan Red Bridge | 156 | 梅山红桥 |
| Guantang Bridge | 158 | 官塘大桥 |
| Daxiaojing Bridge | 162 | 大小井特大桥 |
| Zigui Bridge over Yangtze River | 166 | 秭归长江大桥 |
| Chengdu-Guiyang Railway Bridge over Yachi River | 168 | 成贵铁路鸭池河特大桥 |
| Third Pingnan Bridge | 170 | 平南三桥 |
| Qianwei Bridge over Min River on Renshou-Muchuan-Xinshi Highway | 174 | 仁沐新高速犍为岷江特大桥 |
| Zangmu Bridge over Yarlung Zangbo River | 176 | 藏木雅鲁藏布江大桥 |
| Third Hejiang Bridge over Yangtze River | 178 | 合江长江三桥 |
| Pearl Bay Bridge | 180 | 明珠湾大桥 |
| Dejiang-Yuqing Expresswaya Bridge over Wu River | 182 | 德余高速乌江特大桥 |
| Tian'e Longtan Bridge | 184 | 天峨龙滩特大桥 |

| Chapter 5   Girder Bridges | 189 | 第五篇 / 梁式桥 |

| | | |
|---|---|---|
| Introduction | 190 | 引言 |
| Tianjin Jizhao Bridge | 192 | 天津吉兆桥 |
| Liupanshui-Panxian Expressway Bridge over Beipan River | 194 | 六盘水至盘县高速公路北盘江特大桥 |
| Fudiankou No. 1 Main Bridge over Xi River | 198 | 扶典口西江特大桥1号主桥 |
| Yushan Bridge | 200 | 鱼山大桥 |
| Sanjiangkou Bridge | 204 | 三江口大桥 |
| Yunbao Bridge over Yellow River | 206 | 运宝黄河大桥 |
| Haoji Railway Bridge over Han River | 210 | 浩吉铁路汉江特大桥 |
| Cuijiaying Bridge over Han River on Wuhan-Shiyan Railway | 212 | 汉十铁路崔家营汉江特大桥 |
| Chenggong Bridge | 214 | 成功大桥 |
| Kalasuke Reservoir Bridge | 216 | 喀腊塑克水库特大桥 |
| Hongxi Bridge on Longyou-Lishui-Wenzhou Expressway | 218 | 龙丽温高速洪溪特大桥 |
| Jiantan Bridge over Dong River | 220 | 剑潭东江特大桥 |
| Daoqingzhou Bridge | 222 | 道庆洲大桥 |
| Jiahua Rail Transit Bridge | 224 | 嘉华轨道专用桥 |
| Ganxi Bridge | 226 | 甘溪特大桥 |
| Fuzhou-Pingtan Railway Bridge over Wulong River | 228 | 福平铁路乌龙江特大桥 |
| Liulv Bridge over Yong River | 230 | 六律邕江特大桥 |

## Chapter 6  Urban Bridges  233   第六篇 / 城市桥梁

| | | |
|---|---:|---|
| Introduction | 234 | 引言 |
| Lanzhou Shen'an Bridge over Yellow River | 236 | 兰州深安黄河大桥 |
| Chongqing Shuangbei Bridge over Jialing River | 238 | 重庆双碑嘉陵江大桥 |
| Zhuzhou Fengxi Bridge | 240 | 株洲枫溪大桥 |
| Sixth Luzhou Bridge over Tuo River | 242 | 泸州沱江六桥 |
| Zhangzhou Shazhou Island Bridge | 244 | 漳州沙洲岛大桥 |
| Beijing New Shougang Bridge | 246 | 北京新首钢大桥 |
| Xiamen Hemei Bridge of Shanhai Fitness Trail | 248 | 厦门山海健康步道和美桥 |
| Ningbo Zhongxing Bridge | 252 | 宁波中兴大桥 |
| Ningbo Sanguantang Bridge | 254 | 宁波三官堂大桥 |
| Guangzhou Haixin Bridge | 258 | 广州海心桥 |
| Third Bridge over Ulan Moron River | 262 | 乌兰木伦河 3 号桥 |
| Dongguan Binhai Bay Bridge | 264 | 东莞滨海湾大桥 |
| Hong Kong Tseung Kwan O Cross Bay Bridge | 266 | 香港将军澳跨湾大桥 |

## Appendix  Overseas Bridges Built by China  269  附录 / 中国参建的国外桥梁

| | | |
|---|---:|---|
| Introduction | 270 | 引言 |
| San Francisco-Oakland Bay Bridge New East Span | 272 | 旧金山—奥克兰新海湾东桥 |
| Second Penang Bridge | 276 | 槟城第二跨海大桥 |
| Mohammed VI Bridge | 278 | 穆罕默德六世大桥 |
| China-Maldives Friendship Bridge | 280 | 中马友谊大桥 |
| Katembe Bridge | 282 | 卡腾贝大桥 |
| Halogaland Bridge | 284 | 哈罗格兰德大桥 |
| Third Bridge over Panama Canal | 288 | 巴拿马运河三桥 |
| New Selander Bridge | 292 | 坦桑蓝跨海大桥 |
| Padma Bridge | 294 | 帕德玛大桥 |
| Peljesac Bridge | 296 | 佩列沙茨大桥 |

## Afterword  298  出版后记

中国桥梁　BRIDGES IN CHINA　2013—2023

# Chapter 1

## 第一篇

# 长大桥梁

## Long Major Bridges

# 引言

长大桥梁是指长度长和规模大的铁路桥梁、公路桥梁或公铁两用桥梁。世界长大桥梁建设的历史可以追溯到1884年，这一年美国建成了全长9.3km的跨越庞恰特雷恩湖的诺福克大桥，这是一座铁路桥梁；1965年，法国建成了长18km的戴高乐机场试验线铁路桥；1982年，日本建成了东北新干线高速铁路Kita-Yaita高架铁路桥，全长114.4km；2011年，我国建成了目前全世界最长的铁路桥梁——京沪高铁丹昆特大桥，全长164.85km。一般认为世界长大公路桥梁建设始于1936年建成的美国旧金山—奥克兰海湾大桥，全长6.4km。1956年，美国建成了长38.4km的庞恰特雷恩湖公路桥；2000年，泰国建成了长54km的邦纳高速公路高架桥；2018年，我国建成了目前全世界最长的公路桥梁——港珠澳大桥，全长55km，包括6.7km沉管隧道。

我国长大桥梁建设从20世纪80年代改革开放后起步，第一座10km以上的铁路桥梁是1985年建成的长东黄河大桥，全长10.3km；2006年，建成了长11.7km的青藏铁路清水河大桥；2007年，建成了长35.8km的京津城际铁路杨村特大桥；2008年，建成了长79.7km的郑西高速铁路渭南渭河特大桥；2011年，建成了全长164.85km的京沪高铁丹昆特大桥。在长大公路桥梁建设方面，1991年，建成了长8.4km的上海南浦大桥；2005年，先后建成了长32.5km的东海大桥和长35.7km的润扬长江大桥；2007年，建成了长35.8km的杭州湾大桥；2018年，长55km的港珠澳大桥正式通车。

近10年来，我国建成了30多座长度超过5km的铁路桥梁和公路桥梁。本画册选取了10座长大桥梁，包括5座长大公路桥梁、3座长大铁路桥梁和2座长大公铁两用桥梁。入选的长大铁路桥梁主要以32m和24m跨度预应力混凝土简支箱梁为主，跨越河道和道路的桥孔大到150m左右的都采用预应力混凝土连续梁或连续刚构，公铁两用桥梁则采用双层桥面钢桁梁，跨度更大的则采用拱式桥或斜拉桥。长大公路桥梁特别是跨海大桥的非通航孔桥，采用了钢箱梁、钢-混凝土结合梁和预应力混凝土梁，其中，钢箱梁和钢-混凝土结合梁的跨度已经达到110m，预应力混凝土梁的跨度也达到了85m，环境保护和可持续性已经成为非通航孔桥的主要挑战和创新。通航孔桥大都采用斜拉桥，跨度更大的采用悬索桥，特大跨度悬索桥和斜拉桥抗风问题依然严峻，特别是影响台风多发地区跨海大桥结构和行车抗风安全；为了提高通航孔桥梁的连续跨越能力，多主跨斜拉桥和悬索桥已经成为一种发展趋势，而且跨度越来越大。

长大桥梁作为超级工程，需要用尽可能好的技术来建造，在尽可能短的时间内建成，为尽可能长的时间所使用，用尽可能方便的方式去养护，这些都需要桥梁工程师们共同努力。

# INTRODUCTION

Long major bridges refers to bridges of great length and size. They can carry railway, highway, or both modes of transportation. The history of long major bridge construction can be traced back to 1884 with the construction of the Norfolk Bridge, a railway bridge crossing Lake Pontchartrain in the United States with a total length of 9.3km. Notable works carrying railway include the 18km-long Aérotrain Test Track to Charles de Gaulle Airport in France, built in 1965, and the 1982 Kita-Yaita Viaduct of the Northeast Shinkansen High-speed railway in Japan, with a total length of 114.4km. In 2011, China built the longest railway bridge in the world, the 164.85km-long Danyang-Kunshan Grand Bridge on the Beijing-Shanghai High-speed Railway. Construction of long major highway bridges is generally regarded to have begun in 1936 with the San Francisco-Oakland Bay Bridge, with a total length of 6.4km. Notable long major bridges carrying highway traffice include the 38.4km-long Pontchartrain Lake Highway Bridge, built in the United States in 1956, and the 54km-long Bang Na Expressway Viaduct built in Thailand in 2000. In 2018, China built the longest highway bridge in the world, the Hong Kong-Zhuhai-Macao Bridge, with a total length of 55km, including a 6.7km immersed tunnel.

The construction of long major bridges in China started after the Reform and Opening-up Policy in the 1980s. The first railway bridge over 10km was the Changyuan-Dongming Bridge over Yellow River built in 1985, with a total length of 10.3km. In 2006, the 11.7km-long Qingshuihe Bridge on the Qinghai-Tibet Railway was completed. One year later, the 35.8km-long Yang Village Grand Bridge on the Beijing-Tianjin Inter-Municipal Railway was built. In 2008, the 79.7km-long Weinan Grand Bridge over Wei River on the Zhengzhou-Xi'an High-speed Railway was completed. In 2011, the 164.85km-long Danyang-Kunshan Grand Bridge on the Beijing-Shanghai High-speed Railway was finished. Important long major highway bridges include the 8.4km-long Shanghai Nanpu Bridge, built in 1991, the 32.5km-long Donghai Bridge, built in 2005, and the 35.7km-long Runyang Bridge over Yangtze River, also built in 2005. Two years later, the 35.8km-long Hangzhou Bay Bridge was completed. In 2018, the 55km-long Hong Kong-Zhuhai-Macao Bridge was opened for traffic.

In the past ten years, China has built more than thirty major bridges longer than five kilometers, from which ten representatives are selected in this album, including five long major highway bridges, three long major railway bridges and two long major bridges carrying both highway and railway. The selected long major railway bridges are mainly prestressed concrete simply supported box girder bridges with spans of 32m and 24m. Prestressed concrete continuous girder bridges or continuous rigid frame bridges are used to cross rivers and roads with spans of up to 150m. Double-deck steel truss girders are used for bridges carrying both highway and railway traffic, and arch bridges or cable-stayed bridges are used for even longer spans. Steel box, steel-concrete composite and prestressed concrete girders have been employed in long major highway bridges, especially for non-navigable spans of sea-crossing bridges. Among them, the span length of steel box girders and steel-concrete composite girders has reached 110m, and that of prestressed concrete girders has reached 85m. Environmental protection and sustainability have become the main challenge driving innovation for these bridges. Cable stayed bridges and suspension bridges are commonly used by these bridges to cross navigable spans. Problems arising from wind resistance for long-span suspension bridges and cable-stayed bridges are still severe, especially those pertaining to structure safety and vehicle safety for sea-crossing bridges in typhoon prone areas. In order to improve the total span capacity of navigable span bridges, multi-main-span cable-stayed bridges and suspension bridges have become a developing trend, with longer and longer spans.

As super engineering projects, long major bridges need to be built with the best possible technology, in the shortest possible construction time, for the longest possible service life, and for maximum ease of maintenance. This requires a joint effort from all bridge engineers.

# 丹昆特大桥
Danyang–Kunshan Grand Bridge

丹昆特大桥是京沪高速铁路南京至上海段的特大桥梁，大桥西起丹阳，途径常州、无锡、苏州，东至昆山，全长164.85km，是全世界最长的桥梁。大桥地处经济发达的苏南地区，先后跨越150多条河道和180余条道路，桥上设有常州北站、无锡东站、苏州北站和昆山南站共4个高架车站，全世界独一无二。

丹昆特大桥主要采用了32m和24m标准跨度、整孔预制架设的预应力混凝土简支箱梁，全桥设置了139处特殊结构桥梁，包括正线连续梁88处、道岔连续梁41处、系杆拱桥9处和连续梁－拱组合桥1处。其中，系杆拱桥最大跨度128m，连续梁－拱组合桥跨度为70m+136m+70m。主要墩台类型有：门式墩、实体墩、矩形空心墩、圆端型空心墩、花瓶墩、双柱墩、矩形空心台、框架台等。

丹昆特大桥几乎涵盖客运专线大多数桥型及施工方法，堪称桥型陈列馆，其中阳澄湖区桥梁基础采用"双排桩筑坝围堰"的施工方法，开创了湖区绿色施工的先河。

Danyang-Kunshan Grand Bridge is a extra-long bridge in Nanjing-Shanghai section of Beijing-shanghai High-speed Railway. It starts from Danyang in the west, passing through Changzhou, Wuxi and Suzhou, and ends at Kunshan in the east. With a total length of 164.85km, it is the longest bridge in the world. The bridge is located in the economically developed southern part of Jiangsu Province. It has successively crossed more than 150 rivers and more than 180 roads. There are four elevated stations on the bridge, including Changzhou North Station, Wuxi East Station, Suzhou North Station and Kunshan South Station, which is unique in the world.

Danyang-Kunshan Grand Bridge is composed mainly of prestressed concrete simply supported box girders with the standard span length of 32m and 24m, which were prefabricated and erected on site. There are also 139 different structures set up in the whole bridge, including 88 continuous girder bridges in the main line, 41 continuous girder bridges in the switch section, 9 tied arch bridges and 1 composite continuous girder and arch combined bridge. The maximum span length of the tied arch bridge is 128m, and the span layout of the composite bridge is 70m+136m+70m. There are various substructures in the piers and abutments, including portal pier, solid pier, rectangular hollow pier, round-ended hollow pier, vase-shaped pier, double column pier, rectangular hollow abutment and frame abutment, etc.

Danyang-Kunshan Grand Bridge covers most structure types and construction methods of bridges for passenger dedicated lines, which can be even called a bridge exhibition hall. The construction method of "double row pile cofferdam construction technology" was invented for the foundations of the bridge in Yangcheng Lake district, which has created a precedent for green construction in lake areas.

桥　　名：丹昆特大桥
桥　　型：连续梁拱桥、系杆拱桥、连续梁桥、简支梁桥等
桥梁长度：164.85km
桥　　址：江苏省丹阳市、常州市、无锡市、苏州市和昆山市
建成时间：2011年6月30日
建设单位：京沪高速铁路股份有限公司
设计单位：中铁第四勘察设计院集团有限公司
施工单位：中国交通建设股份有限公司、中铁三局集团有限公司、中铁五局集团有限公司等

**Name:** Danyang-Kunshan Grand Bridge
**Type:** Composite bridge with continuous girder and arch, tied arch bridge, continuous girder bridge and simply supported girder bridge, etc.
**Length:** 164.85km
**Location:** Danyang City, Changzhou City, Wuxi City, Suzhou City, Kunshan City, Jiangsu Province
**Completion:** June 30, 2011
**Owner(s):** Beijing-Shanghai High Speed Railway Co., Ltd.
**Designer(s):** China Railway Siyuan Survey and Design Group Co., Ltd.
**Contractor(s):** China Communication s Construction Co., Ltd., China Railway No.3 Engineering Group Co., Ltd. and China Railway No.5 Engineering Group Co., Ltd., etc.

# 晋陕黄河特大桥
## Shanxi-Shaanxi Bridge over Yellow River

| | |
|---|---|
| 桥　名： | 晋陕黄河特大桥 |
| 桥　型： | 单T刚构加劲钢桁组合梁桥、连续梁桥、简支梁桥等 |
| 桥梁长度： | 9.97km |
| 桥　址： | 山西省永济市、陕西省渭南市 |
| 建成时间： | 2014年5月31日 |
| 建设单位： | 大西铁路客运专线有限责任公司 |
| 设计单位： | 中铁第一勘察设计院集团有限公司 |
| 施工单位： | 中铁上海工程局集团有限公司 |

**Name:** Shanxi-Shaanxi Bridge over Yellow River
**Type:** Single T-shaped rigid frame with stiffening steel truss, continuous girder bridge and simply supported girder bridge, etc.
**Length:** 9.97km
**Location:** Yongji City, Shanxi Province and Weinan City, Shaanxi Province
**Completion:** May 31, 2014
**Owner(s):** Daxi Passenger Dedicated Line Co., Ltd.
**Designer(s):** China Railway First Survey and Design Institute Group Co., Ltd.
**Contractor(s):** Shanghai Civil Engineering Group Co., Ltd. of CREC

晋陕黄河特大桥是大西（大同至西安）客运专线的重点控制工程，跨越黄河。线路东起山西省永济市，向西跨越黄河，穿越洽川国家湿地森林公园，进入陕西省渭南市，全长9.97km，是目前我国高速铁路跨越黄河主桥长度最长的桥梁。

晋陕黄河特大桥采用了简支梁、连续梁和T形刚构等梁桥体系，跨越黄河的主桥采用15联2×108m单T刚构加劲钢桁组合梁，引桥分别采用48m和35m单T刚构，90m和80m中跨连续梁，48m、40m和32m简支梁等。主桥变截面单箱双室混凝土单T刚构采用挂篮悬臂浇筑法施工，三角形加劲钢桁采用预制拼装法架设，上弦节点连接采用插入直埋式、下弦节点采用散装式，加劲钢桁与混凝土T构采用PBL剪力件及普通钢筋连接。

晋陕黄河特大桥穿越洽川国家级风景名胜区和黄河湿地边缘地带，沿线分布有天鹅、灰鹤、白鹤、鸳鸯等60余种珍稀鸟类和飞禽种群，为此，大桥两侧专门设置了长达7.5km的声屏障，防止高速列车与飞鸟相撞，并有效隔绝噪音对鸟类栖息地的惊扰。

Shanxi-Shaanxi Bridge over Yellow River is a key engineering project of the Daxi (Datong-Xi'an) Passenger Dedicated Line crossing the Yellow River. The bridge starts from Yongji City, Shanxi Province in the east, crosses the Yellow River in the west, passes through the Qiachuan National Wetland Forest Park, and enters Weinan City, Shaanxi Province, with a total length of 9.97km. It holds the record of the longest high-speed railway bridge across the Yellow River in China.

Shanxi-Shaanxi Bridge over Yellow River is mainly composed of simply supported girders, continuous girders, T-shaped rigid frames and other girder bridge structures. The main bridge crossing the Yellow River consists of fifteen single T-shaped rigid frames (2×108m) with stiffening steel truss beams, while T-shaped rigid frames with 48m and 35m spans, continuous girders with 90m and 80m mid spans, simply supported girders with 48m, 40m and 32m spans are used for the approach bridge. The concrete T-shaped rigid frames of the main bridge with variable cross sections of single box double chambers were constructed by cast-in-place cantilever construction method with travelling carriages, while the triangular stiffening steel trusses were prefabricated and erected on site. The stiffening steel trusses and concrete T-shaped rigid frames are connected by PBL shear keys and ordinary steel bars.

Shanxi-Shaanxi Bridge over Yellow River passes through the Qiachuan National Scenic Area and the edge of the Yellow River Wetlands. There are more than 60 species of rare birds lives in these areas, such as swans, gray cranes, white cranes, mandarin ducks, etc. Therefore, 7.5km-long sound barriers have been set up on both sides of the bridge, to prevent high-speed trains from colliding with these birds, and effectively restrain noise from disturbing the bird habitat.

# 杭瑞洞庭大桥
## Hangzhou-Ruili Dongting Bridge

杭瑞洞庭大桥是湖南省岳阳市境内连接君山区和岳阳楼区的跨长江通道，是杭州—瑞丽高速公路（国家高速G56）湖南段的重要组成部分。大桥全长23.118km，双向六车道，设计速度100km/h。主桥采用1480m+453.6m两跨连续悬索桥的跨径布置。

杭瑞洞庭大桥主桥采用板桁结合钢桁加劲梁悬索桥，桁高9.0m，桁宽35.4m，节间长度8.4m。主缆垂跨比1/10，两根主缆中心距35.4m，每根主缆由175根通长索股组成，君山侧边跨另增设6根背索。每根索股由127根$\phi$5.35mm的高强镀锌钢丝组成。吊索标准间距为16.8m，跨中处吊索间距为17.6m，并设置5对柔性中央扣。索塔采用门式框架塔，岳阳楼区侧塔高203m，君山区侧塔高207m。两岸锚碇均为地连墙基础重力式锚碇。

杭瑞洞庭大桥在结构选型、高性能材料应用、施工技术等方面取得了一系列创新技术成果：采用超高韧性混凝土的轻型组合桥面结构，减小了正交异性桥面板疲劳开裂风险；应用板桁结合型加劲梁，降低用钢量并节省结构造价；采用葫芦形地下连续墙基础的锚碇，大大节省了混凝土工程数量，并克服了两个不同直径地下连续墙受力不对称的技术难题。

Hangzhou-Ruili Dongting Bridge is a Yangtze River-crossing channel connecting Junshan District and Yueyang Tower District in Yueyang City, Hunan Province, and is an important part of the Hunan section of Hangzhou-Ruili Expressway (National G56 Expressway). The bridge has a total length of 23.118km, carrying a highway traffic of two-way six lanes with design speed of 100km/h. The main bridge is a suspension bridge with two continuous spans of 1480m+453.6m.

The main bridge of Hangzhou-Ruili Dongting Bridge is a suspension bridge with the plate-truss combined steel truss stiffening girder. The truss has a depth of 9.0m and a width of 35.4m, and the section length is 8.4m. The sag ratio of the main cable is 1/10, and the center distance between the two main cables is 35.4m. Each main cable is composed of 175 full-length cable strands, while 6 back cables are added to the side span in Junshan. Each strand consists of 127 $\phi$ 5.35mm high strength galvanized steel wire. The standard spacing of hangers is 16.8m, and the spacing of hangers at mid-span is 17.6m, where 5 pairs of flexible central buckles are installed. The cable tower is a portal frame tower with a height of 203m at Yueyang Tower District side and 207m at Junshan District side. Anchorages on both banks are gravity anchorages with diaphragm wall foundation.

Hangzhou-Ruili Dongting Bridge has made a series of innovative technical achievements in structural selection, application of high-performance materials, construction technology, etc. The use of lightweight composite deck structure with ultra-high toughness concrete reduces the risk of fatigue cracking in orthotropic bridge deck. The plate-truss combined stiffening girder is applied to reduce the steel consumption and save the structural cost. The use of the anchorage with the gourd-shaped diaphragm wall foundation has greatly saved the number of concrete works and overcome the technical problem of asymmetric stress of two diaphragm walls with different diameters.

| 桥　名： | 杭瑞洞庭大桥 | **Name:** Hangzhou-Ruili Dongting Bridge |
| --- | --- | --- |
| 桥　型： | 悬索桥、连续梁桥、简支梁桥等 | **Type:** Suspension bridge, continuous girder bridge and simply supported girder bridge, etc. |
| 桥梁长度： | 23.118km | **Length:** 23.118km |
| 桥　址： | 湖南省岳阳市 | **Location:** Yueyang City, Hunan Province |
| 建成时间： | 2018年2月1日 | **Completion:** February 1, 2018 |
| 建设单位： | 湖南省大岳高速洞庭湖大桥建设开发有限公司 | **Owner(s):** Hunan Dayue Expressway Dongting Lake Bridge Construction and Development Co., Ltd. |
| 设计单位： | 湖南省交通规划勘察设计院有限公司 | **Designer(s):** Hunan Provincial Communications Planning, Survey & Design Institute Co., Ltd. |
| 施工单位： | 湖南路桥建设集团有限责任公司 | **Contractor(s):** Hunan Road & Bridge Construction Group Co., Ltd. |

# 乐清湾大桥
## Yueqing Bay Bridge

乐清湾大桥是连接浙江省温州市与台州市的跨海通道，位于乐清湾水域之上，是浙江省高速公路网的重要组成部分之一。大桥东起芦浦互通，上跨乐清湾、茅埏岛，西至南塘枢纽，全长10.088km。桥面为双向六车道高速公路，设计速度100km/h。

乐清湾大桥主桥为双塔整幅组合梁斜拉桥，半漂浮结构体系，跨径布置为70m+90m+365m+90m+70m；主梁采用分离式双边钢箱与混凝土桥面板组合梁，钢梁外侧设置风嘴，混凝土桥面板通过剪力钉与钢梁共同受力形成组合梁；索塔采用钻石形混凝土塔身，塔柱总高145.35m；全桥共128根斜拉索，平行双索面扇形布置；主塔基础采用桩基接承台的结构形式，钻孔灌注桩基础，梅花形布置，按摩擦桩设计。

在索塔主梁连接处设置了纵向限位挡块，主要是限制全桥承受纵向风荷载、汽车活载（包含制动力）作用时主梁和索塔的相对位移，设置了普通阻尼器，通过改变结构的动力特性并耗散地震能量，达到减震消能的目的。在主梁施工时，由于需要多点同时监控，因此在预制节段时采用双控措施，对多点测量数据进行复核，以保证施工精度。

Yueqing Bay Bridge is a sea-crossing passage connecting Wenzhou City and Taizhou City. It is located above the waters of Yueqing Bay, and is one of the important parts of the expressway network in Zhejiang Province. The bridge runs from Lupu Interchange in the east, crosses Yueqing Bay and Maoyan Island, and reaches Nantang Hub in the west. The total length of the bridge is 10.088 km. The bridge carries a two-way six-lane highway with a design speed of 100 km/h.

The main bridge of Yueqing Bay Bridge is a twin-tower composite-beam cable-stayed bridge with a semi-floating structural system. The span arrangement is 70m+90m+365m+90m+70m. The main girder is combined with two separate flat steel boxes and a concrete deck. A pair of fairings are set on the outside of the steel beam. The concrete bridge deck is connected with the steel beam through shear stubs to form a composite girder. The tower is a diamond-shaped concrete structure and the total height is 145.35m. The bridge has 128 cables set as fan-shaped in two cable planes. The foundation of the main tower adopts the pile foundation with bearing platform. Bored piles are arranged in plum blossom shapes designed as friction piles.

A longitudinal limit stop, and an ordinary damper are set at the connection between the main girder and the tower. The longitudinal limit stop is to restrict the relative displacement of the main girder and the tower when the whole bridge is subjected to longitudinal wind load and vehicle load (including braking force). Ordinary dampers are used to achieve the purpose of shock absorption and energy dissipation by changing the dynamic characteristics of the structure and dissipating seismic energy when

the whole bridge is subjected to seismic actions. During the construction of the main girder, due to the need for simultaneous monitoring of multiple points, it is necessary to ensure construction accuracy. Therefore, dual control measures are adopted in segment prefabrication to check the multi-point measurement data.

桥　　名：乐清湾大桥
桥　　型：斜拉桥、连续梁桥、简支梁桥等
桥梁长度：10.088km
桥　　址：浙江省温州市和台州市
建成时间：2018年9月
建设单位：浙江省交通投资集团有限公司
设计单位：浙江省交通规划设计研究院有限公司
　　　　　（现更名为浙江数智交院科技股份有限公司）
施工单位：中交一公局集团有限公司、中交第二公路工程局有限公司等

**Name:** Yueqing Bay Bridge
**Type:** Cable-stayed bridge, continuous girder bridge, simply supported girder bridge, etc.
**Length:** 10.088 km
**Location:** Wenzhou City and Taizhou City, Zhejiang Province
**Completion:** September, 2018
**Owner(s):** Zhejiang Communications Investment Group Co., Ltd.
**Designer(s):** Zhejiang Institute of Communications Co., Ltd.
**Contractor(s):** CCCC Frist Highway Engineering Group Co., Ltd., CCCC Second Highway Engineering Group Co., Ltd., etc.

# 港珠澳大桥
Hong Kong-Zhuhai-Macao Bridge

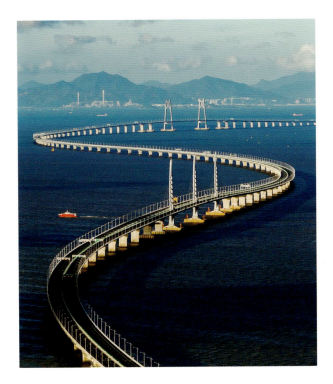

缩短了施工时间,并达到耐久性和高质量的施工目标。九洲航道桥和江海直达船航道桥分别采用风帆式和海豚式桥塔,建筑造型优美、标志性强。

Hong Kong-Zhuhai-Macao Bridge crosses the Lingdingyang Bay at the mouth of the Pearl River. It starts from the artificial island of Hong Kong Port near Hong Kong International Airport in the east, connects Lantau Island in the west and becomes a 12km long Hong Kong connection line. The 29.6km long main line runs westward to the artificial island of Zhuhai and Macao Port, and extends further westward to the Hongwan Interchange in Zhuhai, which is a 13.4km long Zhuhai connection line. The bridge has a total length of 55km, and is the longest sea-crossing bridge and tunnel project in the world.

The main line of Hong Kong-Zhuhai-Macao Bridge consists of a 6.7km immersed tunnel and a 22.9km sea-crossing bridge. The sea-crossing bridge is composed of three navigable span bridges, including Qingzhou Channel Bridge, Jianghai Direct Ship Channel Bridge and Jiuzhou Channel Bridge from east to west, as well as non-navigable span bridges in deep and shallow water areas. Qingzhou Channel Bridge is a double tower double cable plane steel box girder cable-stayed bridge with a main span of 458m. Jianghai Direct Ship Channel Bridge is a single cable plane three tower steel box girder cable-stayed bridge with two main spans of 258m each. Jiuzhou Channel Bridge is a double tower single cable plane steel-concrete composite girder cable-stayed bridge with a main span of 298m. The non-navigable span bridges in deep water area are 110m span steel box continuous girder bridges, which consist of single column pier and single box girder, while the non-navigable span bridges in shallow water area are 85m span prestressed concrete continuous girder bridges, which consist of single column pier and double girders.

港珠澳大桥跨越珠江口伶仃洋,东起香港国际机场附近的香港口岸人工岛,西接大屿山岛的部分为长 12km 的香港连接线,向西一直到珠海和澳门口岸人工岛的部分为长 29.6km 的主线,再往西至珠海洪湾立交的部分为长 13.4km 的珠海连接线,大桥全长 55km,是世界上最长的跨海桥隧工程。

港珠澳大桥主线工程由 6.7km 沉管隧道和 22.9km 跨海桥梁组成。跨海桥梁从东到西设置了青州航道桥、江海直达船航道桥和九洲航道桥三座通航孔桥以及深、浅水区非通航孔桥。青州航道桥是一座双塔双索面钢箱梁斜拉桥,主跨 458m;江海直达船航道桥是一座单索面三塔钢箱梁斜拉桥,两个主跨各 258m;九洲航道桥是一座双塔单索面钢-混凝土组合梁斜拉桥,主跨 298m;深水区非通航孔桥为 110m 跨径钢箱连续梁桥,采用独柱墩整幅梁;浅水区非通航孔桥为 85m 跨径预应力混凝土连续梁桥,采用独柱墩双幅梁。

为了降低深水区非通航孔桥的阻水率,减少环境负面影响,有效保护中华白海豚栖息地,提出采用装配化埋床式全预制墩身和承台(埋入海床),研发了结构构造、设计方法和施工方案,将预制整体承台和墩柱下放到复合桩上,通过临时围堰允许承台在干燥的环境中与桩连接,避免了在海洋环境中湿接施工,

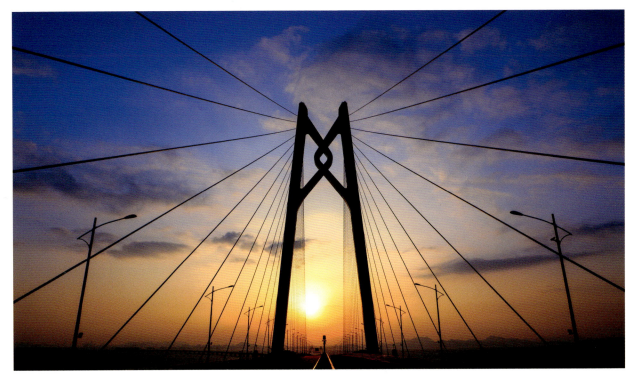

In order to reduce the water blocking rate of non-navigable bridges in deep-water area, and to restrain the negative impact on the environment and effectively protect the habitat of Chinese white dolphins, fully prefabricated and embedded pier shafts and pile caps (buried in the seabed) were proposed, designed and developed. The fully prefabricated pile caps and pier columns were placed on composite piles, then the pile caps were connected to the piles in a dry environment through temporary cofferdams. Thus, the wet joint construction in the marine environment has been avoided, the construction time was shortened, and the construction objectives of durability and high quality have been achieved. Jiuzhou Channel Bridge and Jianghai Direct Ship Channel Bridge adopt sail style and dolphin style bridge towers respectively, with beautiful architectural shape and strong visual impact.

桥　　名：港珠澳大桥
桥　　型：斜拉桥、连续梁桥、简支梁桥、沉管隧道等
桥梁长度：55km
桥　　址：香港、珠海和澳门
建成时间：2018 年 10 月 24 日
建设单位：港珠澳大桥管理局
设计单位：中交公路规划设计院有限公司、中铁大桥勘测设计院集团有限公司、丹麦 COWI 公司等
施工单位：中国交通建设股份有限公司、中铁大桥局股份有限公司、保利长大公路工程有限公司等

**Name:** Hong Kong-Zhuhai-Macao Bridge
**Type:** Cable-stayed bridge, continuous girder bridge, simply supported girder bridge, immersed tunnel, etc.
**Length:** 55km
**Location:** Hong Kong, Zhuhai and Macao
**Completion:** October 24, 2018
**Owner(s):** Hong Kong-Zhuhai-Macao Bridge Authority
**Designer(s):** CCCC Highway Consultants Co., Ltd., China Railway Major Bridge Reconnaissance & Design Institute Co., Ltd. and COWI, etc.
**Contractor(s):** China Communication Construction Co., Ltd., China Railway Major Bridge Engineering Group Co., Ltd. and Poly Changda Highway Engineering Co., Ltd., etc.

# 石济铁路客运专线济南黄河公铁两用桥

## Jinan Highway and Railway Bridge over Yellow River on Shijiazhuang-Jinan Railway Passenger Dedicated Line

石家庄至济南铁路客运专线连接京广高速铁路和京沪高速铁路两大高铁大动脉,其关键控制性工程是济南黄河公铁两用桥。大桥全长14.03km,上层桥面为双向六车道公路,设计速度80km/h,北起崔寨南立交,上跨黄河河道、裕华路,南至华山北互通;下层桥面为设计速度250km/h的石济铁路客运专线双线和设计速度120km/h的邯济胶济铁路联络线双线铁路。

大桥主桥采用128m+3×180m+128m五跨一联刚性悬索加劲连续钢桁梁,引桥分别采用了90m+132m+90m预应力混凝土连续刚构桥,125m简支钢桁梁以及30m、32m和52m预应力混凝土简支箱梁等。刚性悬索加劲连续钢桁梁采用工厂化制造,现场整体拼装后单向顶推施工,黄河水中墩及基础采用双壁钢围堰防护及栈桥辅助施工。

主桥设计采用了刚性悬索加劲钢桁梁的公铁两用桥型,开展了加劲弦钢拉杆锚固节点足尺模型试验研究,解决了多项设计关键技术。主桥施工形成了钢桁梁带加劲弦三桁多点同步顶推成套施工技术、三桁结构高差控制技术、高速铁路公铁两用桥智能建造技术、绿色施工技术等成果。

Shijiazhuang-Jinan Railway Passenger Dedicated Line connects the two major high-speed rail arteries—Beijing-Guangzhou High-speed Railway and Beijing-Shanghai High-speed Railway. The key project is Jinan Highway and Railway Bridge over Yellow River. The total length of the bridge is 14.03km, and the upper deck is a two-way six-lane highway with a design speed of 80 km/h, which starts from Cuizhai South Interchange in the north, crosses the Yellow River and Yuhua Road, and ends at Huashan North Interchange in the south. The lower deck is Shijiazhuang-Jinan Railway Passenger Dedicated Line with a design speed of 250km/h and the link line of Handan-Jinan High-speed Railway and Qingdao-Jinan High-speed Railway with a design speed of 120km/h.

The main bridge has 128m+3×180m+128m five-span continuous steel truss girder with stiffening rigid suspension cables, and the approach bridges consist of

90m+132m+90m prestressed concrete continuous rigid frames, 125m simply supported steel truss girders, and 30m, 32m and 52m prestressed concrete simply supported box girders. Rigid suspension cable stiffened continuous steel truss girders are factory-manufactured, constructed by one-way incremental launching method after being assembled on site. The piers and foundations in the Yellow River are protected by double-walled steel cofferdams and constructed with the aid of trestle bridge.

The design of the main bridge adopts the combined highway and railway bridge type of rigid suspension cable stiffened steel truss girder. The full-scale model test research of stiffened chord steel rod anchor joint has been carried out, and a number of key design technologies have been developed. The construction of the main bridge has gained various technical achievements, such as multi-point incremental launching method for steel truss girder with stiffening chord, elevation difference control technology for three truss structures, high-speed combined highway and railway bridge intelligent construction technology, and green construction technology.

桥　　名：石济铁路客运专线济南黄河公铁两用桥
桥　　型：刚性悬索加劲连续钢桁架桥、连续刚构桥、简支梁桥等
桥梁长度：14.03km
桥　　址：山东省济南市
建成时间：2020 年 9 月 1 日
建设单位：石济铁路客运专线有限公司
设计单位：中国铁路设计集团有限公司
施工单位：中铁四局集团有限公司

**Name:** Jinan Highway and Railway Bridge over Yellow River on Shijiazhuang-Jinan Railway Passenger Dedicated Line
**Type:** Continuous steel truss girder bridge with stiffening suspension cables, continuous rigid frame bridge and simply supported girder bridge, etc.
**Length:** 14.03km
**Location:** Jinan City, Shandong Province
**Completion:** September 1, 2020
**Owner(s):** Shijiazhuang-Jinan Passenger Dedicated Line Co., Ltd.
**Designer(s):** China Railway Design Group Co., Ltd.
**Contractor(s):** China Railway No.4 Engineering Group Co., Ltd.

# 平潭海峡公铁两用大桥
## Pingtan Strait Highway and Railway Bridge

平潭海峡公铁两用大桥是福建省福州市连接大陆和平潭岛的跨海通道，也是北京至台北铁路通道福平铁路段的关键控制性工程。作为我国第一座跨海公铁两用大桥，线路北起松下收费站，上跨元洪航道、鼓屿门水道、大小练岛水道和北东口水道，南至苏澳收费站，全长16.323km。上层桥面为双向六车道高速公路，设计速度100km/h；下层桥面为双线铁路，设计速度200km/h。

大桥共有四座通航孔桥，其中，元洪航道桥、鼓屿门水道桥和大小练岛水道桥统一采用双塔双索面钢桁架–混凝土混合梁斜拉桥，主跨分别为532m、364m和336m；北东口水道桥为2×168m双主跨连续刚构桥；其他非通航孔桥和引桥根据墩高、水深及地质条件分别采用跨度88m和80m的简支钢桁组合梁，跨度64m、48m和40m的预应力混凝土箱梁。

大桥建造于风浪流及地质条件极端复杂的风暴潮海峡中，施工克服了恶劣自然条件，突破了6级风停工规定，制定了7级和8级风作业规定，增加有效工作时间近一倍。基础采用"先平台后围堰"施工方案，以减少波浪和水流的影响。桥塔采用全封闭液压爬模降低大风干扰，非通航孔钢桁梁架设采用"双孔连做"节段梁架桥机施工提高工效，确保了大桥施工组织安全、有序、高效和优质。大桥的成功建设标志着我国铁路桥梁从内陆走向海洋。

Pingtan Strait Highway and Railway Bridge is a sea-crossing passage connecting the mainland and Pingtan Island in Fuzhou City, Fujian Province, which is a key project of the Fuzhou-Pingtan Railway section of the Beijing-Taipei Railway. As the first sea-crossing highway and railway bridge in China, the bridge starts from Songxia toll station in the north, crossing Yuanhong Waterway, Guyumen Waterway, Daxiaoliandao Waterway and Beidongkou Waterway, reaching Su'ao toll station in the south, with a total length of 16.323km. The upper deck is designed to carry a highway traffic of two-way six-lane with a design speed of 100km/h, while the lower deck is designed as a double-track railway with a designed speed of 200km/h.

There are totally four navigable channel bridges. Among which, Yuanhong Waterway Bridge, Guyumen Waterway Bridge and Daxiaoliandao Waterway Bridge are steel truss and concrete hybrid girder cable-stayed bridges with double towers and double cable planes, with the main spans of 532m, 364m and 336m, respectively. Beidongkou Waterway Bridge is a 2×168m continuous rigid frame bridge with two main spans. Non-navigable channel bridges and approach bridges are simply supported steel truss composite girders with span lengths of 88m and 80m, and prestressed concrete box girders with span lengths of 64m, 48m and 40m, respectively, which were chosen accordingly with pier height, water depth and geological conditions.

The bridge was built in a storm prone strait with extremely complex wind, wave and geological conditions. The construction of the bridge has overcome the harsh natural conditions, increased the construction limit wind condition from wind force scale level 6 to level 8, which has almost doubled the effective working time. As for the construction of foundations, the construction scheme of "platform before cofferdam" has been adopted to reduce the influence of wave and current. During the erection of towers, fully enclosed hydraulic climbing formwork was developed to reduce the interference of strong wind. "Double-span continuous construction scheme" has been used in the construction of non-navigable steel truss girders to improve work efficiency, and ensure the safety, ordering, efficiency and high-quality of the bridge construction. The successful construction of Pingtan Strait Highway and Railway Bridge marks the growth of China railway bridges from inland to the ocean.

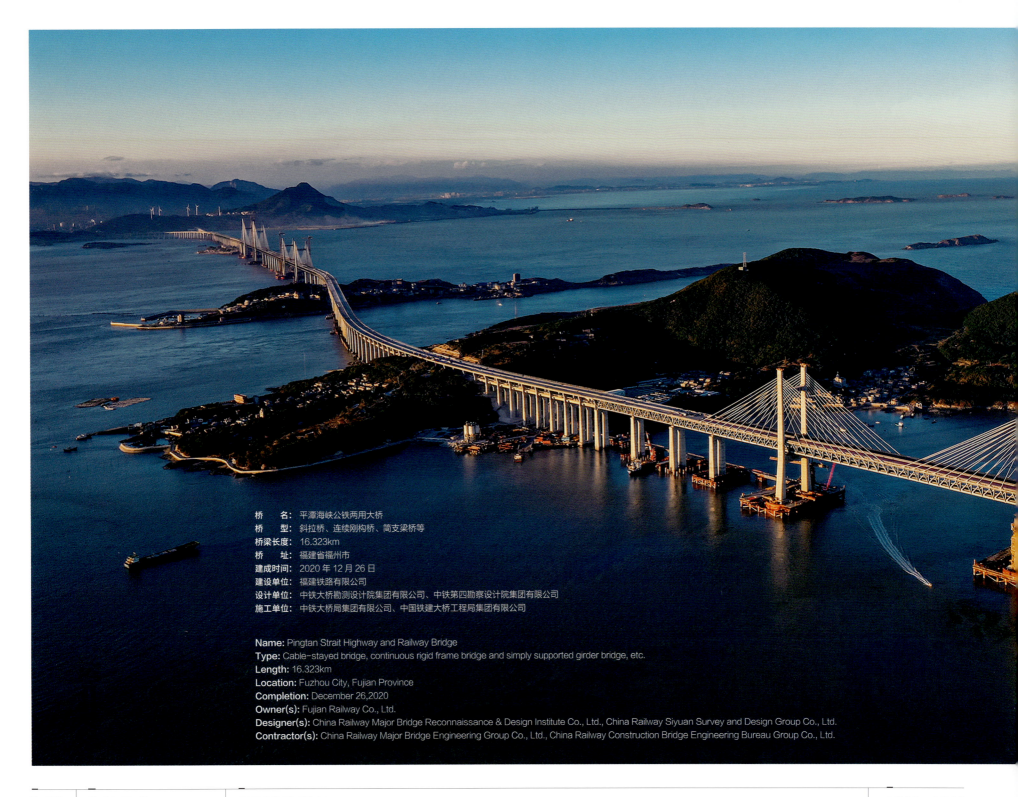

桥　　名：平潭海峡公铁两用大桥
桥　　型：斜拉桥、连续刚构桥、简支梁桥等
桥梁长度：16.323km
桥　　址：福建省福州市
建成时间：2020年12月26日
建设单位：福建铁路有限公司
设计单位：中铁大桥勘测设计院集团有限公司、中铁第四勘察设计院集团有限公司
施工单位：中铁大桥局集团有限公司、中国铁建大桥工程局集团有限公司

**Name:** Pingtan Strait Highway and Railway Bridge
**Type:** Cable-stayed bridge, continuous rigid frame bridge and simply supported girder bridge, etc.
**Length:** 16.323km
**Location:** Fuzhou City, Fujian Province
**Completion:** December 26, 2020
**Owner(s):** Fujian Railway Co., Ltd.
**Designer(s):** China Railway Major Bridge Reconnaissance & Design Institute Co., Ltd., China Railway Siyuan Survey and Design Group Co., Ltd.
**Contractor(s):** China Railway Major Bridge Engineering Group Co., Ltd., China Railway Construction Bridge Engineering Bureau Group Co., Ltd.

CHAPTER 1　　LONG MAJOR BRIDGES　　长大桥梁　　第一篇　　P-023

# 舟岱大桥
## Zhoushan–Daishan Bridge

宁波舟山港主通道舟岱大桥是浙江省舟山市连接定海区与岱山县的跨海通道。大桥主线位于灰鳖洋海域，南起岑港互通，穿马目山后设南通航孔桥、主通航孔桥和北通航孔桥依次跨越长白西航道、舟山中部港域西航道和岱山南航道，设长白海上互通及其接线连接长白岛，主线北止双合互通，全长28km。

南通航孔桥为主跨390m的双塔双索面钢箱梁斜拉桥，主通航孔桥为主跨2×550m的三塔双索面钢箱梁斜拉桥，北通航孔桥为主跨260m的钢-混凝土混合梁连续刚构桥，深水区非通航孔桥为跨径70m的预应力混凝土连续箱梁桥，采用整孔预制和架设，近岸区非通航孔桥为跨径62.5m的预应力混凝土节段预制拼装箱梁桥。

陆域段桥梁采用墩梁全预制一体化绿色拼装技术，以显著减少桥梁建造活动对环境的影响；海域段主通航孔桥承台采用"内层钢套箱整体安装+外层钢套箱逐块安装"快速施工工艺；钢管桩沉桩采用北斗卫星导航定位基准服务系统实现沉桩精度校核；预制墩身拼装大规模采用新型自锚式预应力体系，有效减少了海上作业时间和工序；超高性能混凝土（UHPC）提升跨海桥梁工程性能的技术研究，直接应用于海洋环境组合结构梁桥。

**Name:** Zhoushan-Daishan Bridge
**Type:** Cable-stayed bridge, continuous rigid frame bridge and simply supported girder bridge，etc.
**Length:** 28km
**Location:** Zhoushan City, Zhejiang Province
**Completion:** December 29, 2021
**Owner(s):** Ningbo Zhoushan Port Main Channel Project Engineering Construction Headquarters
**Designer(s):** Zhejiang Institute of Communications Co., Ltd., CCCC Highway Consultants Co., Ltd.
**Contractor(s):** Zhejiang Communications Construction Group Co., Ltd., China Railway Major Bridge Engineering Group Co., Ltd., China Communications Construction Group Co., Ltd., etc.

| | |
|---|---|
| 桥　　名： | 舟岱大桥 |
| 桥　　型： | 斜拉桥、连续刚构桥、简支梁桥等 |
| 桥梁长度： | 28km |
| 桥　　址： | 浙江省舟山市 |
| 建成时间： | 2021年12月29日 |
| 建设单位： | 宁波舟山港主通道项目工程建设指挥部 |
| 设计单位： | 浙江数智交院科技股份有限公司、中交公路规划设计院有限公司 |
| 施工单位： | 浙江交工集团股份有限公司、中铁大桥局集团有限公司、中国交通建设集团有限公司等 |

Zhoushan-Daishan Bridge is a sea-crossing passage connecting Dinghai District and Daishan County in Zhoushan City, Zhejiang Province. The main bridge is located in Huibieyang Sea area, starting from Cengang Interchange in the south, passing through Mamu Mountain, crossing the west navigation channel of Changbai, the west channel of Zhoushan Central Port Region and the south channel of Daishan with south navigable bridge, main navigable bridge and north navigable bridge respectively, and connects Changbai Island with Changbai Sea Interchange, finally ends at Shuanghe Interchange in the north, with a total length of 28km.

The south navigable bridge is a 390m double-tower double-cable plane steel box girder cable-stayed bridge. The main navigable bridge is a 2×550m three-tower double-cable plane steel box girder cable-stayed bridge. The north navigable bridge is a 260m continuous rigid-frame bridge with steel-concrete hybrid girders. The non-navigable bridge in deep water area consists of 70m prestressed concrete continuous box girders, which are pre-cast and erected on site. The non-navigable bridge in the nearshore area is composed of 62.5m prestressed concrete precast segmental box girders.

In order to significantly reduce the environmental impact of bridge construction activities, fully prefabricated piers and girders with green integration assembly technology have been adopted in land area. The rapid construction technology of "integral installation of inner steel boxed cofferdam plus block-by-block installation of outer steel boxed cofferdam" has been developed for the pile caps of the main navigable bridge in the sea area. Beidou satellite navigation and positioning reference service system has been used to verify the accuracy of steel pipe pile driving. A new type of self-anchored prestressed system was adopted to assemble the precast pier on a large scale, which has effectively reduced the time and working procedures at sea. The research on the technology of UHPC to improve the engineering performance of sea-crossing bridges has also been directly applied to the composite girder bridges in marine environment.

# 泉州湾跨海大桥
## Quanzhou Bay Sea-crossing Bridge

泉州湾跨海大桥是福厦高速铁路的重点控制性工程，全长 20.287km，跨海段桥长超过 8km，分为南岸陆地区引桥、南岸浅水区引桥、蚶江互通主线桥、南岸深水区引桥、通航主桥、北岸深水区引桥、北岸浅水区引桥、秀涂互通主线桥九个区段。

泉州湾跨海大桥主桥采用双塔双索面钢-混凝土组合梁半漂浮斜拉桥，其跨径布置为 70m+130m+400m+130m+70m=800m；塔梁之间设置纵向阻尼器，横向于索塔塔柱之间设置抗风支座。主梁采用混凝土桥面板+槽形钢箱梁的封闭箱形断面形式，共由 77 个节段组成，含风嘴全宽 21m，梁高 4.25m。桥塔采用曲线 H 形塔，贝壳分瓣的圆弧造型融入了泉州地域海洋元素，造型新颖轻盈，与并行公路桥塔形式相近，与景观相协调。

大桥深水区引桥采用了 21 联无支座连续刚构，该形式在国内铁路施工中尚属首次。桥梁建设者研发了多联无支座交接墩主梁挂篮悬臂浇筑施工技术，解决了搭设难度大、工程量大的难题，实现了跨海高铁无支座连续刚构桥全挂篮悬臂浇筑施工，提高了施工安全性及工效。

Quanzhou Bay Sea-crossing Bridge is a key project in the Fuzhou-Xiamen High-speed Railway, with a total length of 20.287km and more than 8km over sea. It is divided into nine sections, namely, the southern-shore land area approach, the southern-shore shallow water area approach, the Hanjiang River Interchange, the southern-shore shallow water area approach, the southern-shore deep water area approach, the navigational main bridge, the northern-shore deep water area approach, the

northern-shore shallow water area approach, and the Xiutu Interchange.

The main bridge of Quanzhou Bay Sea-crossing Bridge is a semi-floating cable-stayed bridge with steel-concrete composite girders, double towers and double cable planes. The layout of the bridge span is 70m+130m+400m+130m+70m=800m. Longitudinal dampers and transverse wind-resistant bearings are installed between tower and girder. The main girder, longitudinally divided into 77 segments, has a closed box section consists of concrete deck slab and steel tub-girder, with a total width of 21m including the wind fairings and a depth of 4.25m. The bridge tower has a curved H-shape. The circular arc shape of the tower column, originated from the shape of a shell fish which represents the marine environment of Quanzhou City, is similar to the parallel highway bridge and integrated well with the landscape.

The approach bridge in deep water area is composed of 21 continuous rigid frames without bearings, which is pioneering in domestic railway construction. The cantilever casting construction technology with travelling carriages has been developed for the multiple continuous rigid frames with bearing-free piers, which has solved the problems of erection difficulties and large quantities, realized the cantilever casting construction with travelling carriages for the continuous rigid frame bridge of the sea-crossing high-speed railway, and improved the construction safety and efficiency.

桥　　名：泉州湾跨海大桥
桥　　型：斜拉桥、连续刚构桥和简支梁桥
桥梁长度：20.287km
桥　　址：福建省泉州市
建成时间：2022 年 8 月 25 日
建设单位：东南沿海铁路福建有限责任公司
设计单位：中铁第四勘察设计院集团有限公司
施工单位：中交第二航务工程局有限公司

**Name:** Quanzhou Bay Sea-crossing Bridge
**Type:** Cable-stayed bridge, continuous rigid frame bridge and simply supported girder bridge
**Length:** 20.287km
**Location:** Quanzhou City, Fujian Province
**Completion:** August 25, 2022
**Owner(s):** Dongnan Coastal Railway Fujian Co., Ltd.
**Designer(s):** China Railway Siyuan Survey and Design Group Co., Ltd.
**Contractor(s):** CCCC Second Harbor Engineering Co., Ltd.

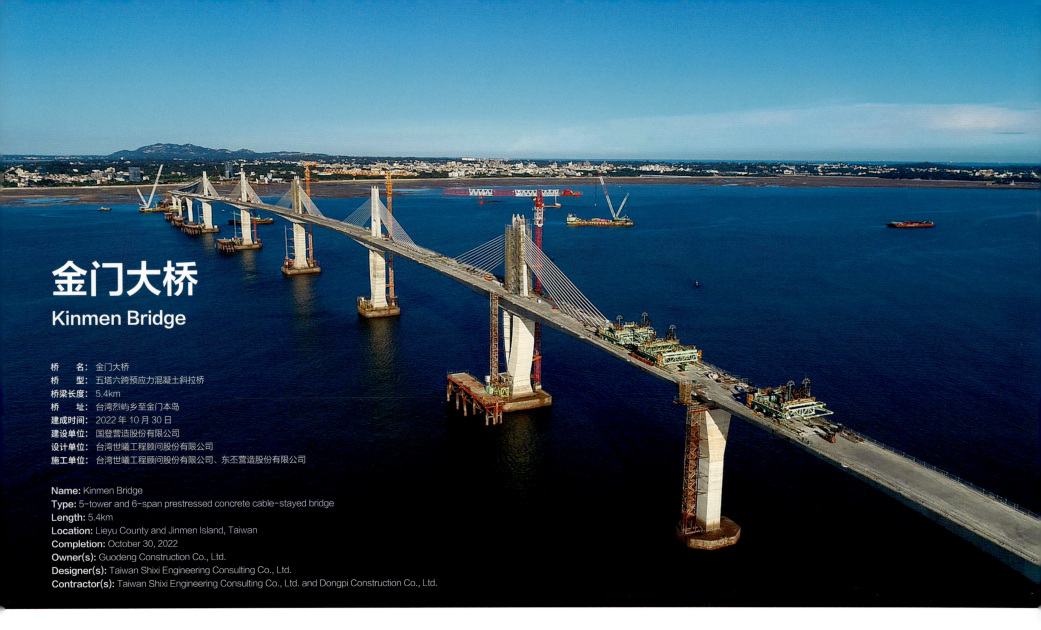

# 金门大桥
## Kinmen Bridge

桥　名：金门大桥
桥　型：五塔六跨预应力混凝土斜拉桥
桥梁长度：5.4km
桥　址：台湾烈屿乡至金门本岛
建成时间：2022 年 10 月 30 日
建设单位：国登营造股份有限公司
设计单位：台湾世曦工程顾问股份有限公司
施工单位：台湾世曦工程顾问股份有限公司、东丕营造股份有限公司

**Name:** Kinmen Bridge
**Type:** 5-tower and 6-span prestressed concrete cable-stayed bridge
**Length:** 5.4km
**Location:** Lieyu County and Jinmen Island, Taiwan
**Completion:** October 30, 2022
**Owner(s):** Guodeng Construction Co., Ltd.
**Designer(s):** Taiwan Shixi Engineering Consulting Co., Ltd.
**Contractor(s):** Taiwan Shixi Engineering Consulting Co., Ltd. and Dongpi Construction Co., Ltd.

　　金门大桥是连接大金门和小金门的跨海通道，是中国台湾地区首座跨海大桥。大桥西起台湾烈屿乡（小金门）后头湖埔路，东到金门本岛（大金门）金宁乡湖下慈湖路，全长 5.4km，包括主桥、左右边桥、左右引桥及两岛立交等。该桥为双向四车道，主桥宽度 18.8m，设计速度 60km/h。

　　主桥为五塔六跨斜拉桥，跨径布置为 125m+4×200m+125m，主塔采用曲线形混凝土墩柱，每座桥塔设置 11 对斜拉索，单索面扇形布置，中间 3 塔采用塔墩梁固结体系，两边各 1 塔采用半漂浮结构体系，主梁采用预应力混凝土箱梁。左右边桥为三跨预应力混凝土连续箱梁，跨径布置为 110m+150m+100m。左右引桥和两岛立交采用 35m 到 50m 跨径预应力混凝土简支箱梁。

　　金门大桥在设计过程中考虑了涨落潮及海浪带来的水位变化影响，基础上端高程设计在最低潮位以下 1m；在施工过程中，针对桥梁所处深槽地段花岗岩岩层深度变化剧烈的特点，采用钢围堰现浇基础；主梁则采用预制节段悬臂拼装施工。

Kinmen Bridge is a sea-crossing channel connecting the Greater Kinmen and the Lesser Kinmen as the first sea-crossing bridge in Taiwan. The bridge starts from Houtou Hupu Road in Lieyu County of Taiwan (Lesser Kinmen) in the west and ends at Huxia Cihu Road in Jinning County, Jinmen Island (Greater Kinmen) in the east. The total length of the bridge is 5.4km, including the main bridge, left and right side bridges, left and right approaches, and two overpasses in both islands. The bridge is a two-way four-lane bridge with a total width of 18.8m and a design speed of 60km/h.

The main bridge is a 5-tower and 6-span cable-stayed bridge with the span arrangement of 125m+4×200m+125m. The main towers are curved concrete pier columns, and each tower is equipped with 11 pairs of stay cables, with single cable plane fan-shaped layout. The middle three towers adopt tower-pier-beam consolidation system, and both side towers adopt semi-floating structural system. The main girder is prestressed concrete box girder. The left and right side bridges are three span prestressed concrete continuous box girders, with the span of 110m+150m+100m. The left and right approaches and the overpasses in two islands adopt prestressed concrete simply supported box girders with the spans of 35m to 50m.

During the design of Kinmen Bridge, the influence of water level changes caused by rising and falling tides and waves was carefully considered, and the elevation of the top of the foundation was designed to be 1m below the lowest tide level. During the construction, the cast-in-situ steel cofferdam foundation was adopted in view of the dramatic change in the depth of granite rock stratum in the deep groove section where the bridge is located. The main girder was assembled with prefabricated segmental cantilever method.

中国桥梁　BRIDGES IN CHINA　2013—2023

# Chapter 2

第二篇

# 悬索桥

Suspension Bridges

# 引言

悬索桥也称吊桥，是由中国人发明的一种古老桥型，现有历史记载的最古老的铁链悬索桥是我国陕西省汉中地区的樊河铁索桥，该桥以铁链作为主要承重构件，建于公元前206年。全世界第一座跨度突破百米的桥梁是我国1705年建成的大渡河泸定桥，全长103.67m，宽3m，由13根铁链承重。国外第一座悬索桥是1741年在英国蒂斯河上建成的跨度21.3m的铁索桥。

现代悬索桥以钢丝编制主缆为主要特征，可以追溯到1883年美国建成的跨度486m的布鲁克林大桥。此后，美国分别于1903年、1924年、1926年和1929年四次改写悬索桥跨度纪录。1931年，美国建成了跨度1067m的乔治·华盛顿大桥，成为全世界第一座跨度突破千米的桥梁。1937年和1964年，美国又分别建成了跨度1280m的金门大桥和跨度1298m的韦伦札诺海峡大桥。所有这些美式悬索桥都采用了主缆钢丝纺线法（air-spinning，AS法）和钢桁架加劲梁。1981年和1998年，英国和丹麦分别建成了跨度1410m的亨伯大桥和跨度1624m的大海带桥，均采用了闭口钢箱加劲梁。1998年，日本建成了1991m的明石海峡大桥，采用了主缆索股架设法（prefabricated paralle-wire strands，PPWS法）。2022年，土耳其建成了跨度2023m的1915恰纳卡莱大桥，采用了分体双箱梁提高抗风稳定性。

我国现代大跨度悬索桥建设始于20世纪90年代，1994年，率先建成了跨度452m的汕头海湾大桥，采用了预应力混凝土加劲梁；此后又先后建成了西陵长江大桥、丰都长江大桥、虎门大桥、厦门海沧大桥、江阴长江大桥等钢箱梁悬索桥，使得我国悬索桥跨度突破了千米。进入21世纪后，我国又先后建成润扬长江大桥、阳逻长江大桥、黄埔大桥、贵州坝陵河大桥、舟山西堠门大桥等跨度超千米的悬索桥，特别是2009年建成的西堠门大桥，曾经是全世界跨度最大的钢箱梁悬索桥，也是世界上第一座分体钢箱梁悬索桥。2012年和2013年，我国先后建成了两座跨度超千米的双主跨悬索桥，泰州长江大桥和马鞍山长江大桥，揭开了双主跨悬索桥建设序幕。2019年和2023年，我国又先后建成了跨度1700m的钢桁梁悬索桥武汉杨泗港长江大桥和跨度1756m的钢箱梁悬索桥南京仙新路长江大桥，进一步提升了两种加劲梁悬索桥跨度。2022年，在全世界已经建成的48座跨度超千米的悬索桥中，我国有26座，占一半以上。

近10年来，我国建成了近百座悬索桥，包括大跨度悬索桥、多主跨悬索桥、自锚式悬索桥等。本画册选取了19座悬索桥，包括15座大跨度悬索桥、2座双主跨悬索桥和2座自锚式悬索桥。相比《中国桥梁 2003—2013》，入选悬索桥的跨度有所增长，公路悬索桥的跨度钢箱梁增长至1756m，钢桁梁增长至1700m，铁路悬索桥的跨度首次突破了千米，达到1092m，自锚式悬索桥的跨度不仅提升到了600m，而且建成了428m双主跨自锚式悬索桥。悬索桥主缆钢丝强度研发取得突破，连续提升到1960MPa和2100MPa两个等级强度，已经或将要在后续超大跨度悬索桥中推广应用。

# INTRODUCTION

The suspension bridge is an ancient type of bridge developed by Chinese many centuries ago. According to historical records, the world's oldest suspension bridge is the Fanhe Bridge, located in Hanzhong District of Shaanxi Province, China. It was designed to use iron chains as the main load-carrying components and was completed in 206 BC. The world's first bridge with a span longer than 100m is the Luding Bridge over the Dadu River, which was completed in 1705 in China. It has a total length of 103.67m, a width of 3m, and uses 13 iron chains as the main load-carrying components. The first suspension bridge built outside of China is an iron-chain bridge spanning 21.3m built in 1741 cross the Tees River in England.

Modern suspension bridges are characterized by main cables fabricated from steel wires. The first bridge of this type was the Brooklyn Bridge, completed in 1883 in the United States, with a main span of 486m. Following this, the span record was broken four times, in 1903, 1924, 1926 and 1929, by bridges in the United States. The George Washington Bridge completed in 1931 with a span of 1067m, became the world's first bridge with a span longer than 1000m. The Golden Gate Bridge with a span of 1280m and the Verrazano-Narrows Bridge with a span of 1298m were then completed in 1937 and 1964, respectively. All of these American suspension bridges used the air-spinning method and steel truss stiffening girders. The Humber Bridge, completed in 1981 in England with a span of 1410m and the Great Belt Bridge, built in 1998 in Denmark with a span of 1624m, both employed a steel box stiffening girder. In 1998, the Akashi Kaikyo Bridge, which has a main span of 1991m and which used prefabricated parallel-wire strands, was completed in Japan. In 2022, the Canakkale 1915 Bridge, which has a main span of 2023m and which incorporates a twin-box stiffening girder to enhance the stability under wind loads, was completed in Turkey.

China started building modern suspension bridges in the 1990s. In 1994, the Shantou Bay Bridge, with a span of 452m and a prestressed concrete stiffening girder, was completed. Following this, many suspension bridges with steel box girders were built, including the Xiling Bridge over the Yangtze River, the Fengdu Bridge over the Yangtze River, the Humen Bridge, the Haicang Bridge in Xiamen, and the Jiangying Bridge over the Yangtze River. These bridges included main spans longer than 1000m. In the 21st century, suspension bridges with span lengths over 1000m were commonly built in China, including the Runyang Bridge over the Yangtze River, the Yangluo Bridge over the Yangtze River, the Huangpu Bridge over the Pearl River, the Baling River Bridge in Guizhou, and the Xihoumen Bridge in Zhoushan. The Xihoumen Bridge held the record for the world's longest steel box suspension bridge when completed in 2009 and was also the first suspension bridge with a steel twin-box design. Two double-main-span suspension bridges, the Taizhou Bridge over the Yangtze River and the Ma'anshan Bridge over the Yangtze River, were completed in 2012 and 2013, respectively. This ushered in the construction of additional single-main-span suspension bridges in China, including, the 2019 Yangsigang Bridge over the Yangtze River in Wuhan, with a main steel truss girder span of 1700m and the 2023 Xianxin Road Bridge over the Yangtze River in Nanjing, with a main steel box girder span of 1756m. These bridges further pushed forward the span record for suspension bridges with these two types of stiffening girders. Among 48 suspension bridges with main spans longer than 1000m around the world in 2022, more than half of them (26) are located in China.

In the last decade, China finished the construction of nearly one hundred suspension bridges, including long-span suspension bridges, multi-main-span suspension bridges and self-anchored suspension bridges. This album showcases nineteen suspension bridges, including fifteen long-span suspension bridges, two double-main-span suspension bridges, and two self-anchored suspension bridges. The main span lengths of the suspension bridges included in this album show increases compared with the ones in the previous edition. Main span length increased to 1756m for highway steel box suspension bridges, to 1700m for highway steel truss suspension bridges, and to 1092m for railway suspension bridges. Self-anchored suspension bridges not only saw an increase in main span length to 600m, but also the construction of a double-main-span self-anchored structure with two spans of 428m. The strength for steel wire used in the main cables underwent important developments. Wires with tensile strength of 1960MPa and 2100MPa standard strength steel wires were produced and are likely to be widely used in future super-long-span suspension bridges.

# 鹦鹉洲长江大桥

## Yingwuzhou Bridge over Yangtze River

鹦鹉洲长江大桥位于湖北省武汉市，是连接汉阳区和武昌区的过江通道，大桥西起江城大道，上跨长江水道，东至梅家山立交，全长 3.42km，设双向八车道。

鹦鹉洲长江大桥主桥为三塔四跨吊悬索桥，主跨跨径 2×850m。钢－混凝土组合加劲梁桥面宽 38m，中心梁高 3m。主缆跨径为 225m+850m+850m+225m，垂跨比 1/9，采用 127φ5.25mm 预制平行钢丝索股，每根主缆由 114 根索股组成，标准强度 1770MPa。南、北边塔采用 I 形混凝土结构，高 126.2m。中塔采用钢－混凝土混合结构，边、中塔塔顶高差为 18m。桥塔下部采用钻孔灌注桩基础。两岸均采用重力式锚碇，南锚碇基础采用地下连续墙结构，北锚碇基础采用沉井结构。大桥四跨加劲梁均为简支体系，边、中塔及边墩处设上、下游竖向拉压支座、横向抗风支座，中塔、边墩处设纵向固定支座。

鹦鹉洲长江大桥在加劲梁架设过程中采取了不对称架梁、无水平牵引力荡移、高低支架拼装台座等新技术。鹦鹉洲长江大桥中塔设计为纵向人字形的钢－混凝土混合结构，钢塔高度方向划分 15 节，节段之间连接设置五处调整接头，钢塔与混凝土桥塔结合段采用承压板后压浆的施工方法，保证结合段的施工质量。中塔墩基础采用双壁钢套箱围堰和"先围堰后平台"的总体施工方案，减小了施工风险和对河床防护的干扰。

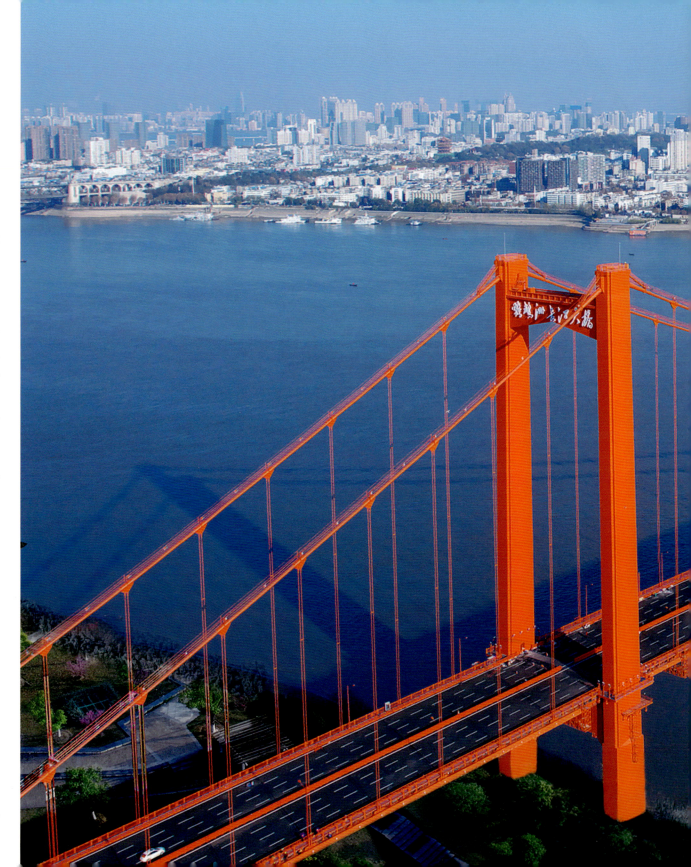

Yingwuzhou Bridge over Yangtze River, located in Wuhan City of Hubei Province, is a river-crossing passage connecting Hanyang District and Wuchang District. The bridge starts from Jiangcheng Avenue in the west and ends at Meijiashan Interchange in the east, having a total length of 3.42km and eight traffic lanes in dual direction.

The main bridge of Yingwuzhou Bridge over Yangtze River is a three-tower four-suspended-span suspension bridge with main span lengths of 2×850m. The steel-concrete composite stiffening girder has a 38m width and a 3m central depth. The span of the main cable is 225m+850m+850m+225m. The sag-to-span ratio is 1/9. Both main cables are prefabricated with 114 parallel wire bundles, and each bundle consists of 127 $\phi$ 5.25mm steel wires with standard strength of 1770MPa. The north and south side towers are I-shaped concrete structures with heights of 126.2m. The middle tower is a steel-concrete hybrid structure, and the height difference between the side towers and the middle tower is 18m. The lower parts of the towers are supported by bored piles. Gravity-type anchorages are used on both banks. The south anchorage is supported by diaphragm walls, and the north anchorage is supported by caisson structures. The four-span stiffening girder is simply supported; vertical tension-resistant bearings in upstream and downstream directions together with transversal wind-resistant bearings are set at the side, middle towers and side piers; longitudinal fixed bearings are set at the middle tower and side piers.

桥　　名：鹦鹉洲长江大桥
桥　　型：三塔四跨吊悬索桥
主跨跨径：2×850m
桥　　址：湖北省武汉市
建成时间：2014 年 12 月
建设单位：武汉市城市建设投资开发集团有限公司
设计单位：中铁大桥勘测设计院集团有限公司
施工单位：中铁大桥局集团有限公司

**Name:** Yingwuzhou Bridge over Yangtze River
**Type:** Three-tower four-suspended-span suspension bridge
**Main Span:** 2×850m
**Location:** Wuhan City, Hubei Province
**Completion:** December, 2014
**Owner(s):** Wuhan Construction Investment Development Group Co., Ltd.
**Designer(s):** China Railway Major Bridge Reconnaissance & Design Institute Co., Ltd.
**Contractor(s):** China Railway Major Bridge Engineering Group Co., Ltd.

The main features of the bridge are: 1) New construction techniques, including asymmetrical erection, swing without transversal traction forces, assembling pedestal with support brackets of various heights and etc., were developed for the girder erection. 2) The middle tower was designed as a steel-concrete hybrid structure with a herringbone shape longitudinally. The steel part was divided into 15 sections vertically; five adjustment joints were set for the connection between the sections. The post-grouting technique with the bearing plate was adopted for the construction of the joint section of the steel and concrete tower parts, ensuring the construction quality. 3) The foundation of the middle tower was designed as a double-walled steel box cofferdam and an overall construction plan of "cofferdam before platform" was adopted, reducing the construction risk and interference to riverbed protection.

# 贵瓮高速公路清水河大桥

## Guiyang-Weng'an Expressway Bridge over Qingshui River

| | |
|---|---|
| 桥　名： | 贵瓮高速公路清水河大桥 |
| 桥　型： | 双塔单跨吊悬索桥 |
| 主跨跨径： | 1130m |
| 桥　址： | 贵州省贵阳市 |
| 建成时间： | 2015 年 12 月 |
| 建设单位： | 贵州中交贵瓮高速公路有限公司 |
| 设计单位： | 中交公路规划设计院有限公司 |
| 施工单位： | 中交第二公路工程局有限公司 |

**Name:** Guiyang-Weng'an Expressway Bridge over Qingshui River
**Type:** Double-tower single-suspended-span suspension bridge
**Main Span:** 1130m
**Location:** Guiyang City, Guizhou Province
**Completion:** December, 2015
**Owner(s):** Guizhou CCCC Guiweng Highway Co., Ltd.
**Designer(s):** CCCC Highway Consultants Co., Ltd.
**Contractor(s):** CCCC Second Highway Engineering Co., Ltd.

贵瓮高速公路清水河大桥位于贵州省境内，横跨清水河峡谷，连接贵阳市开阳县与黔南布依族苗族自治州瓮安县。全长2.17km，设双向四车道。

贵瓮高速公路清水河大桥主桥为双塔单跨吊悬索桥，主跨跨径1130m。加劲梁采用板桁组合体系，主桁架桁高7m，两片主桁架弦杆中心间距27m。主缆跨径为258m+1130m+345m，垂跨比1/10，采用91ϕ5.25mm预制平行钢丝索股，每根主缆179股，标准强度1770MPa，开阳侧边跨另设8根背索。吊索顺桥向间距15.2m。桥塔采用钢筋混凝土门式框架结构，开阳岸桥塔高230m，瓮安岸桥塔高236/220m。两岸桥塔基础均采用嵌岩桩基础。两岸锚碇采用扩大基础结构形式。大桥加劲梁在桥塔处设置竖向支座及横向抗风支座。

贵瓮高速公路清水河大桥采用桥面板与主桁梁组合的加劲梁结构，全跨范围内桥面与桁架刚性连接，板-桁焊接构造省去高强度的拼接板和螺栓，更为经济。施工中采用自主研制的山区特大桥自行式主缆检修车设备，其抗偏载和抗风能力强，能实现在主缆上26°角爬升和自动过吊索功能。

Guiyang-Weng'an Expressway Bridge over Qingshui River is located in Guizhou Province and crosses the Qingshui River Valley. The bridge connects Kaiyang County of Guiyang City and Weng'an County of Qiannan Buyei and Miao Autonomous Prefecture, having a total length of 2.17km and four traffic lanes in dual direction.

The main bridge of Guiyang-Weng'an Expressway Bridge over Qingshui River is a double-tower single-suspended-span suspension bridge with a main span of 1130m. The stiffening girder adopts the plate-truss composite system. The main truss is 7m deep, and the center distance between two main truss chords is 27m. The span of the main cable is 258m+1130m+345m. The sag-to-span ratio is 1/10. Both main cables are prefabricated with 179 parallel wire bundles, and each bundle includes 91ϕ5.25mm steel wires with standard strength of 1770MPa. 8 additional back cables are set at the side span of Kaiyang bank. The longitudinal spacing between hangers is 15.2m. The towers are portal frame reinforced concrete structures. The

height of the tower near Kaiyang and that near Weng'an are 230m and 236/220m, respectively. Rock socketed pile foundations are used for the bridge towers, and spread foundations are used for the anchorages on both banks. Vertical bearings and transversal wind resistant bearings are set for the stiffening girder at the towers.

The main features of the bridge are: 1) The stiffening girder was designed as plate-truss composite structures. The

bridge deck is rigidly connected to the truss within the full span; the welding of the deck plate and the truss waives the high-strength splice plates and bolts, improving the economic performance. 2) New self-propelled vehicle equipment was developed and adopted for the main-cable maintenance for super-long-span suspension bridges in mountainous areas. The vehicle equipment has stronger resistance to eccentric loads and wind loads, and is able to climb on the main cable over 26 degrees and automatically pass through the sling.

# 保腾高速公路龙江大桥

## Baoshan-Tengchong Expressway Bridge over Long River

保腾高速公路龙江大桥位于云南省西部，跨越保山市龙陵县与腾冲县之间的龙川江河谷，全长2.47km，设双向四车道。

保腾高速公路龙江大桥主桥为双塔单跨吊悬索桥，主跨跨径1196m，桥面距谷底280m。加劲梁采用流线型扁平钢箱梁，箱梁宽33.5m，梁中心高3m。主缆跨径为320m+1196m+320m，垂跨比1/10.5，采用91∅5.25mm预制平行钢丝索股，每根主缆169股，标准强度1770MPa。吊索采用钢丝绳吊索，每个吊点设2根吊索，吊索钢丝绳公称直径为52mm。桥塔采用内倾式混凝土门式框架结构，钻孔灌注桩基础。保山岸桥塔高169.7m，腾冲岸桥塔高129.7m。两岸锚碇采用重力式锚碇+扩大基础的结构形式。大桥在加劲梁两端共设4套横向抗风支座，4套竖向拉压支座，在索塔和加劲梁之间共设4套纵向黏滞阻尼器。

保腾高速公路龙江大桥进行了强震山区千米级悬索桥抗震设计和全桥地震模拟试验研究，建立了强震山区高边坡综合平均稳定性评价技术与监测。大桥采用包括无人飞行器牵引先导索过江、索股入鞍段预成型及架设、喷洒葡萄糖酸钠作为缓凝剂等多项新施工技术，解决了山区千米级悬索桥的施工难题。

桥　　名：保腾高速公路龙江大桥
桥　　型：双塔单跨吊悬索桥
主跨跨径：1196m
桥　　址：云南省保山市
建成时间：2016年5月
建设单位：云南省交通投资建设集团有限公司
设计单位：云南省交通规划设计研究院有限公司、中交公路规划设计院有限公司
施工单位：中交第二公路工程局有限公司、中交路桥建设有限公司

Name: Baoshan-Tengchong Expressway Bridge over Long River
Type: Double-tower single-suspended-span suspension bridge
Main Span: 1196m
Location: Baoshan City, Yunnan Province
Completion: May, 2016
Owner(s): Yunnan Communications Investment & Construction Group Co., Ltd.
Designer(s): Broadvision Engineering Consultants Co., Ltd. and CCCC Highway Consultants Co., Ltd.
Contractor(s): CCCC Second Highway Engineering Co., Ltd. and CCCC Road & Bridge International Co., Ltd.

Baoshan-Tengchong Expressway Bridge over Long River is located in the western part of Yunnan Province and crosses the Longchuan River Valley between Longling County and Tengchong County of Baoshan City. The bridge has a total length of 2.47km and four traffic lanes in dual direction.

The main bridge of Baoshan-Tengchong Expressway Bridge over Long River is a double-tower single-suspended-span suspension bridge with a main span of 1196m and a 280m distance from the deck to the bottom of the valley. The stiffening girder is a streamlined flat steel box girder. The width of the stiffening girder is 33.5m, and the center depth is 3m. The span of the main cable is 320m+1196m+320m. The sag-to-span ratio is 1/10.5. Both main cables are prefabricated with 169 parallel wire bundles, and each bundle consists of 91 $\phi$ 5.25mm galvanized steel wires with standard strength of 1770MPa. The hangers are made of steel wire rope slings, and 2 rope slings are set for each lifting point. The nominal diameter of the steel wire rope slings is 52mm. The towers are inward-inclined portal frame reinforced concrete structures, supported by bored piles. The height of the tower at the Baoshan side and that at the Tengchong side are 169.7m and 129.7m, respectively. Gravity-type anchorages with spread foundations are used on both blocks. 4 sets of transversal wind resistant bearings together with vertical tension-resistance bearings are designed for both ends of the stiffening girder; 4 sets of longitudinal viscous dampers are also designed between the tower and the stiffening girder.

The main features of the bridge are: 1) The anti-seismic design together with the bridge seismic experiment for the kilometer-length-level suspension bridge in mountainous regions with strong earthquake risks were studied. The general stability evaluation and monitoring techniques have been established for the high slopes in mountainous regions with strong earthquake risks. 2) New construction technologies were used during construction, including unmanned aerial vehicle towing the pilot cable across the river, pre-forming and erection of cable strands into the saddle and spraying sodium gluconate as a retarder; the construction challenges for the kilometer-length-level suspension bridge in mountainous areas were solved.

# 几江长江大桥
## Jijiang Bridge over Yangtze River

| | |
|---|---|
| 桥　名： 几江长江大桥 | **Name:** Jijiang Bridge over Yangtze River |
| 桥　型： 双塔单跨吊悬索桥 | **Type:** Double-tower single-suspended-span suspension bridge |
| 主跨跨径：600m | **Main Span:** 600m |
| 桥　址： 重庆市 | **Location:** Chongqing City |
| 建成时间：2016年7月 | **Completion:** July, 2016 |
| 建设单位：重庆市江津区人民政府 | **Owner(s):** The People's Government of Jiangjin District, Chongqing City |
| 设计单位：中铁第四勘察设计院集团有限公司 | **Designer(s):** China Railway Siyuan Survey and Design Group Co., Ltd. |
| 施工单位：中国建筑第六工程局有限公司 | **Contractor(s):** China Construction Sixth Engineering Bureau Co., Ltd. |

几江长江大桥位于重庆市江津区长江水道，南起江津几江街道，北至滨江新城，全长1.9km，设双向六车道。

几江长江大桥主桥为双塔单跨吊悬索桥，主跨跨径600m。钢箱梁宽33m，梁中心高3m。主缆跨径组合为176m+600m+140m，垂跨比1/9.09，采用127∅5.2mm预制平行钢丝索股，每根主缆65股，标准强度1670MPa。吊索纵向间距12m，采用平行钢丝束索股。桥塔采用钢筋混凝土门式框架结构，南塔、北塔塔柱高分别为112.7m和106.1m，桥塔下部采用分离式承台、钻孔灌注桩基础。南岸采用重力式锚碇，北岸采用隧道式锚碇。大桥加劲梁在桥塔处设黏滞阻尼器和横向限位装置。

几江长江大桥北岸锚碇采用隧道锚周边岩体植入型钢剪力键，大幅提高了锚体抗拔能力，锚体体量较常规隧道锚减小18%；采用了自主研发的锚固系统洞外拼装成型、整体滑移入洞工法。南岸锚碇采用锚体深嵌沉井的新型组合锚碇结构，大幅减少了地面构筑物体量。钢箱梁架设采用"高低栈桥+二次荡移+二次平移"组合施工技术，克服了山区地形高差与河流水位变化大的难题。

Jijiang Bridge over Yangtze River, located in Yangtze River Waterway of Jiangjin District, Chongqing City, starts from Jijiang Road in the south and ends at New Binjiang Town in the north. The bridge has a total length of 1.9km and six traffic lanes in dual direction.

The main bridge of Jijiang Bridge over Yangtze River is a double-tower single-suspended-span suspension bridge with a main span length of 600m. The steel box girder is designed with a 33m width and a 3m central depth. The span of the main cable is 176m+600m+140m. The sag-to-span ratio is 1/9.09. Both main cables are prefabricated with 65 parallel wire bundles, and each bundle includes 127 $\phi$ 5.2mm steel wires with standard strength of 1670MPa. The hangers are also made of parallel wire bundles, and the longitudinal spacing between hangers is 12m. The towers are portal frame reinforced concrete structures. The heights of the southern tower and northern tower are 112.7m and 106.1m, respectively. The towers are supported by bored piles with separated pile caps. A gravity-type anchorage and a tunnel-type anchorage are used in the southern and northern anchor blocks, respectively. Viscous dampers and transversal displacement-limiting devices are set for the stiffening girder at the tower.

The main features of the bridge are: 1) The northern anchor block adopts the steel shear keys that are embedded into the rock mass near the tunnel-type anchorage, significantly improving the pullout-resistance capacity of the anchorage; the size of the anchorage has been reduced by 18% compared with the traditional tunnel-type anchorage. A new construction method, which enables the anchoring system to be assembled outside the tunnel and to slide into the place for the anchorage, was developed and adopted. 2) The southern anchor block adopts a new type of composite anchor structure that embeds the anchor block deeply into the caisson foundation. The size of the anchorage above the ground has been significantly reduced. 3) "Trestles with different heights cooperated with a secondary-swing and secondary-translational-motion" method were developed for the box-girder erection, which solved the construction problem incurred by the difference among the terrain heights and river water levels.

# 驸马长江大桥
## Fuma Bridge over Yangtze River

驸马长江大桥位于重庆市万州区境内，跨越长江水道，北起驸马镇吊龙村，南接太龙镇向坪村，全长2km，设双向四车道。

驸马长江大桥主桥为双塔单跨吊悬索桥，主缆跨径1050m。梁宽32m，中心梁高3.2m。主缆跨径为285m+1050m+345m，垂跨比1/10，采用127ϕ5.2mm预制平行钢丝索股，每根主缆108股，标准强度1770MPa。吊索纵向标准间距16m，采用127ϕ5.0mm镀锌高强钢丝，标准强度1670MPa。桥塔采用钢筋混凝土门式框架结构，北岸塔高210.5m，南岸塔高167.8m。北岸采用重力锚方案，南岸采用隧道锚方案。

驸马长江大桥采用永久吊索＋接长吊索长距离多次荡移架设钢箱梁，解决了荡移距离与角度限制问题，并且避免了搭设岸边支架，减少了对环境的影响。大桥北岸重力锚深基坑开挖过程中，采取抗滑桩+锚索支护治理，浇筑了78根抗滑桩，每隔4m设一根锚索，有效地控制了岩体的位移。南岸隧道锚进行围岩注浆，并在隧道锚底部建纵向排水导洞，使隧道锚整体处于干燥防护状态，延长其使用寿命。

Fuma Bridge over Yangtze River, located in Wanzhou District of Chongqing City, crosses the Yangtze River Waterway, starts from Diaolong Village of Fuma Town in the north and ends at Xiangping Village of Tailong Town in the south. The bridge has a total length of 2km and four traffic lanes in dual direction.

The main bridge of Fuma Bridge over Yangtze River is a double-tower single-suspended-span suspension bridge

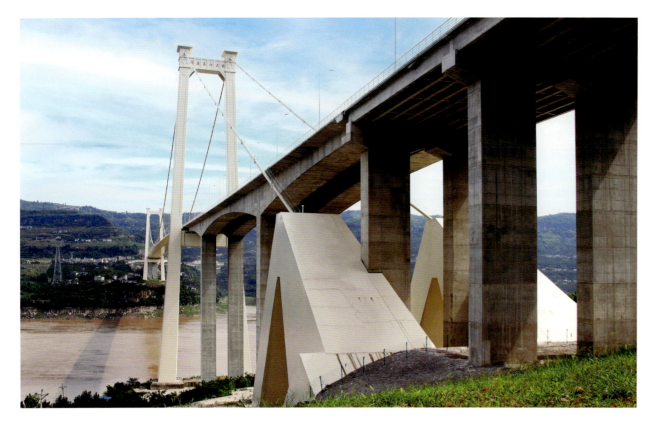

with a main span of 1050m. The steel box girder is designed with a 32m width and a 3.2m central depth. The span of the main cable is 285m+1050m+345m. The sag-to-span ratio is 1/10. Both main cables are prefabricated with 108 parallel wire bundles, and each bundle includes 127$\phi$5.2mm steel wires with standard strength of 1770MPa. The hangers are made of 127$\phi$5.0mm steel wires with standard strength of 1670MPa, having a 16m longitudinal standard spacing. The towers are portal frame reinforced concrete structures. The heights of the northern tower and southern tower are 210.5m and 167.8m, respectively. A gravity-type anchorage and a tunnel-type anchorage are used in the northern and southern anchor blocks, respectively.

The main features of the bridge are: 1) Permanent hangers and extension hangers were used for repeated swing erection of the steel box girder, addressing the limitation for the swing distance and angle, also avoiding the shoreside trestle and protecting the environment. 2) 78 anti-sliding piles and anchor cables with a spacing of 4m were applied for the northern gravity-type anchorage during the construction, effectively mitigating the displacement of the rock mass. 3) The surrounding rock was grouted in the southern tunnel-type anchorage; drainage pilot tunnel was also constructed at the tunnel bottom, making the anchorage in a dry condition and therefore extending the service life.

桥　名：驸马长江大桥
桥　型：双塔单跨吊悬索桥
主跨跨径：1050m
桥　址：重庆市
建成时间：2017 年 12 月
建设单位：重庆万利万达高速公路有限公司
设计单位：中交公路规划设计院有限公司、中交一公局公路勘察设计院有限公司（现更名为中交综合规划设计院有限公司）、重庆市交通规划勘察设计院（现更名为中铁长江交通设计集团有限公司）
施工单位：中交一公局集团有限公司

**Name:** Fuma Bridge over Yangtze River
**Type:** Double-tower single-suspended-span suspension bridge
**Main Span:** 1050m
**Location:** Chongqing City
**Completion:** December, 2017
**Owner(s):** Chongqing Wanli Wanda Highway Co., Ltd
**Designer(s):** CCCC Highway Consultants Co., Ltd., CCCC Comprehensive Planning and Design Institute Co., Ltd. and China Railway Changjiang Transport Design Group Co., Ltd.
**Contractor(s):** CCCC First Highway Engineering Group Co., Ltd.

# 兴康大桥
## Xingkang Bridge

　　兴康大桥位于四川省甘孜藏族自治州境内，是川藏高速公路的组成部分，东西横跨大渡河，全长1.41km，设双向四车道。

　　兴康大桥主桥为双塔单跨吊悬索桥，主跨跨径1100m。钢桁加劲梁采用钢筋混凝土组合桥道系，桁宽27m，桁高8.2m。主缆跨径为220m+1100m+253m，垂跨比1/9，采用91Φ5.3mm预制平行钢丝索股，每根主缆187股，标准强度1860MPa，横向中心间距27m。纵向吊索间距10m。两岸桥塔采用钢筋混凝土门式框架结构，波形钢腹板混凝土组合横梁，桥塔高度188m。桥塔下部采用群桩基础。雅安岸采用隧道式锚碇，康定岸采用重力式锚碇。大桥加劲梁在桥塔处各设1对竖直向支座、2对横向抗风支座和1对纵向阻尼装置。

　　兴康大桥设计采用防屈曲钢支撑中央扣，用于抵抗地震。桥塔横梁采用波形钢腹板与混凝土顶底板的组合结构，提高了混凝土横梁和钢横梁的抗震性能，同时简化了塔柱和横梁的连接构造。钢桁梁分为57个节段吊装，单节段最大吊重达200.5t。

Xingkang Bridge is located in Ganzi Tibetan Autonomous Prefecture of Sichuan Province, forming a part of Chengdu-Lhasa Expressway. The bridge crosses the Dadu River from east to west, having a total length of 1.41km and four traffic lanes in dual direction.

The main bridge is a double-tower single-suspended-span suspension bridge with a main span of 1100m. The steel truss stiffener girder adopts a steel-concrete composite deck system, with a width of 27m and a depth of 8.2m. The span of the main cable is 220m+1100m+253m. The sag-to-span ratio is 1/9. Both main cables are prefabricated with 187 parallel wire bundles, and each bundle includes 91Φ5.3mm steel wires with standard strength of 1860MPa. The lateral spacing between the main cable centers is 27m. The longitudinal spacing between hangers is 10m. The towers on both sides are portal frame reinforced concrete structures, and the cross beam is made of prestressed concrete combined with corrugated steel webs. The towers are 188m high, supported by bored piles. A tunnel-type anchorage is used for the anchor block on the Ya'an bank, and a gravity-type anchorage is used for the kangding bank. A pair of vertical bearings, two pairs of transversal wind-resistance bearings and a pair of longitudinal damping devices are set for the stiffening girder at the tower.

The main features of the bridge are: 1) The central buckle with buckling-restrained steel brace was designed for enhancing the earthquake resistance. 2) The cross beam of the tower adopts a composite structure that combines the corrugated steel webs and concrete slabs, improving the seismic performance of the cross beam and also simplifying

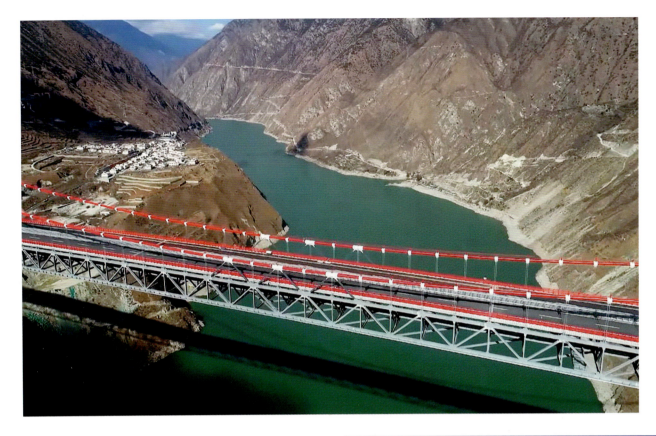

**Name:** Xingkang Bridge
**Type:** Double-tower single-suspended-span suspension bridge
**Main Span:** 1100m
**Location:** Ganzi Tibetan Autonomous Prefecture, Sichuan Province
**Completion:** December, 2018
**Owner(s):** Sichuan Transportation Investment Group Co. Ltd.
**Designer(s):** Sichuan Highway Planning, Survey, Design and Research Institute Co. Ltd.
**Contractor(s):** Sichuan Road & Bridge (Group) Co. Ltd.

the connection structure. 3) The steel truss girder was divided into 57 segments, and the maximum lifting weight of a single segment is up to 200.5t.

桥　　名：兴康大桥
桥　　型：双塔单跨吊悬索桥
主跨跨径：1100m
桥　　址：四川省甘孜藏族自治州
建成时间：2018年12月
建设单位：四川省交通投资集团有限责任公司
设计单位：四川省公路规划勘察设计研究院有限公司
施工单位：四川公路桥梁建设集团有限公司

# 南沙大桥
## Nansha Bridge

南沙大桥位于广东省珠江水域，西接广州市南沙区，东连东莞市沙田镇，由坭洲水道桥、大沙水道桥两座悬索桥与连接线组成。大桥全长12.89km，设双向八车道。

南沙大桥坭洲水道桥为双塔双跨吊悬索桥，主跨跨径1688m。钢箱梁全宽47.9m，梁高4m。主缆跨径为658m+1688m+520m，垂跨比1/9.5，采用127ϕ5mm预制平行钢丝索股，每根主缆252股，标准强度1960MPa。主缆间距42.1m，吊索标准纵向间距12.8m。桥塔采用钢筋混凝土门式框架结构，设上、中、下三道横梁，塔高260m，基础采用群桩，锚碇为重力式锚碇。大桥纵向采用静力限位-动力阻尼约束体系，竖向和横向采用碟形弹簧与动力阻尼组合的新型减震抗风支座。

南沙大桥大沙水道桥为双塔单跨吊悬索桥，主跨跨径1200m。钢箱梁断面与坭洲水道桥相同。主缆跨径为360m+1200m+480m，垂跨比1/9.5，采用127ϕ5.2mm预制平行钢丝索股，每根主缆252股，标准强度1770MPa。桥塔采用钢筋混凝土门式框架结构，设上、下两道横梁，塔高193.1m，基础采用群桩，锚碇为重力式锚碇。

南沙大桥坭洲水道桥大规模应用了我国自主研发生产的1960MPa级镀锌铝钢丝主缆，主缆钢丝外缠绕S形钢丝、涂覆全新铠装系统，并配备新型空气除湿系统。南沙大桥吊索采用了成套减振装置，控制了吊索各方向及各阶次的振动。南沙大桥建设中提出了复合地连墙锚碇基础设计方法及整套施工监控、质量检测措施，开发了基于建筑信息模型（BIM）的建养一体化信息平台。

Nansha Bridge, located on the Pearl River Waterway of Guangdong Province, starts from Nansha District of Guangzhou City in the west and ends at Shatian Town of Dongguan City in the east. Nansha Bridge consists of two suspension bridges—Nizhou Waterway Bridge, Dasha Waterway Bridge and approach bridges. The total length of Nansha Bridge is 12.89km with eight traffic lanes in dual direction.

Nizhou Waterway Birdge of Nansha Bridge is a double-tower double-suspended-span suspension bridge with a main span length of 1688m. The steel box girder is designed with a 47.9m width and a 4m central depth. The span of the main cable is 658m+1688m+520m. The sag-to-span ratio is 1/9.5. Both main cables are prefabricated with 252 parallel wire bundles, and each bundle includes 127ϕ5mm steel wires with standard strength of 1960MPa. The spacing between cables is 42.1m, and the longitudinal spacing between hangers is 12.8m. The towers are portal frame reinforced concrete structures with three crossbeams. The towers are 260m high and supported by pile-group foundations. Both anchorages are gravity-type. Nizhou Waterway Bridge adopts a restraint system that limits the displacement under static loads and sets viscous dampers for dynamic loads. A new seismic-reduction and wind-resistant bearing, which combines disc springs and viscous dampers, is applied in the vertical and transversal directions.

Dasha Waterway Bridge of Nansha Bridge is a double-tower single-suspended-span suspension bridge with a main span length of 1200m. The same steel box girder is applied as Nizhou Waterway Bridge. The span of the main cable is 360m+1200m+480m. The sag-to-span ratio is 1/9.5. Both main cables are prefabricated with 252 parallel wire bundles, and each bundle includes 127 $\phi$ 5.2mm steel wires with standard strength of 1770MPa. The towers are portal frame reinforced concrete structures with two crossbeams. The towers are 193.1m high and supported by pile-group foundations. Both anchorages are gravity-type.

The main features of the bridge are: 1) The 1960MPa Al-Zn alloy coated steel wires developed by China were applied in Nizhou Waterway Bridge with S-shaped steel wires wrapping, a new armor coating and dehumidification system. 2) Vibration suppression devices were systematically applied; the vibration of hangers has been mitigated. 3) The design method together with the construction monitoring and quality control measures were developed for the underground diaphragm wall-anchorage composite foundation; a BIM-based integrated construction and maintenance management system was also developed.

桥　　名：南沙大桥
桥　　型：双塔双跨吊悬索桥（坭洲水道桥）；双塔单跨吊悬索桥（大沙水道桥）
主跨跨径：坭洲水道桥1688m；大沙水道桥1200m
桥　　址：广东省广州市、东莞市
建成时间：2019年4月
建设单位：广东省交通集团有限公司
设计单位：中交公路规划设计院有限公司、
　　　　　广东省交通规划设计研究院集团股份有限公司
施工单位：中交第二公路工程局有限公司、中交第二航务工程局有限公司、
　　　　　保利长大工程有限公司

**Name:** Nansha Bridge
**Type:** Double-tower double-suspended-span suspension bridge (Nizhou Waterway Bridge); double-tower single-suspended-span suspension bridge (Dasha Waterway Bridge)
**Main Span:** Nizhou Waterway Bridge 1688m; Dasha Waterway Bridge 1200m
**Location:** Guangzhou City and Dongguan City, Guangdong Province
**Completion:** April, 2019
**Owner(s):** Guangdong Province Traffic Group Co., Ltd.
**Designer(s):** CCCC Highway Consultants Co., Ltd. and Guangdong Communication Planning & Design Institute Group Co., Ltd.
**Contractor(s):** CCCC Second Highway Engineering Co., Ltd., CCCC Second Harbor Engineering Co., Ltd. and Poly Changda Engineering Co., Ltd.

# 杨泗港长江大桥

## Yangsigang Bridge over Yangtze River

杨泗港长江大桥位于武桥水道河段、鹦鹉洲长江大桥和白沙洲大桥之间,全长 4.13km,上层设六车道城市快速路,下层设四车道城市主干路和两条非机动车道,上、下层桥面两侧均设置人行道。

杨泗港长江大桥主桥为双塔单跨吊悬索桥,主跨跨径 1700m。加劲梁采用华伦式钢桁梁,桁高 10m,两片主桁中心距 28m,标准节间距 9m。主缆跨径为 465m+1700m+465m,垂跨比 1/9,采用 91∅6.2mm 预制平行钢丝索股,每根主缆 271 股,标准强度 1960MPa。吊索与索夹为骑跨式连接,与钢加劲梁为销接式连接。桥塔采用钢筋混凝土门式框架结构,

桥塔高 243.9m。桥塔基础采用圆端形沉井结构，锚碇基础采用圆形地下连续墙结构。大桥主桥加劲钢桁梁两端在两主塔立柱上设置竖向支座和横向抗风支座，加劲梁端设置纵向液压阻尼器，塔梁之间设置纵向限位支座。

杨泗港长江大桥应用直径 6.2mm、强度 1960MPa 的主缆钢丝，研发了索夹螺杆同步张拉设备和工艺以解决索夹滑移问题。钢桁加劲梁采用千吨级整体吊装和全焊接结构技术。锚碇基础施工采用坚硬土层条件下超大沉井下沉新技术，大桥 2 号塔底节钢沉井下水质量高达 6200t。

Yangsigang Bridge over Yangtze River is located between Yingwuzhou Bridge over Yangtze River and Baishazhou Bridge, crossing the Wuqiao Waterway and having a total length of 4.14km. Six urban expressway traffic lanes are set on the upper level of the deck; four urban trunk lanes and two non-motorized traffic lanes are set on the lower level of the deck; sidewalks are set on both deck levels.

The main bridge of Yangsigang Bridge over Yangtze River is a double-tower single-suspended-span suspension bridge with a main span of 1700m. The stiffening girder adopts the Warren type steel truss with a 10m depth. The central distance between the two main trusses is 28m, and the standard section spacing is 9m. The span of the main cable is 465m+1700m+465m. The sag-to-span ratio is 1/9. Both main cables are prefabricated with 271 parallel wire bundles, and each bundle includes 91 $\phi$ 6.2mm steel wires with standard strength of 1960MPa. The hanger is connected with the cable clamp in a straddle type, and connected with the steel stiffening beam in a pin type. The towers are portal frame reinforced concrete structures with heights of 243.9m. Circular caisson structures are used for the tower foundation, and circular diaphragm walls are used for the anchorage foundation. Vertical bearings and transversal wind resistant bearings are set for the stiffening girder at the columns of both towers; longitudinal hydraulic dampers are set at the ends of the stiffening girder, and longitudinal limit bearings are set between the tower and girder.

The main features of the bridge are: 1) The main cable steel wire of 6.2mm diameter and 1960MPa standard strength was developed. Synchronous tension equipment and the corresponding construction technique were developed for solving the cable clamp slip problem. 2) The steel truss stiffening girder adopts kiloton-level integral hoisting and all-welded structures. 3) The anchorage foundation construction adopts a new technique of super large caisson sinking under the condition of hard soil; the weight of steel caisson at the bottom of the No. 2 tower is up to 6200t.

桥　　名：杨泗港长江大桥
桥　　型：双塔单跨吊悬索桥
主跨跨径：1700m
桥　　址：湖北省武汉市
建成时间：2019 年 10 月
建设单位：武汉市城市建设投资开发集团有限公司
设计单位：中铁大桥勘察设计院集团有限公司
施工单位：中铁大桥局集团有限公司

**Name:** Yangsigang Bridge over Yangtze River
**Type:** Double-tower single-suspended-span suspension bridge
**Main Span:** 1700m
**Location:** Wuhan City, Hubei Province
**Completion:** October, 2019
**Owner(s):** Wuhan Urban Construction Investment and Development Group Co., Ltd.
**Designer(s):** China Railway Major Bridge Reconnaissance & Design Institute Group Co., Ltd.
**Contractor(s):** China Railway Major Bridge Engineering Group Co., Ltd.

# 鹅公岩轨道大桥
## Egongyan Rail Transit Bridge

桥　　名：鹅公岩轨道大桥
桥　　型：五跨连续钢-混凝土混合梁自锚式悬索桥
主跨跨径：600m
桥　　址：重庆市
建成时间：2019年12月
建设单位：重庆市轨道交通（集团）有限公司
设计单位：上海市政工程设计研究总院（集团）有限公司、林同棪国际工程咨询（中国）有限公司
施工单位：中国铁建大桥工程局集团有限公司

**Name:** Egongyan Rail Transit Bridge
**Type:** Five-span continuous steel-concrete hybrid girder self-anchored suspension bridge
**Main Span:** 600m
**Location:** Chongqing City
**Completion:** December, 2019
**Owner(s):** Chongqing Rail Transit (Group) Co., Ltd.
**Designer(s):** Shanghai Municipal Engineering Design Institute (Group) Co., Ltd. and T.Y. Lin International Engineering Consulting (China) Co., Ltd.
**Contractor(s):** China Railway Construction Bridge Engineering Bureau Group Co., Ltd.

鹅公岩轨道大桥位于重庆市九龙坡区，跨越长江水道，南起南岸区，北至九龙坡区，全长1.65km，设双向轨道及人行道。

为保证相邻的既有鹅公岩大桥的运营安全并保持二者造型统一，鹅公岩轨道大桥主桥采用五跨连续钢-混凝土混合梁自锚式悬索桥，主跨跨径600m，建成时为世界上主跨跨径最大的自锚式悬索桥。大桥采用钢-混凝土混合梁；主缆锚固段和锚跨段采用预应力混凝土箱梁，锚跨梁高4.5~10m，宽17m；其余部分采用钢箱梁，梁高4.5m，宽22m。主缆跨径为210m+600m+210m，垂跨比1/10，采用127φ5.3mm锌铝合金镀层预制平行钢丝索股，每根主缆92股，标准强度1860MPa。吊索纵向间距15m，采用φ7mm平行钢丝束索股。桥塔采用钢筋混凝土门式框架结构，桥塔下部采用灌注嵌岩桩基础。大桥主梁与主塔连接处采用竖向支承及纵向阻尼约束，与桥墩连接处采用竖向支承及横向限位约束。

鹅公岩轨道大桥采用"先斜拉后悬索"的施工方法，既满足了自锚式悬索桥"先梁后缆"的施工要求，又避免了在航道水域设置临时支撑对通航的影响。钢箱梁体量大，边跨钢箱梁无法通过水路运输，因此采用了研发的"多点同步步履式顶推施工技术"，以解决边跨钢箱梁架设难题。

Egongyan Rail Transit Bridge is located in Jiulongpo District of Chongqing City and crosses the Yangtze River Waterway. The bridge starts from Nan'an District in the south and ends at Jiulongpo District in the north, having a total length of 1.65km with rail transit lines in dual direction and pedestrian walkways.

In order to keep the consistency in the bridge appearance and ensure the operational safety considering the existing adjacent Egongyan Bridge, the main bridge of Egongyan Rail Transit Bridge is a five-span continuous steel-concrete hybrid girder self-anchored suspension bridge with a main span length of 600m, which is the world's longest self-anchored suspension bridge at the time of completion. The bridge adopts the steel-concrete hybrid girder. The prestressed concrete box girder is used at the anchorage section and span of main cable, with a 4.5-10m depth and a 17m width; the steel box girder is adopted in other sections, with a 4.5m depth and a 22m width. The span of the main cable is 210m+600m+210m. The sag-to-span ratio is 1/10. Both main cables are prefabricated with 92 parallel wire bundles, and each bundle includes 127 φ5.3mm steel wires with Zn-Al alloy coating and standard strength of 1860MPa. The hangers are made of φ7mm steel wires, having a longitudinal spacing of 15m. The towers are portal frame reinforced concrete structures, supported by rock-embedded bored-pile foundations. Vertical bearings

and longitudinal damping devices are set for the girder at the tower, vertical bearings and transversal displacement-limiting devices are set for the girder at the pier.

The main features of the bridge are: 1) The construction method of cable-staying before suspension was adopted, satisfying the construction requirements of deck before cable for self-anchored suspension bridges and also avoiding interfering the waterway navigation due to setting temporary supports. 2) The steel box girder volume is large, and the side span steel box girder cannot be transported by waterway. Therefore, a steel-box girder-erection construction technique called multi-point synchronous walking-pedrail launching construction technology was developed to address the challenge incurred by the unavailability of shipping transportation in the side span.

# 赤水河红军大桥
## Hongjun Bridge over Chishui River

赤水河红军大桥位于四川省泸州市与贵州省遵义市交界处，西连四川省古蔺县，东接贵州省习水县，全长 2.01km，设双向四车道。

赤水河红军大桥主桥为双塔单跨吊悬索桥，主跨跨径 1200m。钢桁加劲梁梁高 7m，桥面宽 27m。主缆跨径为 325m+1200m+205m，垂跨比 1/9.6，采用 91$\phi$5.35mm 预制平行钢丝索股，每根主缆 169 股，标准强度 1860MPa。桥塔采用钢筋混凝土门式框架结构，桥塔下部采用钻孔灌注桩基础。四川岸、贵州岸塔柱高度分别为 228.5m 和 243.5m。四川岸采用隧道式锚碇，贵州岸采用重力式锚碇。大桥桁架梁端部采用对称约束，每侧设置 2 个竖向支座及 4 个横向抗风支座；梁端顺桥向每侧安装 2 套限位黏滞阻尼器。

赤水河红军大桥形成了"塔梁异步 + 鞍梁同步"索塔施工工艺、钢桁梁"找形刚接法"、基于多基准丝多基准索股的主缆架设方法等施工技术，解决了峡谷超高墩悬索桥施工难题。结合大桥锚碇及地形地质特点，创新性地解决了锚碇排水难题。开发了悬索桥 BIM 模型模块化设计成套技术，搭建了基于 BIM 技术的建设管理平台，为桥梁的快速建设提供了支撑。

Hongjun Bridge over Chishui River, located on the border of Luzhou City of Sichuan Province and Zunyi City of Guizhou Province, connects Gulin County of Sichuan Province in the west and Xishui County of Guizhou Province in the east. The bridge has a total length of 2.01km and four traffic lanes in dual direction.

The main bridge of Hongjun Bridge over Chishui River is a double-tower single-suspended-span suspension bridge with a main span of 1200m. The steel truss stiffening girder is designed with a 7m depth and a 27m width. The main cable span is 325m+1200m+205m. The sag-to-span ratio is 1/9.6. Both main cables are prefabricated with 169 parallel wire bundles, and each bundle includes 91 $\phi$ 5.35mm

steel wires with standard strength of 1860MPa. The towers are portal frame reinforced concrete structures, supported by bored-pile foundations. The tower on the Sichuan bank and that on the Guizhou bank are 228.5m and 243.5m, respectively. A tunnel-type anchorage is used for the anchor block on the Sichuan bank, and a gravity-type anchorage is used for the Guizhou bank. Symmetric constraints are set at the ends of the stiffening girder; 2 vertical bearings and 4 transversal wind-resistance bearings are set at each side; 2 sets of displacement-limiting viscous dampers are also set longitudinally at each side.

The main features of the bridge are: 1) New construction techniques were developed, for instance, the tower-girder asynchronous construction with saddle-girder synchronous construction method, the form-finding and rigid connection method for the steel truss girder, the erection construction method for main cable based on multi-datum-wire-strands and multi-datum-cable-strands, which solved the construction problems for suspension bridges with super-high piers in the canyons. 2) Based on the anchorage design and the topographic and geographic features, the challenge for the anchorage drainage has been addressed. 3) A systematic BIM-based modular design method was developed for suspension bridges, and a BIM-based construction management system was established, supporting the rapid construction of the bridge.

桥　　名：赤水河红军大桥
桥　　型：双塔单跨吊悬索桥
主跨跨径：1200m
桥　　址：贵州省遵义市
建成时间：2020年1月
建设单位：蜀道投资集团有限责任公司
设计单位：四川公路桥梁建设集团有限公司勘察设计分公司
施工单位：四川公路桥梁建设集团有限公司

**Name:** Hongjun Bridge over Chishui River
**Type:** Double-tower single-suspended-span suspension bridge
**Main Span:** 1200m
**Location:** Zunyi City, Guizhou Province
**Completion:** January, 2020
**Owner(s):** Shudao Investment Group Co., Ltd.
**Designer(s):** Survey and Design Company of Sichuan Road & Bridge (Group) Co., Ltd.
**Contractor(s):** Sichuan Road and Bridge (Group) Co., Ltd.

# 五峰山长江大桥
## Wufengshan Bridge over Yangtze River

五峰山长江大桥位于江苏省镇江市境内，是连镇高速铁路、江宜高速公路共同跨越长江的通道，全长 6.41km，上层设双向八车道高速公路，下层设双向四线高速铁路。

五峰山长江大桥主桥为双塔单跨吊悬索桥，主跨跨径 1092m。钢桁梁立面采用华伦桁式，横断面采用带副桁的直主桁式，主桁中心桁宽 30m，桁高 16m，节间距 14m，材质为 Q370qE 钢。主缆跨径为 350m+1092m+350m，垂跨比 1/10，采用 127$\phi$5.5mm 预制平行钢丝索股，每根主缆 352 股，标准强度 1860MPa。吊索采用标准强度 1770MPa 的镀锌高强钢丝，纵向间距 14m。桥塔采用钢筋混凝土门式框架结构，桥塔基础为桩基础。北塔高 203m，南塔高 191m。北锚碇采用大型沉井基础，南锚碇采用不等深圆形地连墙基础。大桥每个主塔及桥墩处主桁下均设有竖向刚性支座、纵向活动支座，在两主塔处钢梁底设纵向液压阻尼器。

作为高速铁路悬索桥，五峰山长江大桥设计荷载达每米 124t，主缆直径达 1.3m。研发的专用紧缆设备可满足大直径主缆的紧缆需求；通过改进设备及工艺，主缆索股以平均 7 根 / 天的速度快速牵引架设。钢梁架设施工采用自主研发的 900t 缆载吊机及两节间大节段钢梁整体安装技术，提高了架设安全性，加快了施工进度。

Wufengshan Bridge over Yangtze River, located in Zhenjiang City of Jiangsu Province, is the passage crossing Yangtze River for both Lianyungang-Zhenjiang High-speed Railway and Jiangdu-Yixing Expressway. The bridge has a total length of 6.41km. Eight expressway lanes in dual direction are set on the upper level of the deck and four high-speed railway lanes in dual direction are set on the lower level of the deck.

The main bridge of Wufengshan Bridge over Yangtze River is a double-tower single-suspended-span suspension bridge with a main span of 1092m. The stiffening girder is designed as a Warren truss type, with the cross section adopting straight main trusses and subsidiary trusses. The central width between the main trusses is 30m; the truss depth is 16m and the section spacing is 14m; Q370qE grade steel is used. The span of the main cable is 350m+1092m+350m. The sag-to-span ratio is 1/10. Both main cables are prefabricated with 352 parallel wire bundles, and each bundle consists of 127 $\phi$ 5.5mm steel wires with standard strength of 1860MPa. The hangers are also made of parallel wire bundles with standard strength of 1770MPa, and the longitudinal spacing between hangers is 14m. The towers are portal frame reinforced concrete structures, supported by bored piles. The heights of the northern tower and southern tower are 203m and 191m, respectively. The north anchorage is supported by a caisson foundation, and the south anchorage is supported by a circular diaphragm wall foundation with various depths. Vertical rigid bearings and longitudinal movable bearings are set for the steel girder at each tower and pier; hydraulic dampers are set longitudinally for the steel girder at the two towers.

The main features of the bridge are: 1) As a suspension bridge carrying high-speed railway, the design load for the bridge is up to 124t per meter, and the diameter of the main cable is up to 1.3m. 2) Special cable tightening equipment was developed to meet the requirement for the main cable with a large diameter. By improving the equipment and construction method, the main cable strands can be quickly towed and erected at an average speed of 7 strands per day. 3) A 900t super-heavy cable-carrying crane and the installation technique for large-size steel girder segments of two intersections were developed for the girder erection, improving the erection safety and facilitating the construction progress.

桥　　名：五峰山长江大桥
桥　　型：双塔单跨吊悬索桥
主跨跨径：1092m
桥　　址：江苏省镇江市
建成时间：2020年12月
建设单位：中国铁路上海局集团有限公司
设计单位：中铁大桥勘测设计院集团有限公司
施工单位：中铁大桥局集团有限公司、中交第二航务工程局有限公司

**Name:** Wufengshan Bridge over Yangtze River
**Type:** Double-tower single-suspended-span suspension bridge
**Main Span:** 1092m
**Location:** Zhenjiang City, Jiangsu Province
**Completion:** December, 2020
**Owner(s):** China Railway Shanghai Group Co., Ltd.
**Designer(s):** China Railway Major Bridge Reconnaissance & Design Institute Co., Ltd.
**Contractor(s):** China Railway Major Bridge Engineering Group Co., Ltd. and CCCC Second Harbor Engineering Co., Ltd.

# 金安金沙江大桥
## Jin'an Bridge over Jinsha River

| | |
|---|---|
| 桥　名：金安金沙江大桥 | Name: Jin'an Bridge over Jinsha River |
| 桥　型：双塔单跨吊悬索桥 | Type: Double-tower single-suspended-span suspension bridge |
| 主跨跨径：1386m | Main Span: 1386m |
| 桥　址：云南省丽江市 | Location: Lijiang City, Yunnan Province |
| 建成时间：2020 年 12 月 | Completion: December, 2020 |
| 建设单位：中国交通建设股份有限公司 | Owner(s): China Communications Construction Co., Ltd. |
| 设计单位：云南省交通规划设计研究院有限公司 | Designer(s): Broadvision Engineering Consultants Co., Ltd. |
| 施工单位：中交第二公路工程局有限公司、中交第二航务工程局有限公司 | Contractor(s): CCCC Second Highway Engineering Co., Ltd. and CCCC Second Harbor Engineering Co., Ltd. |

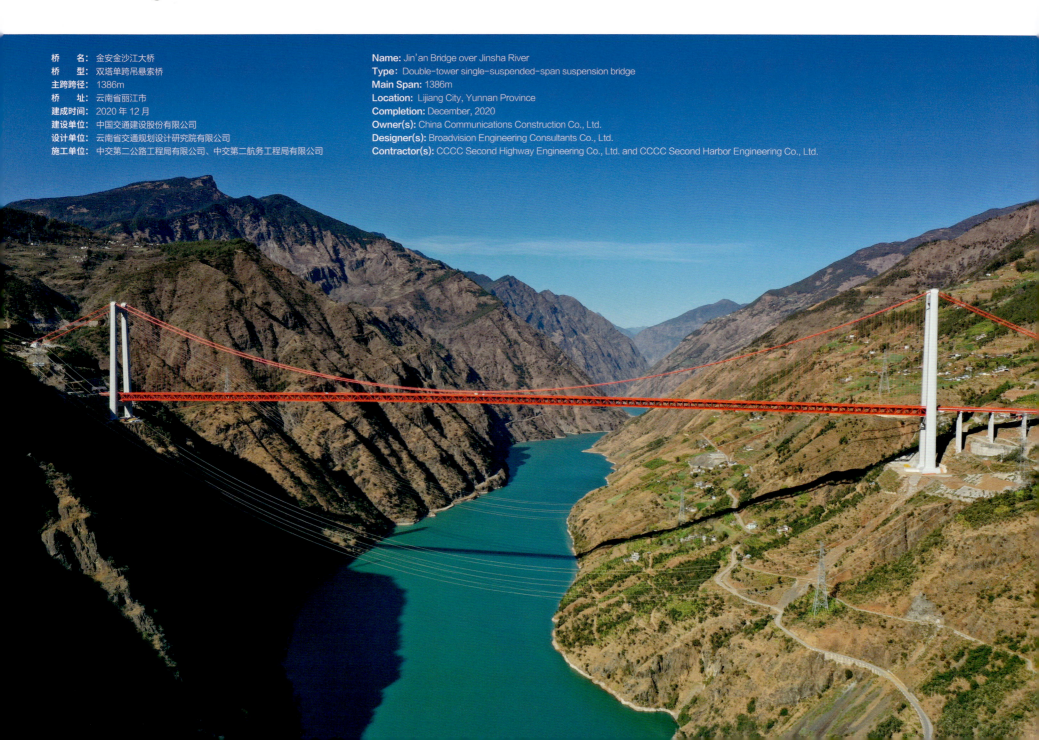

金安金沙江大桥位于云南省丽江市，在金安桥水电站上游跨越金沙江，全长1.68km，设双向四车道。

金安金沙江大桥主桥为双塔单跨吊悬索桥，主跨跨径1386m。采用板桁组合加劲梁，中心间距宽27m，桁高9.5m。主缆跨径为330m+1386m+205m，垂跨比1/10，采用127$\phi$5.25mm预制平行钢丝索股，每根主缆169股，标准强度1770MPa。吊索与索夹为骑跨式连接，纵向间距10.8m，采用标准强度1670MPa、公称直径$\phi$54mm的钢芯钢丝绳。桥塔采用钢筋混凝土门式框架结构，下部采用分离式承台及挖孔灌注桩基础。华坪岸索塔高222m，丽江岸索塔高186m。两岸锚碇均为隧道式锚碇。大桥跨中设置3对柔性中央扣，加劲梁两端上、下弦杆横向共设8套横向抗风支座，下弦共设4套竖向支座，在索塔下横梁和加劲梁之间共设4套黏滞阻尼器。

金安金沙江大桥地处云贵高原的深切峡谷地带，海拔高、地震烈度大，对此，进行了隧道锚与公路隧道三维群洞效应研究与优化。施工中，全桥正交异性板采用U肋全熔透焊接工艺，延长板桁组合加劲梁钢桥面板使用寿命；采用"八"字形分离式倾斜下稳定抗风措施，提高深切峡谷大风攻角下板桁组合加劲梁悬索桥的颤振临界风速；对两岸锚碇排水采用明排方式，解决隧道锚防水难的问题。研发了1500米级悬索桥重载缆索吊快速装配化施工技术及适用于超重钢桁梁的板桁分离式缆索吊装施工技术，开发了一种缆索吊作业自动化集中控制系统。

Jin'an Bridge over Jinsha River is located in Lijiang City of Yunnan Province and crosses the Jinsha River in the upstream side of Jin'anqiao Hydropower Station. The bridge has a total length of 1.68km and four traffic lanes in dual direction.

The main bridge of Jin'an Bridge over Jinsha River is a double-tower single-suspended-span suspension bridge with a main span of 1386m. The stiffening girder is designed as the plate-truss composite girder with a 27m central distance and a 9.5m depth. The span of the main cable is 330m+1386m+205m. The sag-to-span ratio is 1/10. Both main cables are prefabricated with 169 parallel wire bundles, and each bundle includes 127 $\phi$5.25mm steel wires with standard strength of 1770MPa. The hangers are made of $\phi$54mm steel rope slings with standard strength of 1670MPa, connected to the cable clamp in a straddle type and having a longitudinal spacing of 10.8m. The towers are portal frame reinforced concrete structures, supported by pile foundations with separated pile caps. The tower on the Huaping bank is 222m high, and the one on the Lijiang bank is 186m high. Tunnel-type anchorages are used on both banks. 3 pairs of flexible central buckles are designed in the mid-span; 8 sets of transversal wind-resistance bearings are designed for the upper and lower chords; 4 sets of vertical bearings are designed for the lower chords; 4 sets of viscous dampers are designed between the lower crossbeams of the tower and the stiffening girder.

The main features of the bridge are: 1) The bridge is located in the deep canyon area of the Yunnan-Guizhou Plateau with high altitudes and seismic intensities. The tunnel-type anchorage and three-dimensional group cavern effect for the highway tunnel have been studied and optimized. 2) During the construction process, the full-penetration welding construction technique for U-ribs was developed to extend the service life of the plate-truss composite deck; figure-eight-pattern separated tilt-down wind resistance measures were taken to improve the critical wind speed; an open drainage way was developed for both anchorages to address the waterproofing challenge for the tunnel-type anchorage. 3) New techniques, which enable fast assembly construction using the cable crane for 1500m-length suspension bridges and facilitate separated erection of the ultra-heavy steel truss girder using cable crane, were developed; a new automatic centralized system was also developed to control the cable crane operation.

## 虎跳峡金沙江大桥
### Tiger Leaping Gorge Bridge over Jinsha River

| | |
|---|---|
| 桥　名： | 虎跳峡金沙江大桥 |
| 桥　型： | 单塔单跨吊悬索桥 |
| 主跨跨径： | 766m |
| 桥　址： | 云南省丽江市 |
| 建成时间： | 2021年2月 |
| 建设单位： | 云南省建设投资控股集团有限公司 |
| 设计单位： | 云南省交通规划设计研究院有限公司 |
| 施工单位： | 中铁大桥局集团第八工程有限公司 |

| | |
|---|---|
| **Name:** | Tiger Leaping Gorge Bridge over Jinsha River |
| **Type:** | Single-tower single-suspended-span suspension bridge |
| **Main Span:** | 766m |
| **Location:** | Lijiang City, Yunnan Province |
| **Completion:** | February, 2021 |
| **Owner(s):** | Yunnan Construction and Investment Holding Group Co., Ltd. |
| **Designer(s):** | Broadvision Engineering Consultants Co., Ltd. |
| **Contractor(s):** | The 8th Engineering Co., Ltd., MBEC |

虎跳峡金沙江大桥位于云南省虎跳峡景区内,在上虎跳上游跨越金沙江,是香丽高速公路连接香格里拉和丽江两岸的纽带,全长1.02km,设双向四车道。

虎跳峡金沙江大桥主桥为独塔单跨吊悬索桥,主跨跨径为766m。钢桁梁高6m,宽26m,标准节间长11.5m。主缆跨径为766m+160m,垂跨比1/10,采用127ϕ5.4mm预制平行钢丝索股,每根主缆97股,标准强度1770MPa,丽江岸设2根背索。吊索纵向间距11.5m,采用平行钢丝束索股。香格里拉岸有107m长的无吊索区,该区域内布置了2对地锚吊索。丽江岸桥塔采用钢筋混凝土门式框架结构,塔高137.3m,下部采用正方形承台加群桩基础。香格里拉岸采用隧道式锚碇,丽江岸采用重力式锚碇。大桥跨中设置3对柔性中央扣,并设梁端纵向阻尼器,减少了加劲梁纵向位移。加劲梁两端上、下弦杆横向共设8套横向抗风支座,下弦共设4套竖向支座,在索塔下横梁和加劲梁之间共设4套黏滞阻尼器。

虎跳峡金沙江大桥具有"跨径大、独塔单跨、高度非对称、塔梁分离"的特点,设计采用独塔单跨地锚式悬索桥结构和复合索鞍。对香格里拉岸塔-梁分离区主缆布置"钢拉杆+重力锚"的地锚式索鞍锚固系统,有效降低吊索应力幅。施工采用"缆索吊机跨江吊运+拽拉到滑移支架+横向顶推+门架提升、滑移+调整就位"组合技术,解决了山区高陡斜坡复合索鞍的运输及安装难题。

Tiger Leaping Gorge Bridge over Jinsha River is located in the scenic area of Tiger Leaping Gorge of Yunnan Province and crosses the Jinsha River in the upstream side of the Upper Tiger Leaping Gorge. The bridge is a key part of the Shangri-La- Lijiang Expressway that connects Shangri-La City and Lijiang City. The bridge has a total length of 1.02km and four traffic lanes in dual direction.

The main bridge of Tiger Leaping Gorge Bridge over Jinsha River is a single-tower single-suspended-span suspension bridge with a main span of 766m. The steel truss stiffening girder is 6m deep, 26m wide and the length of a standard segment is 11.5m. The span of the main cable is 766m+160m. The sag-to-span ratio is 1/10. Both main cables are prefabricated with 97 parallel wire bundles, and each bundle includes 127ϕ5.4mm steel wires with standard strength of 1770MPa; 2 back cables are set at the Lijiang side span. The hangers are also made of parallel steel wires, having a longitudinal spacing of 11.5m. 2 earth-anchored hangers are set in a 107m non-suspended area on the Shangri-La bank. The tower on the Lijiang bank is a portal frame reinforced concrete structure with a 137.3m height, supported by a group pile foundation with square pile caps. A tunnel-type anchorage is applied for the anchor block on the Shangri-La bank, and a gravity-type anchorage is applied for the anchor block on the Lijiang bank. 3 pairs of flexible central buckles are set in the mid-span, and longitudinal dampers at set at the ends of the girder to reduce the longitudinal displacement. 8 sets of transversal wind-resistance bearings are designed for the upper and lower chords at the ends of the girder; 4 sets of vertical bearings are designed for the lower chords; 4 sets of viscous dampers are installed between the lower crossbeam of the tower and the stiffening girder.

The main features of the bridge are:1) The bridge has the characteristics of "large span length, single tower with single span, asymmetric heights, tower-girder separation", and therefore was designed as a single-tower single-span earth-anchored suspension bridge with a composite cable saddle. 2) An anchorage system, which combines the steel tie and gravity-type anchorage, was designed for earth-anchored hangers in the tower-girder separation area on the Shangri-La bank, efficiently reducing the hanger stress amplitude. 3) Construction techniques, combining "cable crane lifting across the river, pulling to the sliding bracket, lateral pushing, gantry lifting and sliding-adjusting in place", were developed; the transportation and construction challenges for the composite cable saddle on high and steep slopes in mountainous areas have been addressed.

# 伍家岗长江大桥
## Wujiagang Bridge over Yangtze River

伍家岗长江大桥是位于湖北省宜昌市的越江通道,南侧为点军区艾家镇,北侧为伍家岗区,全长2.8km,设双向六车道。

伍家岗长江大桥主桥为双塔单跨吊悬索桥,主跨跨径1160m。钢箱梁宽34.7m,梁中心高2.8m。主缆跨径为209m+1160m+402m,垂跨比1/9,主缆采用新型复合索股,由85股127丝索股和6根91丝索股混合编缆形成,直径为714mm。吊索采用平行钢丝束索股。桥塔采用钢筋混凝土门式框架结构,两塔塔柱高度分别为157m、155m,桥塔下部采用分离式承台的大直径群桩基础。南岸采用浅埋式柔性扩大基础锚碇,北岸采用浅埋软岩隧道式锚碇。大桥加劲梁在主塔处设上、下游竖向拉压支座,横向抗风支座及纵向限位支座;加劲梁端部纵向与主塔间设液压阻尼器。

伍家岗长江大桥施工采用自主研发的整体式自适应智能顶升桥塔平台"造塔机",提升了桥塔施工安全性、质量与效率。钢箱梁节段采用"两两对接、焊架同步"新技术,实现吊装焊接同步,降低了施工成本,缩短了施工工期。

| | |
|---|---|
| 桥　名 | 伍家岗长江大桥 |
| 桥　型 | 双塔单跨吊悬索桥 |
| 主跨跨径 | 1160m |
| 桥　址 | 湖北省宜昌市 |
| 建成时间 | 2021年7月 |
| 建设单位 | 中建宜昌伍家岗大桥建设运营有限公司 |
| 设计单位 | 中铁大桥勘测设计院集团有限公司 |
| 施工单位 | 中交第二航务工程局有限公司、中国建筑第三工程局有限公司 |

Wujiagang Bridge over Yangtze River, located in Yichang City of Hubei Province, starts from Aijia Town of Dianjun District in the south and ends at Wujiagang District in the north. The bridge has a total length of 2.8km and six traffic lanes in dual direction.

The main bridge of Wujiagang Bridge over Yangtze River is a double-tower single-suspended-span suspension bridge with a main span of 1160m. The steel box stiffening girder is 34.7m wide and 2.8m deep. The span of the main cable is 209m+1160m+402m. The sag-to-span ratio is 1/9. The main cable adopts a new design of composite cable strands, formed by 85 bundles of 127 wire strands and 6 bundles of 91 wire strands. The diameter of the main cable is 714mm. The hangers are made of parallel wire strands. The towers are portal frame reinforced concrete structures. The heights of the two towers are 157m and 155m respectively, supported by group pile foundations with separated pile caps. The anchorage with a shallowly buried flexible spread foundation is used on the southern bank; the tunnel-type anchorage shallowly buried in soft rock is used on the northern bank. Vertical tension-resistant bearings in both upstream and downstream directions, together with transversal wind-resistant bearings and longitudinal displacement-limiting bearings, are set for the stiffening girder at the tower. Hydraulic dampers are set between the end of the stiffening girder and the tower.

The main features of the bridge are: 1) An adaptive intelligent holistic lifting-up tower-construction platform, "tower-building-machine", was developed, improving the construction safety, quality and efficiency. 2) A new technique, "alignment at both ends, welding and erection synchronously", was developed for the girder erection, achieving the synchronization between lifting and welding, reducing the construction cost and period.

**Name:** Wujiagang Bridge over Yangtze River
**Type:** Double-tower single-suspended-span suspension bridge
**Main Span:** 1160m
**Location:** Yichang City, Hubei Province
**Completion:** July, 2021
**Owner(s):** CSCEC Yichang Wujiagang Bridge Construction and Operation Co., Ltd.
**Designer(s):** China Railway Major Bridge Reconnaissance & Design Institute Co., Ltd.
**Contractor(s):** CCCC Second Harbor Engineering Co., Ltd. and China Construction Third Engineering Bureau Group Co., Ltd.

# 瓮开高速公路开州湖大桥
## Weng'an-Kaiyang Expressway Bridge over Kaizhou Lake

瓮开高速公路开州湖大桥位于贵州省贵阳市开阳县境内，横跨洛旺河峡谷，连接瓮安县和开阳县两岸，全长 1.26km，设双向四车道。

瓮开高速公路开州湖大桥主桥为双塔单跨吊悬索桥，主跨跨径1100m。采用板桁组合结构形式的加劲梁，主桁为带竖杆的华伦式桁架，桁高7.2m，标准节间长7.2m，两片主桁中心间距27m。主缆跨径为302m+1100m+143m，垂跨比1/10，采用91∅5.3mm预制平行钢丝索股，每根主缆173股，标准强度1860MPa。吊索采用103∅5.0mm镀锌铝合金高强钢丝，标准强度1860MPa。桥塔采用钢筋混凝土门式框架结构，瓮安岸塔柱高139m，开阳岸塔柱高141m，两塔柱均设两道横梁，主塔承台采用左右分离的基础形式。瓮安岸采用重力锚，开阳岸采用隧道锚。

瓮开高速公路开州湖大桥采用了新型分体式散索鞍设计，降低了散索鞍运输重量，克服了山区崎岖道路环境下索鞍运输困难的问题。大桥开阳岸堆积体覆盖范围较广，施工中对坡体采取抗滑桩、局部清方、锚索等综合防护措施。针对桩孔爆破作业、隧道锚与接线隧道协同施工展开了专项施工技术研究，保障了工程安全与质量。

Weng'an-Kaiyang Expressway Bridge over Kaizhou Lake, located in Kaiyang County of Guiyang City of Guizhou Province, connects Weng'an County and Kaiyang County by crossing the Luowang River Gorge. The bridge has a total length of 1.26km and four traffic lanes in dual direction.

The main bridge of Weng'an-Kaiyang Expressway Bridge over Kaizhou Lake is a double-tower single-suspended-span suspension bridge with a main span length of 1100m. The plate-truss composite stiffening girder is applied. The Warren truss is 7.2m deep and has a standard segment length of 7.2m. The distance between the center lines of the two main trusses is 27m. The span of the main cable is 302m+1100m+143m. The sag-to-span ratio is 1/10. Both main cables are prefabricated with 173 parallel wire bundles, and each bundle includes 91∅5.3mm steel wires with standard strength of 1860MPa. The hangers are made of 103∅5.0mm steel wires with zinc aluminum alloy coating and 1860MPa standard strength. The towers are portal frame reinforced concrete structures. The heights of the tower near the Weng'an and the one near the Kaiyang are 139m and 141m, respectively. Each tower is equipped with two crossbeams and two tower legs are supported by separated foundations. A gravity-type anchorage and a tunnel-type anchorage are used for the anchor blocks on the Weng'an bank and Kaiyang bank, respectively.

The main features of the bridge are: 1) A new type of separated splay saddle was designed and applied, reducing the transportation weight and addressing the problems of splay saddle transportation in mountainous and rugged roads. 2) Due to the relatively wide area of accumulation on the Kaiyang bank, the anti-sliding piles, partial earthwork clearance, and anchor cables were used for slope supporting during the construction. 3) Construction techniques have been specially studied for the pile hole blasting, the collaborative construction of the tunnel-type anchorage and the linking tunnel, guaranteeing the safety and quality of the project.

| | |
|---|---|
| 桥　名： | 瓮开高速公路开州湖大桥 |
| 桥　型： | 双塔单跨吊悬索桥 |
| 主跨跨径： | 1100m |
| 桥　址： | 贵州省贵阳市 |
| 建成时间： | 2021年12月 |
| 建设单位： | 贵州中交贵瓮高速公路有限公司 |
| 设计单位： | 贵州省交通规划勘察设计研究院股份有限公司 |
| 施工单位： | 中铁广州工程局集团有限公司、<br>贵州省公路工程集团有限公司 |

**Name:** Weng'an-Kaiyang Expressway Bridge over Kaizhou Lake
**Type:** Double-tower single-suspended-span suspension bridge
**Main Span:** 1100m
**Location:** Guiyang City, Guizhou Province
**Completion:** December, 2021
**Owner(s):** Guizhou CCCC Guiweng Highway Co., Ltd.
**Designer(s):** Guizhou Transportation Planning Survey and Design Academe Co., Ltd.
**Contractor(s):** China Railway Guangzhou Engineering Group Co., Ltd. and Guizhou Highway Engineering Group Co., Ltd.

# 凤凰黄河大桥
## Fenghuang Bridge over Yellow River

| | |
|---|---|
| 桥　名： | 凤凰黄河大桥 |
| 桥　型： | 三塔六跨自锚式悬索桥 |
| 主跨跨径： | 2×428m |
| 桥　址： | 山东省济南市 |
| 建成时间： | 2022年1月 |
| 建设单位： | 济南城市建设集团有限公司 |
| 设计单位： | 上海市政工程设计研究总院（集团）有限公司 |
| 施工单位： | 中交第二航务工程局有限公司、中铁十二局集团有限公司 |

**Name:** Fenghuang Bridge over Yellow River
**Type:** Three-tower six-span self-anchored suspension bridge
**Main Span:** 2×428m
**Location:** Ji'nan City, Shandong Province
**Completion:** January, 2022
**Owner(s):** Ji'nan City Construction Group Co., Ltd.
**Designer(s):** Shanghai Municipal Engineering Design Institute (Group) Co., Ltd.
**Contractor(s):** CCCC Second Harbor Engineering Co., Ltd. and China Railway 12th Bureau Group Co., Ltd.

凤凰黄河大桥位于山东省济南市境内，跨越黄河连接济阳区和历城区，全长6.66km，设双向八车道。

凤凰黄河大桥主桥为三塔六跨空间索面自锚式悬索桥，主跨跨径2×428m。组合梁宽61.7m、中心梁高4m，采用正交异性组合桥面板。主缆跨径为171.5m+428m+428m+171.5m，中跨垂跨比1/6.15，边跨垂跨比1/15.6，采用127Φ6.2mm预制平行钢丝索股，每根主缆61股，标准强度1960MPa。吊索标准纵向间距9m，采用平行钢丝束索股。桥塔采用上部钢结构、下部钢-混凝土组合结构，中塔塔高126m，边塔塔高116.1m，桥塔下部采用钻孔灌注桩基础，桩直径2m，桩长100m。大桥主梁在桥塔、边墩处设竖向支座和横向钢阻尼器，并在桥塔处设纵向液体黏滞阻尼器。

北侧跨大堤引桥采用变高度组合梁桥，跨径布置为154m+245m+154m。组合梁采用正交异性组合桥面板，高从墩顶处的10m过渡到跨中的4.8m，桥面宽从54m过渡至61.7m。墩柱采用多边形截面空心墩，矩形承台，钻孔灌注桩基础。

凤凰黄河大桥主桥设计采用上部钢结构、下部钢-混凝土组合结构的A形塔柱，协调优化了结构刚度和主缆抗滑系数的要求，并设置刚性三角桁架中央扣，改善桥塔受力。采用超宽闭口钢箱梁，允许交通同层布置，降低了接线道路布置的难度；在机动车道及缆吊区铺设纤维钢筋混凝土桥面板，改善了箱梁受力性能，提高了结构耐久性。通过钢箱梁大节段工厂化制造、智能化运输及提升、信息化多点步履式顶推等施工方式，解决了不通航水域条件下的施工难题。

Fenghuang Bridge over Yellow River, located in Ji'nan City of Shandong Province, connects Jiyang District and Licheng District by crossing the Yellow River. The bridge has a total length of 6.66km and eight traffic lanes in dual direction.

The main bridge of Fenghuang Bridge over Yellow River is a three-tower six-span self-anchored suspension bridge with a spatial cable system and main span lengths of 2×428m. The composite girder is designed with a 61.7m width and a 4m central depth. The ortho-composite slab is applied in the deck system. The span of the main cable

is 171.5m+428m+428m+171.5m. The sag-to-main-span ratio and sag-to-side-span ratio are 1/6.15 and 1/15.6, respectively. Both main cables are prefabricated with 61 parallel wire bundles, and each bundle includes 127 $\phi$ 6.2mm steel wires with standard strength of 1960MPa. The hangers are also made of parallel wire bundles, and the longitudinal standard spacing between hangers is 9m. The upper part of the tower is made of steel and the lower part of the tower is made of steel-concrete. The heights of the middle tower and side tower are 126m and 116.1m, respectively. The towers are supported by bored piles with 2m diameters and 100m lengths. Vertical bearings and transversal steel dampers are set for the girder at the middle tower and at the side towers, respectively. In addition, longitudinal viscous dampers are set for the main girder at the towers.

The approach bridge crossing the northern levee is designed as a composite girder bridge with variable heights. The span arrangement is 154m+245m+154m. The composite girder adopts ortho-composite slabs. The height of the girder transitions from 10m at the top of the pier to 4.8m in the mid-span, and the width transitions from 54m to 61.7m. The piers are designed as polygon hollow concrete structures, supported by bored piles with rectangular pile caps.

The main features of the bridge are: 1) The A-shaped tower was designed as steel structures at the upper part and steel-concrete composite structures at the lower part; the bridge stiffness and the anti-slip performance of the main cable have been compatibly optimized; a rigid triangular-truss central buckle was set to further improve the mechanical condition of the tower. 2) The bridge adopts an ultra-wide steel-box girder that allows the highway and railway to be arranged on the same deck level, easing the arrangement of approach bridges. The fiber-concrete layer was applied at the traffic lanes and cable-hanging area of the deck, improving the mechanical performance and durability of the girder. 3) Through combing the factory fabrication, intelligent transportation, multi-point walking-pedrail incremental launching and etc., the construction challenge incurred by unnavigable conditions has been addressed.

# 瓯江北口大桥
## Beikou Bridge over Ou River

瓯江北口大桥位于温州市境内瓯江北汊入海口，上层高速公路起于黄华镇、止于灵昆岛，接甬台温高速公路，全长7.9km；下层一级公路北接国道G228线乐清段、南连国道G228线灵昆段，全长3.9km；均设双向六车道。

瓯江北口大桥主桥为三塔四跨吊索桥，主跨跨径2×800m。加劲梁采用板桁组合钢桁架，主桁采用华伦式结构，桁高12.5m，标准节间长10m，两片主桁中心间距36.2m。主缆跨径为230m+800m+800m+348m，垂跨比1/10，采用127φ5.4mm预制平行钢丝索股，每根主缆169股，标准强度1860MPa。吊索纵向间距10m，采用平行钢丝束索股。中塔采用A型混凝土中塔、沉井基础，塔高145.5m；南、北塔采用混凝土门式塔、钻孔灌注桩基础，塔高分别为143.5m和147.5m。南、北锚均采用重力锚。大桥加劲梁在边塔设置纵向黏滞阻尼器，桥塔及边墩处置竖向支座，加劲梁上、下弦节点与塔柱间设置横向抗风支座。

瓯江北口大桥在多塔连跨悬索桥中采用刚性的混凝土中塔以提高结构刚度，并在中塔塔顶鞍内设置多个摩擦板，增加接触面积，从而解决了中塔鞍内主缆抗滑移问题。采用板桁组合加劲梁，提出了"缆载吊机+分体式液压提升"架设方法及"缆载吊机荡移卸船+滑移系统"工艺，解决了跨中缆梁相交段吊装及边跨加劲梁转运的难题。针对大桥中塔基础所受弯矩大、船撞力大及基岩埋深大的特点，中塔采用防撞能力强、刚度大、经济性更优的倒圆角矩形沉井基础，形成了成套施工技术。

Beikou Bridge over Ou River is located in the north branch estuary of Ou River in Wenzhou City. The expressway on the upper level of the deck starts from Huanghua Town and ends at Lingkun Island, connecting the Ningbo-Taizhou-Wenzhou Expressway and having a total length of 7.9km. The first-class highway on the lower level of the deck starts from the Yueqing section of the G228 national highway in the north and ends at the Lingkun section of the G228 national highway in the south, having a total length of 3.9km. Six traffic lanes in dual direction are set for both the expressway and first-class highway.

The main bridge of Beikou Bridge over Ou River is a three-tower four-suspended-span suspension bridge with

main spans of 2×800m. The plate-truss composite steel stiffening girder is applied. The Warren truss is 12.5m deep and has a standard segment length of 10m. The distance between the center lines of the two main trusses is 36.2m. The span of the main cable is 230m+800m+800m+348m. The sag-to-span ratio is 1/10. Both main cables are prefabricated with 169 parallel wire bundles, and each bundle includes 127 $\phi$ 5.4mm steel wires with standard strength of 1860MPa. The hangers are also made of parallel wire bundles, and the longitudinal spacing between hangers is 10m. The A-shaped concrete middle tower is 145.5m high and supported by a caisson foundation. The northern and southern towers are portal frame reinforced concrete structures supported by bored piles, with 143.5m and 147.5m heights, respectively. Gravity-type anchorages are used for both the northern and southern banks. Longitudinal viscous dampers are set for the girder at the side towers; vertical bearings are set for the girder at the towers and piers; transversal wind-resistant bearings are set between the upper, lower chords and the towers.

The main features of the bridge are: 1) A rigid concrete middle tower was designed to enhance the structural stiffness; multiple friction plates were set inside the saddle on the middle tower to increase the contact area, therefore addressing the anti-slip problem for the main cable crossing the saddle on the middle tower. 2) The plate-truss composite girder was applied. An erection method that uses cable cranes and separated hydraulic synchronous lifting has been developed to address the girder erection problem in the middle span where the main cable is under the upper deck level; a construction technique that combines the swing-unloading and the skid-steer system has been developed to address the girder transporting problem in the side span. 3) Based on the feature that the foundation of the middle tower is subjected to large bending moments, large ship collision forces and has deep bedrock, the middle tower adopts the chamfered rectangular open caisson foundation, which has a better anti-collision ability, higher stiffness and better economic performance; a complete set of construction techniques have been developed.

| | |
|---|---|
| 桥　名： | 瓯江北口大桥 |
| 桥　型： | 三塔四跨吊悬索桥 |
| 主跨跨径： | 2×800m |
| 桥　址： | 浙江省温州市 |
| 建成时间： | 2022年5月 |
| 建设单位： | 温州瓯江口大桥有限公司 |
| 设计单位： | 浙江省交通规划设计研究院有限公司（现更名为浙江数智交院科技股份有限公司）、中铁大桥勘测设计院集团有限公司 |
| 施工单位： | 中铁大桥局集团有限公司、中交一公局集团有限公司、中交第二航务工程局有限公司 |

**Name:** Beikou Bridge over Ou River
**Type:** Three-tower four-suspended-span suspension bridge
**Main Span:** 2×800m
**Location:** Wenzhou City, Zhejiang Province
**Completion:** May, 2022
**Owner(s):** Wenzhou Oujiangkou Bridge Co., Ltd.
**Designer(s):** Zhejiang Institute of Communications Co.,Ltd. and China Railway Major Bridge Reconnaissance & Design Institute Co., Ltd.
**Contractor(s):** China Railway Major Bridge Engineering Group Co., Ltd., CCCC First Highway Engineering Group Co.,Ltd. and CCCC Second Harbor Engineering Co., Ltd.

# 仙新路长江大桥
## Xianxin Road Bridge over Yangtze River

| | |
|---|---|
| 桥　　名：仙新路长江大桥 | **Name:** Xianxin Road Bridge over Yangtze River |
| 桥　　型：双塔单跨吊悬索桥 | **Type:** Double-tower single-suspended-span suspension bridge |
| 主跨跨径：1760m | **Main Span:** 1760m |
| 桥　　址：江苏省南京市 | **Location:** Nanjing City, Jiangsu Province |
| 建成时间：2023年12月 | **Completion:** December, 2023 |
| 建设单位：南京市公共工程建设中心 | **Owner(s):** Nanjing Public Works Construction Center |
| 设计单位：中铁大桥勘测设计院集团有限公司 | **Designer(s):** China Railway Major Bridge Reconnaissance & Design Institute Co., Ltd. |
| 施工单位：中交第二航务工程局有限公司、中交路桥建设有限公司、中交第二公路工程局有限公司、中铁大桥局集团有限公司 | **Contractor(s):** CCCC Second Harbor Engineering Co., Ltd., CCCC Road & Bridge International Co., Ltd., CCCC Second Highway Engineering Co., Ltd. and China Railway Major Bridge Engineering Group Co., Ltd. |

仙新路长江大桥是江苏省南京市境内跨越长江连接南北城区的重要纽带，南起栖霞区仙新路，北止江北新区，全长13.5km，设双向六车道。

仙新路长江大桥主桥为双塔单跨吊悬索桥，主跨跨径1760m。钢箱梁宽31.5m，中心梁高4m。主缆跨径为580m+1760m+580m，垂跨比1/9，横向间距27.7m。桥塔采用混凝土塔，塔柱高267.3m。主桥加劲梁采用单跨吊形式，两端支承采用单跨双铰简支体系。加劲梁在两主塔下横梁处设置竖向支座，约束主塔处加劲梁的竖向位移；在两侧设置横向抗风支座；设置纵向阻尼器和纵向限位结构，减小伸缩装置的伸缩量。

仙新路长江大桥主缆采用强度等级2100MPa的高强钢丝。大桥开展超大跨度悬索桥锚碇基础-土体受力作用机理研究；考虑土体抗力进行锚碇基础设计，减小了锚碇基础规模。大桥南锚碇地连墙基础基坑开挖深度达57m，采用内外双层双轮铣削式水泥土搅拌墙技术（SMC工法）进行槽壁加固，应用"塔式起重机吊装+新型防离析导管+混凝土泵车"的组合混凝土浇筑施工工艺；北锚碇沉井基础长70m、宽50m、深50m，距离西坝港区铁路专用线仅116m，下沉过程穿过厚度达3.7m的胶结卵砾石层。

Xianxin Road Bridge over Yangtze River, located in Nanjing City of Jiangsu Province, starts from Xianxin Road of Qixia District in the south and ends at Jiangbei New District in the north. The bridge has a total length of 13.5km and six traffic lanes in dual direction.

The main bridge of Xianxin Road Bridge over Yangtze River is a double-tower single-suspended-span suspension bridge with a main span length of 1760m. The steel box girder is designed with a 31.5m width and a 4m central depth. The span of the main cable is 580m+1760m+580m. The sag-to-span ratio is 1/9 and the transversal spacing between two main cables is 27.7m. The towers are concrete structures with heights of 267.3m. The bridge adopts a single-suspended-span stiffening girder simply supported at two ends. Vertical bearings are set for the stiffening girder at the tower crossbeams to constrain the vertical displacement; transversal wind-resistant bearings are set at two ends; longitudinal dampers and displacement-limiting devices are set for reducing the wear of expansion devices.

The main features of the bridge are: 1) The main cables are made of steel wires with 2100MPa standard strength. 2) The mechanical performance and mechanism for the anchorage foundation and the soil mass were studied. The anchorage foundation has been designed considering the resistance from the soil, therefore reducing the foundation size. 3) The diaphragm wall foundation for the southern anchorage is 57m deep; the internal-external soil mixing cutting (SMC) construction method was used for strengthening the wall, and the tower crane hoisting cooperated with a new type of anti-segregation catheter and concrete pump trucks were used for pouring the concrete. The sunk shaft foundation for the northern anchorage is 70m long, 50m wide and 50m deep, with only a 116m distance to the railroad in Xiba Port District, and has penetrated a 3.7m thick layer of colluvial pebbles.

# 钦州龙门大桥

## Qinzhou Longmen Bridge

钦州龙门大桥跨越钦州湾北部的茅尾海，连接钦州市钦南区与钦州港区，全长6.6km，设双向六车道。

钦州龙门大桥主桥为双塔单跨吊悬索桥，主跨跨径1098m。钢箱梁高3.2m，桥面宽38.6m。主缆跨径为251m+1098m+251m，垂跨比1/10，采用127ϕ5.25mm预制平行钢丝索股，每根主缆127股，标准强度1860MPa。吊索纵向间距12.8m，采用平行钢丝束索股。东、西岸均采用重力式锚碇。桥塔采用钢筋混凝土门式框架结构，两塔柱高均为174m。钦州龙门大桥加劲梁在索塔位置采用全漂浮结构体系，过渡墩处设置竖向支座、横向抗风支座、纵向阻尼装置。

钦州龙门大桥钢箱梁采用紊流制振机理的新型钢箱梁断面，可以满足100m/s颤振临界风速的要求，并具有良好的抑制涡振性能。采用"S形钢丝+干燥空气除湿"的主动式主缆防护措施，确保主缆耐久性能。大桥锚碇基础采用大直径桩基+铣接头方案，结构整体性更强，提高了基坑开挖速度，止水效果更优。

| | |
|---|---|
| 桥　　名： | 钦州龙门大桥 |
| 桥　　型： | 双塔单跨吊悬索桥 |
| 主跨跨径： | 1098m |
| 桥　　址： | 广西壮族自治区钦州市 |
| 建成时间： | 2023年12月 |
| 建设单位： | 广西交通投资集团有限公司 |
| 设计单位： | 中交公路规划设计院有限公司、广西交通设计集团有限公司 |
| 施工单位： | 中交路桥建设有限公司、广西路桥工程集团有限公司 |

**Name:** Qinzhou Longmen Bridge
**Type:** Double-tower single-suspended-span suspension bridge
**Main Span:** 1098m
**Location:** Qinzhou City, Guangxi Zhuang Autonomous Region
**Completion:** December, 2023
**Owner(s):** Guangxi Communications Investment Group Co., Ltd.
**Designer(s):** CCCC Highway Consultants Co., Ltd. and Guangxi Communications Design Group Co., Ltd.
**Contractor(s):** CCCC Road & Bridge International Co., Ltd. and Guangxi Road and Bridge Engineering Group Co., Ltd.

Qinzhou Longmen Bridge, crossing Maowei Sea in the north of Qinzhou Bay, connects Qinan District and Qinzhou Port District of Qinzhou City. The bridge has a total length of 6.6km and six traffic lanes in dual direction.

The main bridge of Qinzhou Longmen Bridge is a double-tower single-suspended-span suspension bridge with a main span of 1098m. The steel box stiffening girder is 3.2m deep and 38.6m wide. The span of the main cable is 251m+1098m+251m. The sag-to-span ratio is 1/10. Both main cables are prefabricated with 127 parallel wire bundles, and each bundle includes 127 $\phi$ 5.25mm steel wires with standard strength of 1860MPa. The hanger is made of parallel steel wires, having a longitudinal spacing of 12.8m. Gravity-type anchorages are used for both anchor blocks. The towers are portal frame reinforced concrete structures. The heights of the towers are both 174m. The bridge adopts a full-floating structural system; vertical bearings, transversal bearings and longitudinal dampers are set at the transition piers.

The main features of the bridge are: 1) A new type of steel-box girder section considering the mechanism of turbulence-induced vibration has been adopted; 100m/s critical flutter wind speed can be satisfied, also providing good performance for vortex-induced vibration suppression. 2) The main cable has been actively protected by the measures of S-shaped steel-wire wrapping together with air dehumidification, ensuring the durability of the main cable. 3) The anchorage adopts the large-diameter-pile foundation with milling joins; the structural integrity is better, also improving the excavation speed and providing better waterproofing effects.

中国桥梁　BRIDGES IN CHINA　2013—2023

# Chapter 3

## 第三篇

# 斜拉桥

## Cable-stayed Bridges

# 引言

以悬索桥为代表的索承重桥梁形式起源于我国东周，距今已有2300多年的历史，而斜拉索支承桥梁的概念仅有400多年的历史，起源于欧洲文艺复兴时期。现代斜拉桥主要得益于德国和意大利工程师的开创性工作。1955年建成的瑞典Strömsund桥被公认为第一座现代斜拉桥，主跨跨度183m。由于斜拉桥良好的跨越能力，在诞生后的前5年，跨度就迅速突破300m，20世纪60年代，斜拉桥跨度始终徘徊在300m到400m。随后，现代斜拉桥的建设活动开始遍及世界各地，其中法国和日本对现代斜拉桥的发展特别是跨度的拓展起到了积极的推动作用。20世纪70年代，法国和日本相继使斜拉桥的跨度突破400m，到了20世纪90年代，又推动斜拉桥跨度突破800m。俄罗斯斜拉桥的建设起步稍晚，但是，在独塔斜拉桥建设方面独树一帜，先后建成了两座跨度超过400m的独塔斜拉桥，2012年，建成了连接Russky岛的两座超大跨度斜拉桥——1104m的Russky大桥和737m的Zolotoy大桥，前者创造并保持着斜拉桥跨度的世界纪录。

我国斜拉桥技术研发和建设始于20世纪70年代。1982年，建成了上海泖港大桥，主跨跨度达到了200m。1991年，自主建成了主跨跨度423m的钢-混凝土组合梁斜拉桥——上海南浦大桥，居当时世界斜拉桥跨度第三。1993年，建成了跨度602m的上海杨浦大桥，创造了斜拉桥跨度的世界纪录。21世纪初，我国一步一个脚印，将斜拉桥的跨度推进到628m（南京八卦洲长江大桥）和648m（南京大胜关长江大桥），并且在2008年，再次创造了斜拉桥跨度的世界纪录，建成了跨度1088m的苏通长江公路大桥。2009年和2010年又相继建成了跨度1018m的香港昂船洲大桥和跨度926m的鄂东长江大桥。截至2022年，在全世界已经建成的84座跨度超过500m的斜拉桥中，我国有64座，约占四分之三，我国已经成为名副其实的大跨度斜拉桥建设大国。

近10年来，我国建成了近200座斜拉桥，包括独塔斜拉桥、双塔斜拉桥和三塔斜拉桥等。本画册选取了27座斜拉桥，包括1座独塔斜拉桥、24座双塔斜拉桥和2座三塔斜拉桥。相比《中国桥梁 2003—2013》，入选斜拉桥的跨度有所增长，其中，公铁两用斜拉桥的跨度提高到了1092m，在建的还有跨度1160m的观音寺长江大桥、1176m的常泰长江大桥和2×1120m三塔双主跨的马鞍山公铁两用长江大桥等破跨度纪录的斜拉桥。为了提高斜拉桥连续跨越能力，双主跨或多主跨斜拉桥数量显著增长、跨度不断突破。斜拉桥主要受力构件大量采用新材料和新材料组合。其中，1860MPa和1960MPa的高强钢丝提高了斜拉索强度，轻质粗集料活性粉末混凝土优化了混凝土桥面板厚度并降低了组合梁自重，钢壳-混凝土组合索塔技术不仅提升了施工质量，而且增强了耐久性、降低了成本。斜拉桥正展现出比悬索桥更突出的优点和自身发展的广阔空间。

# INTRODUCTION

Although cable suppoted bridges represented by suspension bridges originated in the Eastern Zhou Dynasty of China and has a history of more than 2,300 years, the concept of cable-stayed bridges was traced back to the European Renaissance and is thus only a little more than 400 years old. Modern cable-stayed bridges have their roots in the pioneering work of German and Italian engineers. The first modern cable-stayed bridge is recognized to be the Swedish Strömsund Bridge, built in 1955, which has a main span of 183m. The high efficiency of the structural system made cable-stayed bridges well suited for long spans. The record span for cable-stayed bridges thus increased quickly, reaching 300m only five years later. In the 1960s, spans were commonly built in the 300m to 400m range. Following this, the construction of modern cable-stayed bridges spread throughout the world. In these years, France and Japan played an active role in promoting the development of modern cable-stayed bridges, especially extending the span range of the system. In the 1970s, both countries constructed cable-stayed bridges with spans in excess of 400m. In the 1990s, the span of cable-stayed bridges exceeded 800m. Although the construction of cable-stayed bridges in Russia started later, Russian engineers developed high-level technology in the construction of single-tower cable-stayed bridges, resulting in the construction of two single-tower cable-stayed bridges with a span of more than 400m. In 2012, they built two ultra-long-span cable-stayed bridges, the Russky Bridge with a main span of 1104m and the Zolotoy Bridge with a main span of 737m. The Russky Bridge currently holds the world record for the span of cable-stayed bridges.

Research and development of cable-stayed bridge technology in China began in the 1970s. In 1982, the 200m main span of the Shanghai Maogang Bridge was completed. In 1991, the Shanghai Nanpu Bridge, a cable-stayed bridge with a composite steel-concrete girder, was independently built with a main span of 423m, giving it the third longest main span in the world. In 1993, the 602m Shanghai Yangpu Bridge was built, setting a world record for the span of a cable-stayed bridge. At the beginning of the 21st century, step by step, the span of the cable-stayed bridges was pushed to 628m by the Nanjing Baguazhou Bridge over the Yangtze River and then to 648m by the Nanjing Dashengguan Highway Bridge over the Yangtze River. In 2008, the 1088m Sutong Bridge over the Yangtze River set a new world record for the span. This was followed in 2009 by the 1018m Stonecutters Bridge in Hong Kong and in 2010 by the 926m Edong Bridge over the Yangtze River. By 2022, among the 84 cable-stayed bridges with a span of more than 500m that have been built in the world, China has 64, accounting for three quarters. China has become a leader in the construction of long-span cable-stayed bridges.

In the past 10 years, China has built nearly 200 cable-stayed bridges, including bridges with single-tower, double-tower and multiple-towers. This album includes 27 cable-stayed bridges, consisting of one single-tower bridge, twenty-four double-tower bridges and two triple-tower bridges. The main span lengths of the cable-stayed bridges included in this album show increases compared with the ones in the previous edition. This group includes a highway and railway cable-stayed bridge with main span of 1092m, as well as several long spans currently under construction: the 1160m span of the Guanyin Temple Bridge over the Yangtze River, the 1176m Changzhou-Taixing Bridge over the Yangtze River, and the Ma'anshan Bridge over the Yangtze River with two spans of 1120m. In order to increase the span, the number of double main span or multiple main span cable-stayed bridges has increased significantly. New materials are increasingly used for the main load-carrying components. Cables now use 1860MPa and 1960MPa high-strength steel wire. Ultra high-performance concrete optimizes the thickness of concrete bridge decks and reduces the self-weight of composite girders. Steel-shell-concrete tower technology not only improves construction quality but also enhances durability and reduces costs. Cable-stayed bridges are showing outstanding advantages over suspension bridges and still hold clear potential for further development.

# 长沙西北上行联络线特大桥
## Changsha Northwest Uplink Connecting Line Bridge

长沙西北上行联络线特大桥位于湖南省长沙市雨花区，为沪昆高铁长沙南枢纽的重要节点。该桥跨越京广高铁，全长1.887km。

大桥为独塔双索面混凝土斜拉桥，塔梁墩固结体系，跨径布置为32m+80m+112m。主梁为预应力混凝土非对称槽形梁；采用A形钢筋混凝土主塔，塔高73.9m。

在建设过程中，采用塔梁墩固结体系及四柱式下塔柱结构设计，增加了塔墩横向和纵向刚度，改善了结构受力性能，降低了转体重量，减小了桥梁规模。为避免对运营中的京广高铁造成影响，采用水平转体法施工，转体梁段长196m、重14500t，转体角度为21°；梁采用转体后直接上墩随即形成稳定结构体系的方案，取消了传统工艺中转体后合龙段现浇施工的环节，大大降低了施工安全风险、缩短了施工周期。研发了针对铁路成品索的哈弗式磁通量索力监测技术，解决了既有桥梁拉索运营期索力长效监测的问题。

桥　　名：长沙西北上行联络线特大桥
桥　　型：独塔双索面混凝土斜拉桥，塔梁墩固结体系
主跨跨径：112m
桥　　址：湖南省长沙市
建成时间：2013年7月
建设单位：沪昆铁路客运专线湖南有限责任公司
设计单位：中铁第四勘察设计院集团有限公司
施工单位：中铁三局集团桥隧工程有限公司

**Name:** Changsha Northwest Uplink Connecting Line Bridge
**Type:** Single-tower double-cable plane concrete cable-stayed bridge, tower-beam-pier consolidation system
**Main Span:** 112m
**Location:** Changsha City, Hunan Province
**Completion:** July, 2013
**Owner(s):** Shanghai-Kunming Railway Passenger Line Hunan Co., Ltd.
**Designer(s):** China Railway Siyuan Survey and Design Group Co., Ltd.
**Contractor(s):** Bridge & Tunnel Engineering Company of the Third Engineering Group Co.,Ltd. of China Railway

Located in Yuhua District, Changsha City, Hunan Province, Changsha Northwest Uplink Connecting Line Bridge is an important node project of Changsha South Hub of Shanghai-Kunming High-speed Railway. The bridge spans the Beijing-Guangzhou High-speed Railway with a total length of 1.887km.

The bridge is a single-tower double-cable plane concrete cable-stayed bridge, with a tower-beam-pier consolidation system, and a span arrangement of 32m+80m+112m. The main beam is a prestressed concrete asymmetric channel beam. The A-shaped reinforced concrete tower is adopted with a height of 73.9m.

In the construction process, the tower beam pier consolidation system and four-column lower tower column structure design are adopted to increase the horizontal and vertical stiffness of the tower pier, improve the mechanical performance of the structure, reduce the swivel weight and the bridge scale. In order to avoid the impact on the Beijing-Guangzhou High-speed Railway in operation, the horizontal swivel method is used for construction. The length of the swivel beam section is 196m, the weight is 14500t, and the swivel angle is 21°. The scheme that the beam is directly mounted on the pier after being rotated to form a stable structural system eliminates the cast-in-situ construction of the closure section after being rotated in the traditional process, greatly reducing the construction safety risk and shortening the construction period. The Haval-type magnetic flux cable force monitoring technology for railway cables has been developed to solve the problem of long-term monitoring of cable force during the operation.

# 琅岐闽江大桥
## Langqi Bridge over Min River

琅岐闽江大桥位于福州市马尾区亭江镇和琅岐岛之间,跨越闽江入海口,是马尾区连接琅岐岛的重要通道。桥面为双向六车道城市主干道,设计速度60km/h,桥下可通航3万吨级海轮。

大桥由主桥、引桥及各立交匝道组成,主桥呈西北至东南方向布置。主桥为双塔双索面钢箱梁斜拉桥,半漂浮结构体系,跨径布置为60m+90m+150m+680m+150m+90m+60m。主梁截面形式采用单箱多室流线型扁平钢箱梁。塔柱采用钻石形钢筋混凝土结构,塔高223m。斜拉索为扇形平行空间索面,每索面布置21对拉索。基础采用钻孔灌注桩。

大桥布置和构件形式避免了主梁架设需要搭设高支架的风险,节省了施工材料,钢箱梁架设快,在多台风地区可合理避开台风期,保证架梁安全。主梁采用流线型扁平钢箱梁,截面倾角采用1:4(约14°),抗风性能优。基础防撞结构采用新型复合材料,可抗3万吨级船舶的撞击。针对岩面起伏较大的特点,采用旋挖钻机成孔,伸入承台的钢护筒呈锯齿板状,便于与承台连接。基础承台采用单壁钢吊箱围堰法施工。

Langqi Bridge over Min River is located between Tingjiang Town of Mawei District and Langqi Island in Fuzhou City. It crosses the estuary of Min River and is an important channel connecting Mawei District to Langqi Island. The bridge has six lanes in dual direction with a design speed of 60km/h, and a 30000-ton sea vessel can sail under the bridge.

The bridge is composed of the main bridge, approach bridge and interchange ramp. The main bridge is in the direction of northwest to southeast. The main bridge is a double-tower cable-stayed bridge with double cable planes and a steel box girder. It is a semi-floating structural system with a span arrangement of 60m+90m+150m+680m+150m+90m+60m. The main beam section adopts multi-chamber single-box streamlined flat steel box form. The tower is diamond-shaped reinforced concrete structure, and is 223m in height. The cable is in a fan-shaped parallel space plane, and 21 pairs of cables are arranged on each plane. The foundation adopts bored piles.

The layout and component form of the bridge avoid the risk of the main beam erection of high falsework, saving construction materials, making erection fast, reasonably avoiding typhoon period in the multi typhoon area, and ensuring the safety of the beam. The main beam is a streamlined flat steel box girder, and the section inclination angle is 1 : 4 (about 14°), with excellent wind resistance. The anti-collision structure of foundation is made of new composite materials, which can resist the impact of 30000-ton ships. In view of the characteristic of large rock surface undulation, the rotary drilling rig is used, and the steel casings extending into the cap is in the shape of sawtooth plate, which is convenient to connect with the cap. The foundation cap is constructed by single-wall steel box cofferdam.

桥　　名： 琅岐闽江大桥
桥　　型： 双塔双索面钢箱梁斜拉桥，半漂浮结构体系
主跨跨径： 680m
桥　　址： 福建省福州市
建成时间： 2014 年 1 月
建设单位： 福州市琅岐路桥建设有限公司
设计单位： 中铁大桥勘测设计院集团有限公司
施工单位： 中铁大桥局集团有限公司、中交第二航务工程局有限公司等

**Name:** Langqi Bridge over Min River
**Type:** Double-tower double-cable plane steel box girder cable-stayed bridge, semi-floating structural system
**Main Span:** 680m
**Location:** Fuzhou City, Fujian Province
**Completion:** January, 2014
**Owner(s):** Fuzhou Langqi Road and Bridge Construction Co., Ltd.
**Designer(s):** China Railway Major Bridge Reconnaissance & Design Institute Co., Ltd.
**Contractor(s):** China Railway Major Bridge Engineering Group Co., Ltd. and CCCC Second Harbor Engineering Company Ltd.,etc.

# 黄冈长江大桥
## Huanggang Bridge over Yangtze River

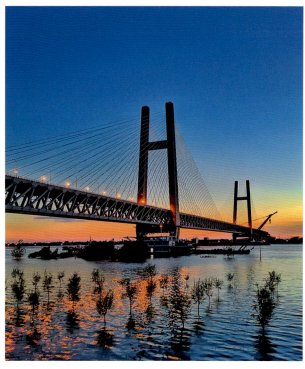

黄冈长江大桥位于湖北省境内，连接黄冈市与鄂州市，为武黄城际铁路、大庆-广州高速公路和武汉-鄂州高速公路的重要通道。大桥采用双层桥面，上层桥面为双向四车道高速公路，设计速度100km/h；下层桥面为双线铁路，设计速度200km/h。跨江大桥全长4.008km，其中公铁合建段长2.568km。

大桥主桥长1215m，为双塔双索面钢桁梁斜拉桥，半漂浮结构体系，跨径布置为81m+243m+567m+243m+81m。主梁采用正N形主桁结构，横截面采用上宽下窄的倒梯形。塔柱为H形混凝土结构，塔高193m。斜拉索为扇形布置，空间双索面，共152根。采用钻孔灌注嵌岩桩、高桩承台基础，使用双壁钢吊箱法围堰施工。

桥塔与主梁间的连接采用塔墩固结、塔梁分离体系，可合理分摊地震、列车制动等特殊荷载产生的结构内力，降低桥塔结构设计内力，减小桥塔基础规模。采用重型冲击钻开孔和大扭矩旋转钻孔机清水钻孔相结合实现快速成桩。采用多角度空间斜腹杆吊具、整体可移动施工脚手架及横向抗风牛腿装置，确保钢桁梁架设的安全及成桥线形流畅。

Huanggang Bridge over Yangtze River is located in Hubei Province, connecting Huanggang City and Ezhou City. It is an important passage of Wuhan-Huanggang Intercity Railway, Daqing-Guangzhou Expressway and Wuhan-Ezhou Expressway. The bridge adopts double-deck. The upper is a four-lane highway in dual direction with a design speed of 100km/h, and the lower is a two-line railway with a design speed of 200km/h. The bridge is 4.008km in length, of which the combined highway and railway section is 2.568km long.

The main bridge is 1215m long and is a double-tower cable-stayed bridge with double cable planes and steel truss girder. It adopts the semi-floating structural system. The span arrangement is 81m+243m+567m+243m+81m. The main beam adopts the N-shaped truss, and the cross section adopts the inverted trapezoid which is wide at the top and narrow at the bottom. The tower is a H-shaped concrete structure with a height of 193m. The stay cables are arranged in fan-shape with double space planes. There are 152 stay cables in total. Rock-socketed pile and high pile cap foundation are used, which are constructed by double wall steel suspension box cofferdam.

The connection between the tower and the main beam adopts the system of pier consolidation and tower-beam separation, which can reasonably share the structural internal forces generated by earthquake, train braking and other special loads, reduce the structural design internal forces of the tower as well as the scale of the tower foundation. The combination of heavy impact drilling and high torque rotary drilling machine are used to achieve rapid pile formation. Multi-angle space diagonal web member spreader, movable construction scaffold and transverse windproof corbel are adopted to ensure the safety of steel truss erection and smooth alignment of the bridge.

桥　　名：黄冈长江大桥
桥　　型：双塔双索面钢桁梁斜拉桥，半漂浮结构体系
主跨跨径：567m
桥　　址：湖北省黄冈市、鄂州市
建成时间：2014年6月
建设单位：湖北城际铁路有限责任公司
设计单位：中铁大桥勘测设计院集团有限公司
施工单位：中铁大桥局集团有限公司、中铁九桥工程有限公司等

**Name:** Huanggang Bridge over Yangtze River
**Type:** Double-tower double-cable plane steel truss girder cable-stayed bridge, semi-floating structural system
**Main Span:** 567m
**Location:** Huanggang City, Ezhou City, Hubei Province
**Completion:** June, 2014
**Owner(s):** Hubei Intercity Railway Co., Ltd.
**Designer(s):** China Railway Major Bridge Reconnaissance & Design Institute Co., Ltd.
**Contractor(s):** China Railway Major Bridge Engineering Group Co., Ltd. and China Railway Jiujiang Bridge Engineering Co., Ltd.,etc.

# 江顺大桥
## Jiangshun Bridge

**桥　名：** 江顺大桥
**桥　型：** 双塔双索面混合梁斜拉桥，半漂浮结构体系
**主跨跨径：** 700m
**桥　址：** 广东省江门市、佛山市
**建成时间：** 2015年6月
**建设单位：** 江门市滨江建设投资管理有限公司
**设计单位：** 广东省交通规划设计研究院集团股份有限公司
**施工单位：** 中国中铁股份有限公司

**Name:** Jiangshun Bridge
**Type:** Double-tower double-cable plane hybrid girder cable-stayed bridge, semi-floating structural system
**Main Span:** 700m
**Location:** Jiangmen City, Foshan City, Guangdong Province
**Completion:** June, 2015
**Owner(s):** Jiangmen Binjiang Construction Investment and Management Co., Ltd.
**Designer(s):** Guangdong Communication Planning & Design Institute Group Co., Ltd.
**Contractor(s):** China Railway Group Limited

江顺大桥位于广东省，是连接江门市蓬江区和佛山市顺德区的跨越西江通道，按双向六车道一级公路标准建设，设计速度80km/h。

大桥主桥为双塔双索面混合梁斜拉桥，桥跨钢-混凝土结合点设在边跨离主塔158m处，结构采用半漂浮结构体系，跨径布置为60m+176m+700m+176m+60m。主梁采用流线型扁平箱梁，其中钢箱梁长1016m，边跨混凝土梁长2×78m。索塔采用H形钢筋混凝土桥塔，塔高186m。全桥共176根斜拉索，采用平面扇形布置。主塔基础采用钻孔灌注桩。

大桥采用了正交异性钢桥面变厚度U肋抗疲劳开裂、索塔先滑后固型钢锚箱防混凝土塔壁开裂、大跨径斜拉桥施工期长悬臂调谐质量阻尼器（TMD）抑震和抗风、混合梁斜拉桥钢-混凝土结合段防钢壳大变形和防混凝土开裂、钢桥面环氧沥青铺装耐久性与抗滑、钢箱梁风嘴内抽湿养护等关键技术。在施工期形成了深水倾斜岩面大直径超长钻孔桩施工、大型钢吊箱围堰计算机控制同步下放、高主塔索导管精密定位、大跨度钢箱梁架设及空间受限条件下长重斜拉索挂设等创新的施工工艺及工法。

Jiangshun Bridge is located in Guangdong Province, crossing Xijiang River and connecting Pengjiang District of Jiangmen City and Shunde District of Foshan City. It is designed as first-class highway with six lanes in dual direction with a design speed of 80km/h.

The main bridge is a double-tower cable-stayed bridge with double cable planes and hybrid girder. The steel-concrete joint of the bridge is located at 158m away from the main tower, and the structure adopts the semi-floating structural system. The span arrangement is 60m+176m+700m+176m+60m. The main beam is a streamlined flat box girder, in which the steel box girder is 1016m long and the side span concrete girder is 2×78m long. The tower adopts a H-shaped reinforced concrete structure with a height of 186m. There are 176 stay cables, which are arranged in a plane fan-shaped way. The foundation of the main tower adopts bored piles.

Key technologies used in the bridge include anti-fatigue cracking of U-rib with variable thickness of orthodontic steel deck, anti-cracking of concrete tower wall with sliding-fixed steel anchor box, anti-earthquake and anti-wind Tuned Mass Damper (TMD) of long cantilever during construction, anti-deformation of steel shell and anti-concrete cracking of steel-concrete joint section, durability and anti-slide of epoxy asphalt pavement of steel deck, and wind fairing dehumidification of steel box girder, etc. During the construction period, some innovative construction techniques and methods have been developed, such as the construction of large-diameter and super-long drilled piles on inclined rock surface in deep water, synchronous lowering of large steel suspension box cofferdam under computer control, precise positioning of cable guide pipe of high pylon, erection of large-span steel box girder, and erection of long heavy stay cable under space limitation.

# 铜陵长江公铁大桥

## Tongling Highway and Railway Bridge over Yangtze River

铜陵长江公铁大桥位于安徽省境内,连接铜陵市义安区与芜湖市无为市,为铜陵—商城高速公路(皖高速S30)的重要节点。公铁合建段总长6.032km,上层桥面为双向六车道高速公路,设计速度100km/h,下层桥面为双向四线铁路。

大桥由主桥、引桥以及各匝道组成,主桥路段呈西北至东南方向布置。主桥为双塔三索面钢桁梁斜拉桥,半漂浮结构体系,跨径布置为90m+240m+630m+240m+90m。主梁采用三片主桁,铁路桥面系采用正交异性整体钢桥面,公路桥面系采用正交异性钢桥面。塔柱采用倒Y形混凝土结构,塔高212m。塔柱两侧斜拉索为扇形布置,各有3×19根钢绞线斜拉索。无为侧主塔墩采用深水沉井基础,铜陵侧主塔墩采用钻孔灌注桩基础。

为改善桥塔附近主桁的受力,在正交异性钢板桥面的基础上,提出了正交异性钢箱桥面的设计。针对大桥建设中沉井下沉、全焊桁片制造精度、钢绞线斜拉索索力误差控制等难题,研发了复杂水文地质条件下大型基础施工、全焊桁片制作与架设、钢绞线斜拉索等值张拉智能控制等一系列新技术。

Tongling Highway and Railway Bridge over Yangtze River is located in Anhui Province, connecting Yi'an District of Tongling City and Wuwei County of Wuhu. It is an important node of Tongling-Shangcheng Expressway (Anhui Expressway S30). The total length of the highway-railway combined section is 6.032km. The upper bridge has six-lane highway in dual direction with a design speed of 100km/h, and the lower has four-line railway in dual direction.

The bridge is composed of main bridge, approach bridge and ramps. The main bridge is arranged in the direction of northwest to southeast. The main bridge is a double-tower cable-stayed bridge with triple cable planes and steel truss girder, semi-floating structural system. It has a span arrangement of 90m+240m+630m+240m+90m. The main beam is composed of three trusses, the railway adopts orthotropic integral steel deck, and the highway adopts orthotropic steel deck. The tower adopts inverted Y-shaped concrete structure, and is 212m in height. There are 3×19 steel strand stay cables on both sides of the tower, and are arranged in fan shape. Deep water caisson foundation is used for tower pier in Wuwei side, and bored pile foundation is used for tower pier in Tongling side.

In order to improve the mechanical performance of the truss near the bottom of the tower, the design of the orthotropic steel box deck is proposed on the basis of the orthotropic steel deck. Aiming at the problems in bridge construction, including sinking of caisson, manufacturing accuracy of all-welded truss units, error control of cable force, a series of new technologies are developed, such as large-scale foundation construction under complex hydrogeological conditions, manufacturing and erection of all-welded truss units, intelligent control of equivalent tensioning of cable.

| | |
|---|---|
| 桥　名： | 铜陵长江公铁大桥 |
| 桥　型： | 双塔三索面钢桁梁斜拉桥，半漂浮结构体系 |
| 主跨跨径： | 630m |
| 桥　址： | 安徽省铜陵市、芜湖市 |
| 建成时间： | 2015年4月 |
| 建设单位： | 京福铁路客运专线安徽有限责任公司 |
| 设计单位： | 中铁大桥勘测设计院集团有限公司 |
| 施工单位： | 中铁大桥局集团有限公司等 |

**Name:** Tongling Highway and Railway Bridge over Yangtze River
**Type:** Double-tower double-cable plane steel truss girder cable-stayed bridge, semi-floating structural system
**Main Span:** 630m
**Location:** Tongling City, Wuhu City, Anhui Province
**Completion:** April, 2015
**Owner(s):** Beijing-Fuzhou Railway Passenger Dedicated Line Anhui Co., Ltd.
**Designer(s):** China Railway Major Bridge Reconnaissance & Design Institute Co., Ltd.
**Contractor(s):** China Railway Major Bridge Engineering Group Co., Ltd.,etc

# 迫龙沟特大桥
## Polonggou Bridge

　　迫龙沟特大桥位于西藏林芝市巴宜区境内，跨越特大型泥石流沟——迫龙沟。大桥全长743m，双向两车道，桥面宽度13.8m（不含风嘴），是川藏公路国道G318线通麦至105道班的关键节点。

　　大桥为双塔双索面混合梁斜拉桥，半漂浮结构体系，跨径布置为156m+430m+156m。该桥边跨采用双肋式预应力混凝土梁，中跨采用钢主梁与混凝土桥面板共同受力的组合梁，梁高2.6m；索塔分别高146.7m和139.7m；桥面以上塔柱为A形，桥面以下合并为单柱形式，采用群桩基础；斜拉索为无黏结钢绞线拉索，主跨标准索距为12m，边跨索距为8.5m，全桥共设置68对，采用扇形布置。

　　该桥边跨采用预应力混凝土主梁，以较好地适应曲线线形兼备压重作用；中跨采用自重相对较轻的组合梁，可减小桥梁下部及基础规模，对桥梁整体抗震有利，且造价适中，工期较短。针对边跨陡峭地形及复杂地质条件，提出边跨混凝土主梁采用挂篮悬臂浇筑、中跨组合梁采用桥面起重机悬臂拼装的不对称悬臂施工方法。为了减小索塔不平衡弯矩，保证主梁线形可控，主梁施工中，采取了边跨设置施工辅助墩、中跨钢梁安装超前边跨1个节段、优化主梁施工步骤、在中跨Z0梁段处设置反拉压重装置、优化边跨现浇段长度等措施，实现了施工风险低、施工工期合理的总体目标。

| | |
|---|---|
| 桥　　名： | 迫龙沟特大桥 |
| 桥　　型： | 双塔双索面混合梁斜拉桥，半漂浮结构体系 |
| 主跨跨径： | 430m |
| 桥　　址： | 西藏林芝市巴宜区 |
| 建成时间： | 2015年12月 |
| 建设单位： | 西藏自治区重点公路建设项目管理中心 |
| 设计单位： | 中交第一公路勘察设计研究院有限公司 |
| 施工单位： | 中铁大桥局集团有限公司 |

Polonggou Bridge is located in Bayi District, Nyingchi City, Tibet, and crosses the extra-large debris flow ditch—Polonggou. The total length of the bridge is 743m, with two lanes in dual directions, and the width of the bridge deck is 13.8m (excluding the tuyere). This bridge is the key node of the Sichuan-Tibet Highway National Highway 318 to 105 Station.

The bridge is a double-tower double-cable plane hybrid cable-stayed bridge, and a semi-floating structural system. The bridge span arrangement is 156m+430m+156m. The side span of the bridge adopts double-ribbed pre-stressed concrete beam, as well as the middle span adopts a composite beam of steel main beam and concrete bridge deck, the beam height is 2.6m. The height of the tower is 146.7m and 139.7m, respectively. The tower column above the bridge deck is A-shaped, and the lower part of the bridge deck is merged into a single column form. The lower part of the tower column adopts a group pile foundation. The stay cable is an unbonded steel strand cable. The

standard cable distance of the main span is 12m, and the side span cable distance is 8.5m. A total of 68 pairs are set up in the whole bridge with a fan-shape arrangement.

The side span of this bridge adopts prestressed concrete main girder to better adapt to the curve linear shape. The main girder also plays a role of weight. The middle span adopts a composite beam with relatively light weight, which can reduce the lower part and foundation scale of the bridge, and is beneficial to the overall seismic resistance of the bridge. The cost can be less and the construction period can be shorter. In view of the steep terrain and complex geological conditions of the side span, the asymmetrical cantilever construction method of hanging basket cantilever pouring for the main concrete beam of the side span and cantilever assembly for the middle span composite beam by bridge deck crane is proposed. In order to reduce the unbalanced bending moment of the tower and ensure the controllable linear shape of the main beam, in the construction of the main beam, 1) the construction auxiliary pier is set on the side span, 2) the middle span steel beam is installed one section ahead of the side span, 3) the construction steps of the main beam are optimized, 4) the reverse tensile compression device is set at the middle span Z0 beam section, and 5) the length of the cast-in-situ section of the side span is optimized, so as to achieve the overall goal of low construction risk and reasonable construction period.

**Name:** Polonggou Bridge
**Type:** Double-tower double-cable plane hybird cable-stayed bridge, semi-floating structural system
**Main Span:** 430m
**Location:** Nyingchi City, Tibet
**Completion:** Decemeber, 2015
**Owner(s):** Tibet Autonomous Region Highway Construction Key Project Management Center
**Designer(s):** CCCC First Highway Consultants Co., Ltd.
**Contractor(s):** China Railway Major Bridge Engineering Group Co., Ltd.

# 贵黔高速鸭池河大桥
## Guiyang-Qianxi Expressway Bridge over Yachi River

贵黔高速鸭池河大桥为贵阳—黔西高速公路（贵黔高速S82）重要节点，地处黔西境，在东风电站上游2km左右跨越鸭池河，起点侧接笔架山隧道，终点侧接龙井沟隧道。桥面为双向四车道高速公路，设计速度80km/h。

大桥为双塔双索面混合梁斜拉桥，半漂浮结构体系，跨径布置为72m+72m+76m+800m+76m+72m+72m。主跨主梁采用钢桁梁加正交异性钢桥面板，边跨主梁为预应力混凝土箱梁，主跨和边跨之间设置钢箱过渡段。塔柱采用H形钢筋混凝土结构，贵阳岸塔高243.2m，黔西岸塔高258.2m。每塔设24根直径3m的混凝土端承桩。全桥共96对斜拉索，采用扇形布置。

大桥采用钢-混凝土组合梁，保证了0.275小边中跨比，结构具有足够的强度和较高的安全储备。大桥建设克服了山区深切峡谷中雨、雪、雾等恶劣天气和场地狭窄等困难。边跨主梁共分为34个块段，采用挂篮结合落地支架进行施工，钢桁梁采用缆索式起重机整体吊装，属于大节段、长悬臂拼装，最大悬臂长度400m，轴线标高偏差控制在10mm以内，满足了控制精度要求。

Guiyang-Qianxi Expressway Bridge over Yachi River is an important node of Guiyang-Qianxi Expressway. It is located at western Guizhou Province, crossing Yachi River about 2km upstream of Dongfeng Power Station, connecting to Bijiashan Tunnel at the starting point and Longjinggou Tunnel at the end. The bridge has four-lane highway in dual direction with a design speed of 80km/h.

The bridge is a double-tower cable-stayed bridge with double cable planes and hybrid girder. It has a span arrangement of 72m+72m+76m+800m+76m+72m+72m, semi-floating structural system. The main span beam is composed of steel truss and orthotropic steel deck. The side span beam is prestressed concrete box girder, and a steel box transition section is set between main span and side span. The tower adopts a H-shaped reinforced concrete structure. The tower in Guiyang is 243.2m in height, and the tower in western Guizhou is 258.2m in height. Each tower has 24 concrete end-bearing piles with a diameter of 3m. There are 96 pairs of stay cables arranged in fan shape.

The steel-concrete composite beam is used to ensure that the structure with small side to mid-span ratio of 0.275 has sufficient strength and high safety margin. The construction of the bridge has overcome the severe weather such as rain, snow and fog in the mountains and deep canyons and the

difficulties of the narrow site. The main beam of the side span is divided into 34 sections, and the construction is carried out by the combination of hanging basket and falsework. The steel truss girder is integrally hoisted by cable cranes, which is assembly of large segment and long cantilever. The longest cantilever is 400m, and the error of axial elevation is controlled under 10mm, which meets the precision requirements.

桥　　名：贵黔高速鸭池河大桥
桥　　型：双塔双索面混合梁斜拉桥，半漂浮结构体系
主跨跨径：800m
桥　　址：贵州省东风电站水库库区
建成时间：2016年5月
建设单位：中交路桥建设有限公司
设计单位：中交第二公路勘察设计研究院有限公司
施工单位：中交路桥华南工程有限公司

**Name:** Guiyang-Qianxi Expressway Bridge over Yachi River
**Type:** Double-tower double-cable plane hybrid girder cable-stayed bridge, semi-floating structural system
**Main Span:** 800m
**Location:** Reservoir area of Dongfeng Power Station, Guizhou Province
**Completion:** May, 2016
**Owner(s):** Road & Bridge International Co., Ltd.
**Designer(s):** CCCC Second Highway Consultants Co., Ltd.
**Contractor(s):** Road & Bridge South China Engineering Co., Ltd.

# 北盘江第一桥
## First Beipan River Bridge

  北盘江第一桥，原名尼珠河大桥或北盘江大桥，是杭瑞高速公路跨越云贵省界的大桥，在云南省曲靖市宣威市普立乡与贵州省六盘水市水城区都格镇间跨越北盘江。桥面为双向四车道，桥面宽度23m，设计速度80km/h。

  大桥主桥为双塔双索面钢桁梁斜拉桥，半漂浮结构体系，跨径布置为80m+88m+88m+720m+88m+88m+80m。主梁采用板桁组合结构，桁高8m，主桁中心距27m。双塔为H形钢筋混凝土框架结构，两岸塔高分别为269m和247m。斜拉索按扇形布置，共设112对。大桥引桥为箱形预应力混凝土连续梁桥，跨径布置为3×34m。索塔、过渡墩、辅助墩、引桥桥墩和桥台均采用桩基础，索塔桩基直径2.8m，其余桩基直径2m，所有桩基持力层均为中风化岩层。

  大桥建设克服了北盘江深切大峡谷地势险峻（桥面至江面垂直距离为565.4m，桥塔顶部至江面垂直距离为740m）、地质条件复杂、自然气候恶劣等不利因素。采用步履式顶推边跨钢桁梁工法，避免了搭设支架，结合纵向移梁桥面起重机悬拼中跨钢桁梁施工方法，实现了边跨钢桁梁顶推与索塔同步施工。悬拼施工中，通过大、小起重机协同施工精准安装，将高差控制在0.5mm以内。利用云技术，研发了集"建设、管理、养护"于一体的桥梁山区大跨度钢桁梁斜拉桥管养综合信息化平台。

First Beipan River Bridge, formerly known as Nizhu River Bridge or Beipan River Bridge, is a bridge on Hangzhou-Ruili Expressway connecting Yunnan Province and Guizhou Province. It crosses the Beipan River between Puli Township, Xuanwei County, Yunnan Province and Duge Town, Shuicheng District, Liupanshui City, Guizhou Province. The bridge has four lanes in dual direction, the deck is 23m in width, and the design speed is 80km/h.

The main bridge is a double-tower cable-stayed bridge with double cable planes and steel truss girder, semi-floating structural system. It has a span arrangement of 80m+88m+88m+720m+88m+88m+80m. The main beam adopts the plate-truss composite structure, the truss is 8m in height, the center spacing of truss is 27m. The towers are H-shaped reinforced concrete frame structures, with a heights of 269m and 247m, respectively. There are 112 pairs of stay cables arranged in fan shape. The approach bridge is a prestressed concrete continuous box girder bridge with a span of 3×34m. The bridge adopts pile foundation. The diameter of the tower pile foundation is 2.8m, and the rest is 2m. The bearing stratum of all piles is moderately weathered rock stratum.

The construction of the bridge overcomes unfavorable factors such as steep terrain (the vertical distance between the bridge deck and the river is 565.4m, and the vertical distance between the top of the tower and the river is 740m), complex geological conditions and harsh natural climate of the deep canyon of the Beipan River. Walking-type incremental launching is used for side span steel truss construction to avoid erection of falsework. Combined with longitudinal moving crane for middle span cantilever erection, the synchronous construction of side span truss and tower is realized. During the cantilever erection, the height difference is controlled within 0.5mm through precise installation of large and small cranes. A comprehensive information platform for "construction, management and maintenance" of long-span steel truss cable-stayed bridge in mountainous areas has been developed using cloud technology.

桥　　名：北盘江第一桥
桥　　型：双塔双索面钢桁梁斜拉桥，半漂浮结构体系
主跨跨径：720m
桥　　址：云南省曲靖市、贵州省六盘水市
建成时间：2016年12月
建设单位：贵州高速公路集团有限公司
设计单位：中交公路规划设计院有限公司
施工单位：中交第二航务工程局有限公司、贵州省公路工程集团有限公司

**Name:** First Beipan River Bridge
**Type:** Double-tower double-cable plane steel truss girder cable-stayed bridge, semi-floating structural system
**Main Span:** 720m
**Location:** Qujing City, Yunnan Province, Liupanshui City, Guizhou Province
**Completion:** December, 2016
**Developer(s):** Guizhou Expressway Group Co., Ltd.
**Designer(s):** CCCC Highway Consultants Co., Ltd.
**Contractor(s):** CCCC Second Harbor Engineering Co., Ltd. and Guizhou Highway Engineering Group Co., Ltd.

# 望东长江公路大桥
## Wangdong Highway Bridge over Yangtze River

望东长江公路大桥位于安徽省境内，是连接安庆市望江县与池州市东至县的过江通道。桥面为双向六车道高速公路，设计速度100km/h。

大桥由主桥、两岸引桥及各立交匝道组成，主桥路段呈西北至东南方向布置。主桥为双塔双索面组合梁斜拉桥，半漂浮结构体系，跨径布置为78m+228m+638m+228m+78m。主梁采用PK型分离式双箱组合梁，钢梁为分离式倒梯形双箱，两箱通过中间的钢横梁连接。塔柱为钻石形混凝土结构，塔高217m。斜拉索为平行钢绞线拉索，采用扇形布置。主塔基础采用钻孔灌注桩。

在设计过程中系统构建了大跨径组合梁斜拉桥"竖向大位移弹性支撑+纵向多阶约束"约束体系，研发了工厂一体化预组合节段梁的设计与制造新技术，提出了基于0.2mm割线刚度理论的剪力钉抗剪刚度计算公式，改善了组合梁长期受力性能，提升了跨江桥梁工业化建造水平。在施工过程中创建了大倾角裸岩面超大异型自适应钢围堰卧拼、卧运、竖转、定位及着床等成套施工技术，解决了特殊地貌和施工环境下的钢围堰施工难题。

Wangdong Highway Bridge over Yangtze River is located in Anhui Province, connecting Wangjiang County, Anqing City and Dongzhi County, Chizhou City. The bridge has six lanes in dual direction with a design speed of 100km/h.

The bridge is composed of main bridge, approach bridge and interchange ramps. The main bridge is arranged in the direction of northwest to southeast. The main bridge is a double-tower cable-stayed bridge with double cable planes and composite girder, semi-floating structural system. It has a span arrangement of 78m+228m+638m+228m+78m. The main beam adopts Pasco Kennewick (PK) type separated double box composite girder. The steel girder is separated double box with inverted trapezoidal cross section, and the two boxes are connected through steel cross beam. The tower is a diamond-shaped concrete structure with a height of 217m. The stay cables are parallel steel strand stay cables and are arranged in fan shape. The foundation of the tower adopts bored piles.

In the design process, the constraint system of "vertical large displacement elastic support + longitudinal multi-order constraints" of the long-span composite girder cable-stayed bridge is systematically established. A new technology for the design and manufacturing of the integrated pre-assembled segment is proposed. A formula for calculating the shear stiffness of shear connections based on the theory of secant stiffness of 0.2mm is established, which improves the long-term mechanical performance of the composite girder and the level of industrial construction of river-crossing bridge. In the construction process, a complete set of technologies such as construction of super-large special-shaped adaptive steel cofferdam on steeply dipping bare rock are created, which solve the construction problems of steel cofferdam under special landform and environment.

| | |
|---|---|
| 桥　　名： | 望东长江公路大桥 |
| 桥　　型： | 双塔双索面组合梁斜拉桥，半漂浮结构体系 |
| 主跨径： | 638m |
| 桥　　址： | 安徽省安庆市、池州市 |
| 建成时间： | 2016年12月 |
| 建设单位： | 安徽省交通控股集团有限公司 |
| 设计单位： | 安徽省交通规划设计研究总院股份有限公司、中交公路规划设计院有限公司等 |
| 施工单位： | 中交第二航务工程局有限公司、中交路桥建设有限公司 |

**Name:** Wangdong Highway Bridge over Yangtze River
**Type:** Double-tower double-cable plane composite girder cable-stayed bridge, semi-floating structural system
**Main Span:** 638m
**Location:** Anqing City, Chizhou City, Anhui Province
**Completion:** December, 2016
**Owner(s):** Anhui Transportation Holding Group Co., Ltd.
**Designer(s):** Anhui Transport Consulting & Design Institute Co., Ltd. and CCCC Highway Consultants Co., Ltd.,etc.
**Contractor(s):** CCCC Second Harbor Engineering Co., Ltd. and Road & Bridge International Co., Ltd.

# 芜湖长江公路二桥
## Second Wuhu Highway Bridge over Yangtze River

芜湖长江公路二桥位于安徽省芜湖市境内，是连接无为市与三山区的过江通道，位于长江水道之上。大桥长13.928km，桥面为双向六车道高速公路，设计速度100km/h。

主桥为双塔四索面斜拉桥，全漂浮结构体系，跨径布置为100m+308m+806m+308m+100m。主梁采用分离式双弧形底钢箱梁，正交异性桥面板，双边箱梁采用箱形横梁连接。塔柱为分肢柱式钢筋混凝土结构，塔高262.48m，外轮廓为倒角式矩形，上塔柱近菱形。全桥共设108对斜拉索，采用扇形布置，梁上锚固间距16m。基础为钻孔灌注桩，直径3~3.4m，采用梅花形布置。

该桥采用了适配柱式桥塔的同向回转鞍座锚索系统，以拉索环抱塔柱，消除传统锚固系统的拉应力，解决锚索易开裂和拉索张拉空间狭窄等问题。主梁顶板采用变厚度设计，慢车道位置顶板厚度为18mm，快车道位置顶板厚度为16mm，可有效缓解重载交通对桥面板疲劳寿命的影响。研发了分肢索塔和四索面分体弧底钢箱梁，塔柱整体具有抗撞抗震优势和适应分体宽梁的特点，有利于控制结构颤振和涡振。在柱形塔上进行优化，将中、下塔柱在横向上分为两肢，以增加整体刚度。采用了四位一体斜置阻尼系统以实现多向抗震。开展了全塔温控工作，通过试验以及理论研究，创新滴灌、管冷、保温、防风、断缝工艺，提出动态温控指标，进行实时温度控制以实现混凝土裂缝的有效管控。

| 桥　名： | 芜湖长江公路二桥 |
| --- | --- |
| 桥　型： | 双塔四索面钢箱梁斜拉桥，全漂浮结构体系 |
| 主跨跨径： | 806m |
| 桥　址： | 安徽省芜湖市 |
| 建成时间： | 2017年10月 |
| 建设单位： | 安徽省交通控股集团有限公司 |
| 设计单位： | 安徽省交通规划设计研究总院股份有限公司 |
| 施工单位： | 中铁大桥局集团有限公司、中交第二航务工程局有限公司 |

**Name:** Second Wuhu Highway Bridge over Yangtze River
**Type:** Double-tower four-cable plane steel box girder cable-stayed bridge, fully floating structural system
**Main Span:** 806m
**Location:** Wuhu City, Anhui Province
**Completion:** October, 2017
**Owner(s):** Anhui Transportation Holding Group Co., Ltd.
**Designer(s):** Anhui Transport Consulting & Design Institute Co., Ltd.
**Contractor(s):** China Railway Major Bridge Engineering Group Co., Ltd. and CCCC Second Harbor Engineering Co., Ltd.

Second Wuhu Highway Bridge over Yangtze River is located in Wuhu City, Anhui Province, the passageway connecting Wuwei City and Sanshan District. The bridge is 13.928km in length, and has six-lane highway in dual direction with a design speed of 100km/h.

The main bridge is a double-tower cable-stayed bridge with four cable planes, fully floating structural system. It has a span arrangement of 100m+308m+806m+308m+100m. The main beam adopts separated double steel box girder with arc bottom plate and orthotropic deck. The two box girders are connected by cross beam. The tower is a column type reinforced concrete structure, and is 262.48m in height. The outer contour is Chamfered rectangle, and the upper tower column is nearly diamond shape. A total of 108 pairs of stay cables are set in fan shape, and the anchorage spacing on beam is 16m. The foundation adopts bored pile of 3-3.4m in diameter, quincuncial layout.

The bridge adopts isodirectionally turning stay cable anchor system for column type tower. The tower is surrounded by cable, which can eliminate the tension stress of the traditional anchoring system, and solve the problems of cracking of anchorage cable and narrow tension space. The top plate of the main beam adopts variable thickness design. The thickness of the top plate in the slow lane is 18mm and that of the fast lane is 16mm, which effectively alleviates the influence of heavy load traffic on fatigue life of deck. The split-limb tower and the steel box girder with four cable planes and arc bottom plate are developed to form the overall resistance against collision and earthquake, which also adapts to the characteristics of the wide separated girder, and can control flutter and vortex vibration. Optimization is carried out on tower by dividing the middle and lower columns into two limbs horizontally to increase the overall stiffness. A four-in-one inclined damping system is used to realize multi-directional seismic performance. Temperature control of the whole tower is carried out, and innovative processes of drip irrigation, pipe cooling, heat preservation, wind protection and break joint are proposed through experiments and theoretical research. Dynamic temperature control indexes are put forward, and real-time temperature control is carried out to achieve effective control of concrete cracks.

# 沌口长江大桥
## Zhuankou Bridge over Yangtze River

桥　名：沌口长江大桥
桥　型：双塔双索面钢箱梁斜拉桥，半漂浮结构体系
主跨跨径：760m
桥　址：湖北省武汉市
建成时间：2017 年 12 月
建设单位：中交城市投资控股有限公司
设计单位：中交第二公路勘察设计研究院有限公司
施工单位：中交第二航务工程局有限公司

**Name:** Zhuankou Bridge over Yangtze River
**Type:** Double-tower double-cable plane steel box girder cable-stayed bridge, semi-floating structural system
**Main Span:** 760m
**Location:** Wuhan City, Hubei Province
**Completion:** December, 2017
**Owner(s):** CCCC Urban Investment Holding Co., Ltd.
**Designer(s):** CCCC Second Highway Consultants Co., Ltd.
**Contractor(s):** CCCC Second Harbor Engineering Co., Ltd.

　　沌口长江大桥位于湖北省武汉市境内，连接蔡甸区与江夏区，是武汉市第九座跨越长江的桥梁。桥面为双向八车道高速公路，设计速度 100km/h。

　　主桥为双塔双索面钢箱梁斜拉桥，半漂浮结构体系，跨径布置为 100m+275m+760m+275m+100m。主梁采用介于整体式断面与分体式之间的 PK 断面钢箱梁，由 2 个流线型扁平边箱、箱间顶板及横隔板组成；塔柱为钻石形混凝土结构，塔高 233.7m；斜拉索采用空间双索面扇形布置，共计 240 根；桥塔基础为整体式群桩基础，按端承桩设计。

　　设计上，按"借助边跨作为高水位期的单孔单向辅助通航孔，以主、边跨结合完全覆盖可通航水域"的思路，拟定通航孔布置方案。建造过程中采用的新技术有：兼顾大桥抗震、静力及疲劳受力性能的大吨位"弹性+阻尼"复合式阻尼器；利用小型智能焊接机器人实现钢桥面板与纵向 U 肋内、外双面角焊缝连接构造；基于几何控制法的桥梁安全监控技术和平台，实现施工与运营全寿命过程监控等。

Zhuankou Bridge over Yangtze River is located in Wuhan City, Hubei Province, connecting Caidian District and Jiangxia District. It is the ninth bridge across the Yangtze River in Wuhan. The bridge deck is a two-way eight-lane expressway with a design speed of 100km/h.

The main bridge is a double-tower double-cable plane steel box girder cable-stayed bridge and a semi-floating structural system. The span arrangement is

100m+275m+760m+275m+100m. The main beam adopts the PK section steel box girder which is between the integral cross section and the split-type cross section. The PK section steel box girder is composed of two streamlined flat side boxes, the top plate between the boxes and the diaphragm. The tower column is a diamond-shaped concrete structure with a height of 233.7m. The stay cables are arranged in a fan-shaped space with double cable planes, a total of 240. The foundation of the bridge tower is an integral pile group foundation, which is designed as end bearing pile.

In terms of design, according to the idea of "using side spans as single-hole one-way auxiliary navigation holes in high water level period, the main and side spans are combined to completely cover the navigable waters", the layout plan of the navigation holes is drawn up. The new technologies used in the construction process include: taking into account the seismic, static and fatigue performance of the bridge, the large-tonnage "elasticity + damping" composite damper, the use of small intelligent welding robots to realize the double fillet weld connection structure between the steel bridge deck and the longitudinal U-rib inner and outer, research and develop the bridge safety monitoring technology and platform based on geometric control method to realire the whole life process monitoring of construction and operation, etc.

# 丰都长江二桥
## Second Fengdu Bridge over Yangtze River

丰都长江二桥连接重庆丰都县长江南北两岸，大桥全长 2.234km，全线采用双向四车道标准建设，主线设计速度 60km/h。

大桥的跨径布置为 70.5m+215.5m+680m+245.5m+70.5m，采用半漂浮结构体系。主梁为流线型扁平钢箱梁，正交异性桥面板。钻石形主塔高 227.1m，采用双塔双索面，扇形拉索布置。

该桥设计和施工特点有：主梁横隔板设计划分为三部分，分别与钢箱梁底板、顶板、外侧纵腹板焊接形成板块单元，然后组拼为整体，改善了横隔板的受力性能及箱梁的疲劳抗裂性能；采用大体积水下封底混凝土一次性浇筑施工技术，使用无钢护筒及部分钢护筒进行钻孔灌注桩施工，解决了深水基础施工难题。

Second Fengdu Bridge over Yangtze River connects the north and south banks of the Yangtze River in Fengdu County, Chongqing, with a total length of 2.234km. The whole line of the bridge adopts the standard criterion for the construction of two-way four-lane, and the design speed of the main line is 60km/h.

The span arrangement is 70.5m + 215.5m + 680m + 245.5m + 70.5m and adopts a semi-floating structural system. The main beam is a streamlined flat steel box girder with orthotropic deck. The diamond-shaped main tower is 227.1m high, and is arranged with double towers, double cable planes and fan-shaped cables.

The design and construction features are: the main beam diaphragm is designed into three parts, which are welded with the steel box girder bottom plate, top plate and outer longitudinal web respectively to form plate units, and then assembled into a whole, which improves the mechanical performance of the diaphragm and the fatigue crack resistance of the box girder. The large-volume underwater bottom-sealing concrete one-time pouring construction technology is used, and the steel-free casing and some steel casings are used for bored pile construction, which solves the problem of deep-water foundation construction.

| | |
|---|---|
| 桥　　名： | 丰都长江二桥 |
| 桥　　型： | 双塔双索面钢箱梁斜拉桥，半漂浮结构体系 |
| 主跨跨径： | 680m |
| 桥　　址： | 重庆市丰都县 |
| 建成时间： | 2016年12月 |
| 建设单位： | 重庆市丰都县长江二桥工程建设有限公司 |
| 设计单位： | 中铁大桥勘测设计院集团有限公司 |
| 施工单位： | 中交路桥建设有限公司 |

**Name:** Second Fengdu Bridge over Yangtze River
**Type:** Double-tower double-cable plane steel box girder cable-stayed bridge, semi-floating structural system
**Main Span:** 680m
**Location:** Fengdu County, Chongqing City
**Completion:** December, 2016
**Owner(s):** Second Chongqing Fengdu Bridge over Yangtze River Construction Co., Ltd.
**Designer(s):** China Railway Major Bridge Reconnaissance & Design Institute Co., Ltd.
**Contractor(s):** China Communications Roads and Bridge Construction Co., Ltd.

# 白沙沱长江大桥
## Baishatuo Bridge over Yangtze River

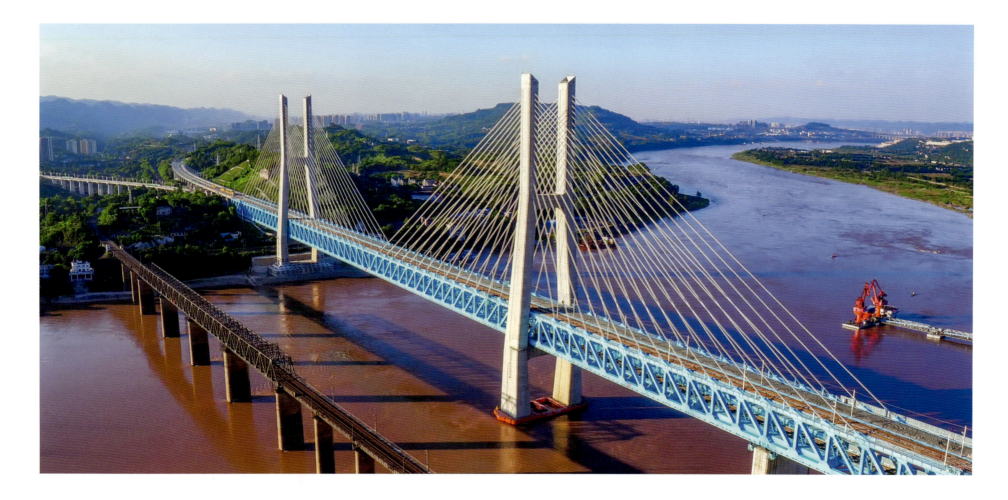

　　白沙沱长江大桥位于重庆市境内长江水道之上，是渝贵客车线、渝贵货车线连接重庆枢纽和渝湘客车线的重要通道。大桥为双层六线铁路桥，全长5.320km；上层为双向四线客运专线，设计速度200km/h，下层为双向二线货车线，设计速度120km/h。

　　大桥主桥为双塔双索面钢桁梁斜拉桥，半漂浮结构体系，跨径布置为81m+162m+432m+162m+81m。主梁为双主桁式结构，采用平弦等高度连续钢桁梁，下层桥面采用纵梁连接的纵横梁桥面结构体系；塔柱为折线H形钢筋混凝土结构，塔高192.45m；斜拉索为平行扇形双索面布置，采用平行钢丝拉索，共224根；基础采用36根直径3.2m的钻孔灌注桩。

　　设计上，基于经济性、景观效果、施工便利性以及桥位条件等因素，采用钢桁梁斜拉桥方案，并根据两端线路条件，确定了六线分层的总体布置方案。建设过程中，研发了深水无覆盖层倾斜岩面基础施工技术，解决了水深流急、河床无覆盖层、主墩承台部分埋入基岩、枯洪水期水位变化大等施工难题。

桥　　名：白沙沱长江大桥
桥　　型：双塔双索面钢桁梁斜拉桥，半漂浮结构体系
主跨跨径：432m
桥　　址：重庆市
建成时间：2019年4月
建设单位：渝黔铁路有限责任公司
设计单位：中铁大桥勘测设计院集团有限公司、中铁二院工程集团有限责任公司
施工单位：中铁大桥局集团有限公司等

Baishatuo Bridge over Yangtze River is located on the Yangtze River Waterway in Chongqing City. It is an important passage for the Chongqing-Guizhou Bus Line and the Chongqing-Guizhou Truck Line to connect the Chongqing Hub and the Chongqing-Hunan Bus Line . The bridge is a double-layer six-track railway bridge with a total length of 5.320km. The upper layer of the bridge is a two-way four-lane passenger dedicated line with a design speed of 200km/h, and the lower layer is a two-way second-line freight train line with a design speed of 120km/h.

The main bridge is a double-tower double-cable plane steel truss-girder cable-stayed bridge, and a semi-floating structural system. The span arrangement is 81m+162m+432m+162m+81m. The main beam is a double main truss structure, using a continuous steel truss girder of equal height with flat chords, and the lower deck adopts a crossing beam deck with longitudinal beams. The tower column is a broken line H-shaped reinforced concrete structure with a tower height of 192.45m. The stay cables are arranged in parallel fan-shaped double-cable planes, using parallel wire cables, with a total of 224 cables. The foundation adopts 36 bored piles with a diameter of 3.2m.

In design, based on factors such as economy, landscape effect, construction convenience and bridge location conditions, the steel truss girder cable-stayed bridge scheme is adopted. According to the line conditions at both ends, a six-line layered general layout scheme is determined. During the construction process, the participant units put forward the construction technology of the inclined rock surface foundation in deep water without overburden, which solves the construction problems such as rapid water depth, no overburden in the river bed, part of the main pier cap buried in the bedrock, and large changes in water level during dry flood periods.

**Name:** Baishatuo Bridge over Yangtze River
**Type:** Double-tower double-cable plane steel truss-girder cable-stayed bridge, semi-floating structural system
**Main Span:** 432m
**Location:** Chongqing City
**Completion:** April, 2019
**Owner(s):** Yu Qian Railway Co., Ltd.
**Designer(s):** China Railway Major Bridge Reconnaissance & Design Institute Co., Ltd. and China Railway Eryuan Engineering Group Co., Ltd.
**Contractor(s):** China Railway Major Bridge Engineering Group Co., Ltd.

# 嘉鱼长江大桥
## Jiayu Bridge over Yangtze River

| | |
|---|---|
| 桥　名： | 嘉鱼长江大桥 |
| 桥　型： | 双塔双索面混合梁斜拉桥，半漂浮结构体系 |
| 主跨跨径： | 920m |
| 桥　址： | 湖北省咸宁市、荆州市 |
| 建成时间： | 2019年5月 |
| 建设单位： | 湖北交通投资集团有限公司 |
| 设计单位： | 湖北省交通规划设计院股份有限公司 |
| 施工单位： | 中交第二公路工程局有限公司、四川公路桥梁建设集团有限公司等 |
| 拉索供应单位： | 柳州欧维姆机械股份有限公司 |

**Name:** Jiayu Bridge over Yangtze River
**Type:** Double-tower double-cable plane hybrid girder cable-stayed bridge, semi-floating structural system
**Main Span:** 920m
**Location:** Xianning City, Jingzhou City, Hubei Province
**Completion:** May, 2019
**Owner(s):** Hubei Communications Investment Group Co., Ltd.
**Designer(s):** Hubei Communication Planning and Design Institute Co., Ltd.
**Contractor(s):** CCCC Second Highway Engineering Co., Ltd. and CCCCSHEC First Engineering Co., Ltd.,etc.
**Cable Vendor:** Liuzhou OVM Co., Ltd.

　　嘉鱼长江大桥位于湖北省长江中游的嘉鱼及燕窝河段，连接荆州市洪湖市与咸宁市嘉鱼县，南起嘉鱼北互通，上跨长江水道，北至燕窝互通，为仙桃—洪湖高速公路（鄂高速S78）重要节点，是湖北沿长江8个市州的重要过江通道。桥面为双向六车道高速公路，设计速度100km/h。

　　主桥为双塔双索面混合梁斜拉桥，采用半漂浮结构体系，主桥长1650m，跨径布置为300m+920m+330m+100m。主梁为预应力混凝土箱梁、混凝土箱梁和钢箱梁，均采用整幅闭口单箱三室断面；塔柱为倒Y形钢筋混凝土结构；全桥拉索为扇形布置，共有240根，钢丝强度1770MPa，拉索疲劳应力幅值250MPa，为解决斜拉索下端密封腐蚀问题，设计采用柔性防水罩和可视化保护罩；主塔基础采用整体式承台配大直径群桩，南塔钻孔灌注桩为摩擦桩，平面按梅花状布置，北塔基础位于岸滩上，枯水期先完成桩基施工，承台基坑采用锁扣钢管桩围护开挖，分层浇筑承台。

　　设计上，为了改善纵向静风荷载及地震荷载作用下的结构性能，在每个索塔处各设置4个纵向黏滞阻尼器，可控制风、地震、汽车制动力等动力荷载引起的主梁位移和速度；在建设过程中，应用小型智能化焊接机器人技术提升了焊缝连接的静力强度和疲劳强度。

Jiayu Bridge over Yangtze River is located in the Jiayu and Swallow's Nest sections of the middle reaches of the Yangtze River in Hubei Province, connecting Honghu County, Jingzhou City and Jiayu County, Xianning City, and connecting Jiayu North Interchange in the south. The bridge spans the Yangtze River Waterway and connects with the Swallow's Nest Interchange in the north. It is an important node of Xiantao-Honghu Expressway (Hubei Expressway S78) and an important river-crossing channel for 8 cities along the Yangtze River in Hubei. The bridge is a two-way six-lane expressway with a design speed of 100km/h.

The main bridge is a double-tower double-cable plane hybrid girder cable-stayed bridge with a semi-floating structural system. The main bridge is 1650m long and has a span arrangement of 300m+920m+300m+100m. The main beam adopts a prestressed concrete box girder, concrete box girder and steel box girder, all of which use the entire closed-open single-box three-chamber section. The tower column is an inverted Y-shaped reinforced concrete structure. The whole bridge has 240 stay cables arranged in a fan shape. The strength of steel wire is 1770MPa, the fatigue stress amplitude of the stay cable is 250MPa. To solve the problem of sealing corrosion at the lower end of the cable, the design adopts a flexible waterproof cover and a visual protective cover. The foundation of the main tower adopts an integral cap and large-diameter piles. The bored piles in the south tower are friction piles, and the plane is arranged in a plum blossom shape. The foundation of the north tower is located on the beach, and the pile foundation construction is completed first in the dry season. The foundation pit of the cap is excavated with locking steel pipe piles, and the cap is poured in layers.

In terms of design, in order to improve the structural performance under longitudinal static wind load and seismic load, 4 longitudinal viscous dampers are installed at each tower. The dampers can control the structural displacement and speed caused by dynamic loads such as dynamic wind, earthquake, and automobile braking force. During the construction process, the application of small intelligent welding robot technology has improved the static strength and fatigue strength of the weld connection.

# 保定乐凯大街南延工程保定南站斜拉桥

## Baoding South Station Cable-stayed Bridge of South Extension Project of Lekai Street

保定乐凯大街南延工程保定南站斜拉桥位于铁路京广线K137+970处以61.8°左右的交角上跨保定南站编组站，由北向南共跨越21条股道。该桥为双向八车道城市主干路，设计速度60km/h。

该桥跨径布置145m+240m+110m，为子母塔单索面预应力混凝土斜拉桥，塔墩梁固结体系。主梁设计采用大悬臂W形腹板截面混凝土箱梁，纵、横、竖三向预应力体系；主塔高68m，子塔高52m，火炬造型混凝土结构；斜拉索采用单索面扇形布置，主塔两侧各布置24对斜拉索，子塔两侧各布置18对斜拉索；基础采用钻孔灌注桩，按扩底桩设计。

设计上，W形主梁截面可以取消传统单箱多室直立内腹板截面中在拉索锚固处设置的横隔板，简化主梁构造的同时大大减轻主梁自重，进一步减少拉索和下部结构的数量；采用母塔段与子塔段双转体施工方法，对边跨主梁的斜腹板、底板进行加厚设计，以此来平衡转体中两侧的不平衡弯矩；采用诸如球面平铰及分块拼接技术等一系列创新设计，解决了转体斜拉桥向超大吨位、超宽方向发展的技术难题。

Baoding South Station Cable-stayed Bridge of South Extension Project of Lekai Street crosses the Baoding South Railway Station marshaling station at an angle of about 61.8° at K137+970 of the Beijing-Guangzhou Railway Line. It crosses 21 pairs of rails from north to south. The bridge is a two-way eight-lane urban arterial road with a design speed of 60km/h.

The span arrangement of the bridge is 145m+240m+110m, which is a single-cable plane prestressed concrete cable-stayed bridge. It forms a tower-pier-beam consolidation system with a taller tower and a lower tower. The main beam design adopts a large cantilever W-shaped web section concrete box girder. The girder applies a three-way (longitudinal, horizontal, and vertical) prestressing system. The taller tower is 68m high, the lower tower is 52m high. Towers are torch-shaped concrete structures. Stay cables are set as single-cable planes with a fan-shaped arrangement. There are 24 pairs of stay cables on each side of the taller tower and 18 pairs on each side of the lower tower. The foundation adopts bored piles and is designed with bottom-expansion piles.

In terms of design, the W-shaped main beam section allow for the elimination of the cross partition set at the cable anchorage in the traditional single-box multi-chamber upright inner web section, which can simplify the main beam structure and greatly reduce the self-weight of the main beam, and further reduce the number of cables and substructures. The double-rotating body construction method is adopted to thicken the oblique web and bottom plate of the side-span, so as to balance the bending moment of the rotating body. Using a series of innovative designs such as spherical flat hinges and block splicing technology, it solves the technical problem of the development of a rotary cable-stayed bridge in the direction of ultra-large tonnage and ultra-wide width.

| | |
|---|---|
| 桥　　名： | 保定乐凯大街南延工程保定南站斜拉桥 |
| 桥　　型： | 子母塔单索面预应力混凝土斜拉桥，塔墩梁固结体系 |
| 主跨跨径： | 240m |
| 桥　　址： | 河北省保定市 |
| 建成时间： | 2019年9月 |
| 建设单位： | 保定市城市管理综合行政执法局 |
| 设计单位： | 中铁工程设计咨询集团有限公司 |
| 施工单位： | 中铁十八局集团有限公司等 |

**Name:** Baoding South Station Cable-stayed Bridge of South Extension Project of Lekai Street
**Type:** Tall and low single-cable prestressed concrete cable-stayed bridge, tower-pier-beam consolidation system
**Main Span:** 240m
**Location:** Baoding City, Hebei Province
**Completion:** September, 2019
**Owner(s):** Baoding Municipal Bureau of Coordinated Administrative Law Enforcement for Urban Management
**Designer(s):** China Railway Engineering Design and Consulting Group Co., Ltd.
**Contractor(s):** China Railway 18th Bureau Group Co., Ltd.,etc.

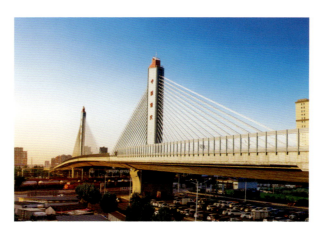

# 池州长江大桥
## Chizhou Bridge over Yangtze River

池州长江大桥位于安徽省境内，是连接池州市与铜陵市的过江通道，是安徽省"五纵九横"高速公路网的重要组成部分。桥梁全长1.448km，桥面为双向六车道高速公路，设计速度100km/h。

大桥为双塔双索面混合梁斜拉桥，全漂浮结构体系，采用3×48m+96m+828m+280m+100m跨径布置。主梁采用混合梁结构，钢箱梁采用整体性及抗风性能较好的扁平流线型断面，桥面为正交异性钢桥面板，主梁横隔板除两端因剪力较大采用实腹板结构外，中间部分采用空腹式桁架结构。混凝土主梁与钢主梁外形一致，采用单箱六室结构。塔柱采用花瓶形钢筋混凝土结构，北塔高237m，南塔高243m。全桥共216根斜拉索，双索面扇形布置。主塔基础采用钻孔灌注桩。

设计上，漂浮结构体系具有较好的动力特性，能大幅度减小温度作用对结构产生的内力，与该桥跨度大、所处地区地震烈度较高的特点相适应。建设过程中，钢混结合段采用纵、横向锁定技术，保证在现浇箱梁混凝土浇筑过程中钢梁始终处于稳定状态；主梁钢混结合段施工采用钢管支架滑移系统，降低了临时设施的搭设和拆除风险；梁段滑移过大堤时，采用可拆卸滑移轨道，减小了施工对大堤交通的影响。

| | |
|---|---|
| 桥　名： | 池州长江大桥 |
| 桥　型： | 双塔双索面混合梁斜拉桥，全漂浮结构体系 |
| 主跨跨径： | 828m |
| 桥　址： | 安徽省铜陵市、池州市 |
| 建成时间： | 2019年12月 |
| 建设单位： | 安徽省交通控股集团有限公司 |
| 设计单位： | 中铁大桥勘测设计院集团有限公司 |
| 施工单位： | 中交路桥华南工程有限公司 |

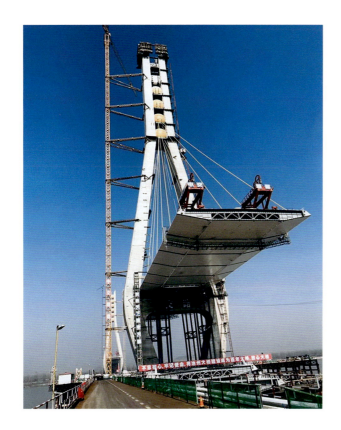

Chizhou Bridge over Yangtze River is a river-crossing passage connecting Chizhou City and Tongling City in Anhui Province. It is an important part of the "five vertical and nine horizontal" expressway network in Anhui Province. The total length of the bridge is 1.448km. It is a two-way six-lane expressway with a design speed of 100km/h.

The bridge is a double-tower double-cable plane hybird girder cable-stayed bridge with a fully floating structural system, and is arranged with a span of 3×48m+96m+828m+280m+100m. The main beam adopts a hybrid beam structure, the steel box girder adopts a flat streamlined section with good integrity and wind resistance, and the bridge deck is an orthotropic steel bridge deck. Except for the solid web structure at both ends of the main beam diaphragm due to the large shear force, the middle part adopts the hollow truss structure. The concrete main beam adopts the same shape as the steel main beam, and adopts a single-box six-chamber structure. The tower is a vase-shaped reinforced concrete structure. The north tower is 237m high and the south tower is 243m high. The 216 stay cables of the whole bridge are arranged in a fan shape with double cable planes. The main tower foundation adopts bored cast-in-place piles.

In terms of design, the floating structural system has good dynamic proporties, which can greatly reduce the internal force generated by the temperature effect on the structure, which is compatible with the characteristics of the bridge's large span and high seismic intensity. During the construction process, the steel-concrete combined section adopts vertical and horizontal locking technology to ensure that the steel beam is always in a stable state during the concrete pouring of the cast-in-place box girder. The steel-concrete joint section of the main beam adopts the steel pipe bracket sliding system, which reduces the risk during the erection and dismantling of temporary facilities. When the beam section was slipping over the embankment, a detachable slip track was utilized to reduce the impact of construction on the traffic of the embankment.

**Name:** Chizhou Bridge over Yangtze River
**Type:** Double-tower double-cable plane hybrid girder cable-stayed bridge, fully floating structural system
**Main Span:** 828m
**Location:** Tongling City, Chizhou City, Anhui Province
**Completion:** December, 2019
**Owner(s):** Anhui Transportation Holding Group Co., Ltd.
**Designer(s):** China Railway Major Bridge Reconnaissance & Design Institute Co., Ltd.
**Contractor(s):** CCCC Road & Bridge South China Engineering Co., Ltd.

# 石首长江大桥
## Shishou Bridge over Yangtze River

石首长江大桥位于湖北省境内，是连接枣阳市与石首市的过江通道、枣阳—石首高速公路（鄂高速S53）重要节点。桥梁全长11.465km，桥面为双向车道高速公路，设计速度100km/h。

大桥由主桥、滩桥、引桥及立交匝道组成，主桥路段呈西南至东北方向布置。主桥为双塔双索面混合梁斜拉桥，半漂浮结构体系，跨径布置为75m+75m+75m+820m+300m+100m。主梁采用钢箱梁与预应力混凝土梁组成的混合梁；南、北塔柱采用倒Y形下柱内收形的钢筋混凝土结构，南塔高234m，北塔高232m，塔柱采用空心箱形断面；全桥采用空间扇形双索面布置，共布置4×26对斜拉索；采用钻孔灌注桩基础。

设计上，桥位所处的碾子湾水道历史上曾发生航槽易位，主跨820m通航净宽为将来航道条件的改善预留一定空间，对通航水域的覆盖及航槽变化的适应性好。同时，为保证深槽摆动的空间，南边跨采用300m+100m的跨径布置。施工新技术包括：钢箱梁顶板U肋采用全自动内焊与顶板连接双面成型熔透焊；北边跨混凝土箱梁采用短线法预制拼装的施工方案；主梁钢混结合段采用带钢格室的部分连接填充混凝土的"后承压板+钢格室+PBL剪力件"构造，填充活性粉末混凝土；索塔基础桩端采用后压浆提高竖向承载力技术；索塔拉索锚固钢锚梁钢壁板与混凝土塔壁结合面采用开孔板连接件的新型结合型式，未设置剪力钉。

Located in Hubei Province, Shishou Bridge over Yangtze River is a river-crossing passage connecting Zaoyang City and Shishou City as an important node of Zaoyang-Shishou Expressway (Hubei Expressway S53). The total length of the bridge is 11.465km. The bridge deck is a two-way lane expressway with a design speed of 100km/h.

The bridge is composed of the main bridge, beach bridge, approach bridge and interchange ramp. The main bridge section is arranged from southwest to northeast. The main bridge is a double-tower double-cable plane hybrid girder cable-stayed bridge.It is a semi-floating structural system with a span arrangement of 75m+75m+75m+820m+300m+100m. The main beam is a composite girder composed of steel box girder and prestressed concrete girder. The south and north towers are reinforced concrete structures with inverted Y-shaped lower columns and internal retraction. The south tower is 234m high and the north tower is 232m high. The towers are designed with hollow box-shaped sections. The whole bridge adopts a spatial sector double cable plane layout, with 4×26 pairs of stay cables in total. The bored pile foundation is adopted.

In design, the Nianziwan channel where the bridge is located has undergone a trough change in history. The net width of the main span of 820m is reserved for the improvement of future channel conditions, the adaptability to the coverage of navigable waters, and the change of navigation channel. The south span needs to reserve 300m + 100m side span, and appropriately reserve space for deep groove swinging. New construction technologies include: steel box girder roof U-rib using automatic internal welding and roof plate connection, double-sided forming penetration welding. The construction scheme of prefabricated assembly of the northern span concrete box girder adopts the short-line method. The steel mixed section of the main beam adopts the structure of "post-pressure plate + steel cell + PBL shear bond" with steel cell partially connected to fill concrete, and fills active powder concrete. The pile end of the tower foundation adopts the technology of post-grouting to improve the vertical bearing capacity. The joint surface of the steel wall plate of the anchor beam of the tower cable and the concrete tower wall adopts a new combination type of perforated plate connection, and no shear nails are provided.

| | |
|---|---|
| 桥　名： | 石首长江大桥 |
| 桥　型： | 双塔双索面混合梁斜拉桥，半漂浮结构体系 |
| 主跨跨径： | 820m |
| 桥　址： | 湖北省石首市 |
| 建成时间： | 2019年4月 |
| 建设单位： | 湖北交通投资集团有限公司 |
| 设计单位： | 中交公路规划设计院有限公司、湖北省交通规划设计院股份有限公司 |
| 施工单位： | 中交第二公路工程局有限公司 |

**Name:** Shishou Bridge over Yangtze River
**Type:** Double-tower double-cable plane hybrid girder cable-stayed bridge, semi-floating structural system
**Main Span:** 820m
**Location:** Shishou City, Hubei Province
**Completion:** April, 2019
**Owner(s):** Hubei Communications Investment Group Co., Ltd.
**Designer(s):** CCCC Highway Consultants Co., Ltd. and Hubei Communications Planning and Design Institute Co., Ltd.
**Contractor(s):** CCCC Second Highway Engineering Co., Ltd.

# 牌楼长江大桥
## Pailou Bridge over Yangtze River

牌楼长江大桥，原称万州长江三桥，位于重庆市万州区境内，距重庆市中心260km，是重庆市行政辖区东北部城市主干道路的重要越江节点。桥面为双向六车道城市主干路，设计速度60km/h。

大桥由主桥、东西两岸引桥及各立交匝道组成，主桥路段呈西南至东北方向布置。主桥为双塔双索面混合梁斜拉桥，采用全漂浮结构体系，跨径布置为4×57.5m+730m+4×57m。主梁中跨采用正交异性桥面板钢箱梁，边跨为单箱多室异型预应力混凝土箱梁；塔柱采用钻石形钢筋混凝土结构，南岸塔高248.18m，北岸塔高208.2m，南岸主桥墩最大水深达57m；斜拉索按扇形布置，两主塔各安装88根斜拉索；桥塔基础采用钻孔灌注桩。

根据桥塔处建设条件，该桥采用刚度差异较大的高低塔形式。综合考虑斜拉桥对抗扭能力的需求以及特殊斜拉索布置形式，最终选择采用上塔柱分开距离较小的钻石形桥塔方案。大桥主要建设难点在于主跨箱梁吊装。主跨钢箱梁采用桥面起重机吊装，针对钢箱梁传统吊装技术因匹配高差产生的附加剪切应力问题，研发了"梁重转移"吊装技术，达到减小匹配高差和附加剪切应力的目的。

桥　　名：牌楼长江大桥
桥　　型：双塔双索面混合梁斜拉桥，全漂浮结构体系
主跨跨径：730m
桥　　址：重庆市万州区
建成时间：2019年5月
建设单位：重庆万州交通建设开发总公司
设计单位：中铁大桥勘测设计院集团有限公司
施工单位：中交路桥华南工程公司、四川公路桥梁建设集团有限公司

Pailou Bridge over Yangtze River, formerly known as Third Wanzhou Bridge over Yangtze River, is located in Wanzhou District, Chongqing City, 260km away from the City center of Chongqing, and is an important river-crossing node of urban trunk roads in the northeast of Chongqing. The bridge deck is a two-way six-lane urban trunk road with a design speed of 60km/h.

The bridge is composed of the main bridge, an approach bridge on both sides of the east and west, and various interchange ramps. The main bridge section is arranged from the southwest to the northeast. The main bridge is a double-tower double-cable plane hybrid girder cable-stayed bridge, which adopts a fully floating structural system. The span arrangement is 4×57.5m+730m+4×57m. The middle span of the main beam is an orthotropic deck steel box girder, and the side span is a single box multi-cell special-shaped prestressed concrete box girder. The tower is a reinforced diamond-shaped concrete structure. The tower height on the south bank is 248.18m, and the tower height on the north bank is 208.2m. The maximum water depth of the main pier on the south bank is 57m. The stay cables are arranged in a sector shape, and 88 stay cables are installed on each tower. The bridge tower foundation adopts bored piles.

According to the construction conditions at the bridge tower, the bridge adopts the form of high and low towers with large differences in stiffness. Considering the requirements of torsion resistance of the bridge and the special layout of stay cables, the diamond-shaped bridge tower with a smaller separation distance of upper tower columns is finally selected. The main construction difficulty of the bridge is the hoisting of the main span box girder. The main span steel box girder is hoisted by bridge cranes. To solve the problem of additional shear stress caused by matching height differences in traditional hoisting technology of steel box girders, the hoisting technology of "beam weight transfer" is developed to reduce matching height difference and additional shear stress.

**Name:** Pailou Bridge over Yangtze River
**Type:** Double-tower double-cable plane hybrid girder cable-stayed bridge, fully floating structural system
**Main Span:** 730m
**Location:** Wanzhou District, Chongqing City
**Completion:** May, 2019
**Owner(s):** Chongqing Wanzhou District Traffic Construction Development Corporation
**Designer(s):** China Railway Major Bridge Reconnaissance & Design Institute Co., Ltd.
**Contractor(s):** CCCC Road & Brdige Southern China Engineering Co., Ltd. and Sichuan Road & Bridge (Group) Co., Ltd.

# 平塘大桥
Pingtang Bridge

桥　　名：平塘大桥
桥　　型：三塔双索面钢-混凝土组合梁斜拉桥，半漂浮结构体系
主跨跨径：2×550m
桥　　址：贵州省黔南布依族苗族自治州
建成时间：2019年9月
建设单位：贵州省公路开发有限责任公司
设计单位：贵州省交通规划勘察设计研究院股份有限公司
施工单位：中铁二十局集团有限公司、珠海市中港路桥建设有限公司等

平塘大桥位于贵州省黔南布依族苗族自治州境内，跨越曹渡河大峡谷，是余庆—安龙高速公路（黔高速S62）重要节点。大桥全长2.135km，主桥全宽30.2m；桥面为双向四车道高速公路，设计速度80km/h。

大桥由主桥、引桥组成，呈西南至东北方向布置。跨径布置为249.5m+550m+550m+249.5m。主桥为三塔双索面钢-混凝土组合梁斜拉桥，采用半漂浮结构体系，主梁采用双工字形钢梁与混凝土桥面板组合梁；塔柱采用折线H形钢筋混凝土结构，三个主塔分别高145.2m、149.2m、145.2m；斜拉索为双索面扇形布置，每个主塔布有22对空间索；基础为挖孔桩基础，桩基按嵌岩桩设计。

桥位地处山区深谷风复杂环境下，桥梁设计根据风洞试验选定了设计基准风速、阵风系数及风攻角，采用空间索塔以适当增加顺桥向中塔刚度，从而提高了三塔斜拉桥整体刚度；并采用中塔塔梁铰接、边塔竖向支承的结构体系，减小了活载作用下主梁挠度及温度作用下塔底弯矩。

Pingtang Bridge is located in Qiannan Buyei and Miao Autonomous Prefecture of Guizhou Province, crossing the Grand Canyon of Caodu River as an important node of Yuqing-Anlong Expressway (Guizhou Expressway S62). The total length of the bridge is 2.135km, and the total width of the main bridge is 30.2m.The bridge deck is a two-way four-lane expressway with a design speed of 80km/h.

The main bridge and approach bridges are arranged from southwest to northeast. The span arrangement is 249.5m+550m+550m+249.5m. The main bridge is a three-tower double-cable plane steel-concrete composite girder cable-stayed bridge with a semi-floating structural system. The main beam is a composite beam of a double I-shaped steel beam and concrete bridge deck. The tower adopts a broken line H-shaped reinforced concrete structure, and the three main towers are 145.2m, 149.2m and 145.2m high, respectively. The stay cables are arranged in a double cable plane sector, and each main tower has 22 pairs of space cables. The foundation is a dug pile foundation, and the pile foundation is designed as rock socketed piles.

The bridge is located in a complex montane environment with deep valley wind. The bridge design has selected the design reference wind speed, gust coefficient, and wind attack angle according to the wind tunnel test. The space cable tower is used to appropriately increase the stiffness of the middle tower along the bridge, thus improving the overall stiffness of the three-tower cable-stayed bridge. The application of a hinge joint between the middle tower and beam reduces the deflection of the main beam under live load and bending moment of the tower bottom under temperature.

**Name:** Pingtang Bridge
**Type:** Three-tower double-cable plane steel-concrete composite girder cable-stayed bridge, semi-floating structural system
**Main Span:** 2×550m
**Location:** Qiannan Buyei and Miao Autonomous Prefecture, Guizhou Province
**Completion:** September, 2019
**Owner(s):** Guizhou Highway Development Co., Ltd.
**Designer(s):** Guizhou Transportation Planning Survey & Design Academe Co., Ltd.
**Contractor(s):** China Railway 20th Bureau Group Co., Ltd. and Zhuhai Zhonggang Road & Bridge Construction Co., Ltd., etc.

# 沪苏通长江公铁大桥

## Shanghai-Suzhou-Nantong Highway and Railway Bridge over Yangtze River

　　沪苏通长江公铁大桥跨越长江江苏段,向北连接渤海湾和京津冀城市群,向南由沪苏通铁路接入上海。大桥全长11.072km,其中公铁合建桥梁长6.989km。大桥采用双层桥面构造,上层为双向六车道通锡高速公路,设计速度100km/h;下层为双向四线铁路,分别为设计速度200km/h的沪苏通铁路和设计速度250km/h的通苏嘉甬高速铁路。

　　大桥由主航道桥、天生港航道桥、横港沙水域桥、跨长江大堤桥梁、两岸引桥组成。主航道桥为双塔三索面钢桁梁斜拉桥,跨径布置为140m+462m+1092m+462m+140m。主梁采用钢箱-桁架双层组合钢梁结构,横向三主桁;塔柱采用钻石形钢筋混凝土结构,承台顶以上塔高330m;斜拉索为扇形布置,采用2000MPa级高强平行钢丝;采用沉井基础。

大桥桥塔自重在塔底截面最大轴力中占比较大，约占54.4%，因此设计上采用高强高性能混凝土以减小桥塔截面尺寸，降低桥塔自重，减小基础规模。建设过程中，通过主塔墩钢沉井整体制造、助浮浮运技术，既保证了钢沉井质量，又可与锚碇同步施工，有效缩短了施工工期；采用超高主塔多索面钢锚梁整体组拼安装技术，保证了钢锚梁和索道管精度，更提高了安装效率；同时通过研制的1800t步履式架梁起重机，解决了大节段钢桁梁高空多杆件对接难题。

桥　　名：沪苏通长江公铁大桥
桥　　型：双塔三索面钢桁梁斜拉桥，半漂浮结构体系
主跨跨径：1092m
桥　　址：江苏省苏州市、南通市
建成时间：2020年6月
建设单位：沪苏通长江公铁大桥建设部
设计单位：中铁大桥勘测设计院集团有限公司
施工单位：中铁大桥局集团有限公司

Shanghai-Suzhou-Nantong Highway and Railway Bridge over Yangtze River spans the Jiangsu section of the Yangtze River, connecting Bohai Bay and the Beijing-Tianjin-Hebei urban agglomeration to the north, and connecting to Shanghai to the south by the Shanghai-Suzhou-Nantong Railway. The total length of the bridge is 11.072km, of which 6.989km is built as the road rail part. The bridge adopts a double-deck structure, and the upper deck is a two-way six-lane expressway, namely Nantong-Wuxi with a design speed of 100km/h. The lower deck is a two-way four-lane railway, namely Shanghai-Suzhou-Tongzhou Railway with a design speed of 200km/h and Nantong-Suzhou-Jiaxing-Ningbo High-speed Railway with a design speed of 250km/h.

The bridge is composed of the main channel bridge, the Tiansheng Port channel bridge, the Henggangsha water bridge, the bridge across the Yangtze River embankment, and the cross-strait approach bridge. The main channel bridge is a double-tower three-cable plane steel truss girder cable-stayed bridge, with a span arrangement of 140m+462m+1092m+462m+140m. The main beam adopts a steel box-truss double-layer combined steel beam structure, and three main trusses transversely. The tower adopts a diamond-shaped reinforced concrete structure, and its height above the top of the bearing platform is 330m. Stay cables are designed with a fan-shaped arrangement, using 2000MPa grade high-strength parallel steel wires. The tower uses a sinking foundation.

The self-weight of the bridge tower accounts for a relatively large proportion of the axial force on the tower bottom section (about 54.4%), so the designer adopts high-strength and high-performance concrete to reduce the cross-sectional size of the bridge tower, the self-weight of the bridge tower and the scale of the foundation. During the construction process, with the overall manufacturing of steel sinking shafts and the assisted floatation technology, the quality of steel sinking shafts is not only guaranteed but also the construction of anchors can be synchronized, which effectively reduces the construction period. The overall assembly and installation technology of the multi-cable plane steel anchor beam of the ultra-high main tower is adopted to ensure the accuracy of the steel anchor beam and the cableway pipe. This kind of application improves installation efficiency. Moreover, through the development of 1800t of walking beam cranes, the problem of high-altitude multi-member docking of large-section steel truss beams is solved.

**Name:** Shanghai-Suzhou-Nantong Highway and Railway Bridge over Yangtze River
**Type:** Double-tower three-cable plane steel truss girder cable-stayed bridge, semi-floating structural system
**Main Span:** 1092m
**Location:** Suzhou City, Nantong City, Jiangsu Province
**Completion:** June, 2020
**Owner(s):** Construction Headquarters of Hutong Yangtze River Bridge
**Designer(s):** China Railway Major Bridge Reconnaissance & Design Institute Co., Ltd.
**Contractor(s):** China Railway Major Bridge Engineering Group Co., Ltd.

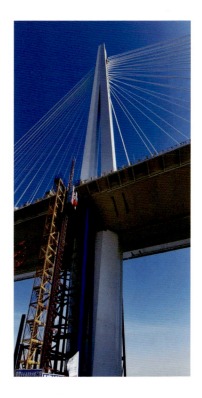

斜拉桥　　第三篇　P-131

南京江心洲长江大桥，又称南京长江第五大桥，位于江苏省南京市境内长江水道之上，是连接浦口区与建邺区的过江通道。桥梁总长 4.400km，主桥长 1796m；桥面为双向六车道城市主干道，设计速度 100km/h。

大桥由北至南分别由北引桥、主桥、南引桥组成。主桥为三塔双索面双主跨组合梁斜拉桥，半漂浮结构体系，跨径布置为 80m+218m+600m+600m+218m+80m；主梁采用轻型钢-混凝土组合结构，将混凝土包裹在钢壳内部；塔柱采用纵向钻石形、横向独柱式的钢-混凝土组合结构，中塔高 175.4m，南、北边塔高 167.7m；采用中央双索面扇形布置，共 240 根斜拉索。

大桥在设计上采用纵向钻石形索塔，设置交叉索结构；索塔具有较大的纵向刚度，与三塔斜拉桥的受力性能高度契合。大桥的建设采用多项新技术，使用粗集料活性粉末混凝土桥面板，在改善传统钢桥面沥青铺装材料性能和克服工艺缺陷的同时，可有效预防钢材疲劳开裂；采用钢壳混凝土组合索塔，提升工厂化制造水平，并实现现场无污染管控；主塔、桥面、桥墩的建设还采用了预制拼装工法，实现了建造过程的高效环保。

Nanjing Jiangxinzhou Bridge over Yangtze River, also known as Nanjing Yangtze River Fifth Bridge, is located on the Yangtze River Waterway in Nanjing, Jiangsu Province. It is a crossing channel connecting Pukou District and Jianye District. The total length of the bridge is 4.400km, the length of the main bridge is 1796m, and the bridge deck is a two-way six-lane urban arterial road with a design speed of 100km/h.

From north to south, the bridge is composed of a north approach bridge, the main bridge, and a south approach bridge. The main bridge is a three-tower double-cable plane double-main span composite girder cable-stayed bridge with a semi-floating structural system. Its span arrangement is 80m+218m+600m+600m+218m+80m. The main beam adopts a light steel-concrete combination structure, which wraps the concrete inside the steel shell. The tower is a longitudinal diamond-shaped, transverse single-column steel-concrete composite structure, with a height of 175.4m in the middle tower and 167.7m in the south and north towers. The bridge adopts a fan-shaped arrangement with a central double cable plane including 240 cables.

The design of the longitudinal single-column diamond-shaped tower with horizontal cross cables assigns the bridge with a large longitudinal stiffness, which highly fits with the force performance of the three-tower cable-stayed bridge. The construction of the bridge adopts a number of new technologies. For example, it utilizes the coarse aggregate active powder concrete bridge deck, which can effectively prevent the steel fatigue cracking and can solve the defects of traditional steel bridge deck asphalt pavement materials and processes. Besides, the use of shell steel-concrete composite towers improves the level of factory manufacturing and realizes pollution-free control on site. Moreover, the construction of the main tower, bridge deck, and piers adopts the prefabricated assembly method to achieve efficient and environmental protection in the construction process.

桥　　名：南京江心洲长江大桥
桥　　型：三塔双索面双主跨组合梁斜拉桥，半漂浮结构体系
主跨跨径：2×600m
桥　　址：江苏省南京市
建成时间：2020年12月
建设单位：南京市公共工程建设中心
设计单位：中交公路规划设计院有限公司
施工单位：中交第二航务工程局有限公司

**Name:** Nanjing Jiangxinzhou Bridge over Yangtze River
**Type:** Three-tower double-cable plane double-main span composite girder cable-stayed bridge, semi-floating structural system
**Main Span:** 2×600m
**Location:** Nanjing City, Jiangsu Province
**Completion:** December, 2020
**Owner(s):** Nanjing Public Project Construction Center
**Designer(s):** CCCC Highway Consultants Co., Ltd.
**Contractor(s):** CCCC Second Harbor Engineering Co., Ltd.

# 芜湖长江三桥
## Third Wuhu Bridge over Yangtze River

| | |
|---|---|
| 桥　名：芜湖长江三桥 | **Name:** Third Wuhu Bridge over Yangtze River |
| 桥　型：高低双塔双索面钢箱-钢桁组合梁斜拉桥，半漂浮结构体系 | **Type:** Double-tower (a high and low tower) double-cable plane double-steel truss girder cable-stayed bridge, semi-floating structural system |
| 主跨跨径：588m | **Main Span:** 588m |
| 桥　址：安徽省芜湖市 | **Location:** Wuhu City, Anhui Province |
| 建成时间：2020年9月 | **Completion:** September, 2020 |
| 建设单位：芜湖长江大桥投资建设有限公司 | **Owner(s):** Wuhu Bridge over Yangtze River Investment and Construction Co., Ltd. |
| 设计单位：中铁大桥勘测设计院集团有限公司 | **Designer(s):** China Railway Major Bridge Reconnaissance & Design Institute Co., Ltd. |
| 施工单位：中铁大桥局集团有限公司 | **Contractor(s):** China Railway Major Bridge Engineering Group Co., Ltd. |

芜湖长江三桥位于安徽省芜湖市境内，是合杭高速铁路和芜湖城市交通网的重要跨江节点。大桥采用双层桥面结构，上层为双向八车道城市主干道，设计速度60km/h，下层为双向四线铁路，设计速度250km/h。

大桥由主桥、南北接线桥及立交匝道组成，主桥呈西北至东南方向布置。主桥为双塔（高低塔）双索面钢箱-钢桁组合梁斜拉桥，半漂浮结构体系，跨径布置为99.3m+238m+588m+224m+85.3m；主梁为箱桁组合结构，下层由钢箱桁架杆件及钢箱桥面系组成整体箱形结构，上层由钢箱杆件及正交异性桥面板构成；塔柱为钻石形混凝土结构，塔高分别为155m、130.5m；斜拉索采用双索面扇形布置，共计76对；基础采用沉井基础。

在建设过程中，克服了多项技术难题。在架设主桥钢梁时，钢梁被划分为89个铁路面梁段单元和94个公路面梁段单元，采用分段吊装施工；考虑柱式框架墩墩帽底部带圆拱的特点，墩帽现浇采用子母式不落地拱架支撑系统+拱形模板的方案施工，将支架的成形结构和承重结构合二为一，优化了支撑系统受力模式。

Third Wuhu Bridge over Yangtze River is located in Wuhu City, Anhui Province, and is an important river-crossing node of Hefei-Hangzhou High-speed Railway and Wuhu City urban transportation network. The bridge adopts a double-deck structure, the upper deck is a two-way eight-lane urban arterial road with a design speed of 60km/h, and the lower deck is a two-way four-lane railway with a design speed of 250km/h.

The bridge consists of the main bridge, the north and south terminal bridges, and the overpass. The main bridge is arranged in a northwest-to-southeast direction. It is a

double-tower (a high and low tower) dowble-cable plane double-steel truss girder cable-stayed bridge, and a semi-floating structural system, with a span arrangement of 99.3m+238m+588m+224m+85.3m. The main beam is a steel box-truss composite structure, the lower layer is composed of steel box truss members and steel box bridge deck system to form an integral box-shaped structure, and the upper layer is composed of steel box members and orthotropic bridge decks. The tower pillars are diamond-shaped concrete structures, with heights of 155m and 130.5m, respectively. Cables are arranged as double-cable planes in a fan shape with a total of 76 pairs. The foundation adopts a sunken foundation.

During the construction process, a number of technical difficulties were overcome. When the steel girder of the main bridge was erected, the steel girder was divided into 89 railway surface beam section units and 94 highway surface beam section units. These units were constructed in sections. Considering the characteristics of the column frame pier cap is designed with a round arch at the bottom, the cast-in-situ construction of the pier cap adopts the scheme of sub-mother type non-floor arch support system with arch formwork, which combines the forming structure and load-bearing structure of the bracket and optimizes the force distribution of the support system.

# 青山长江大桥
## Qingshan Bridge over Yangtze River

桥　　名：青山长江大桥
桥　　型：双塔双索面钢箱梁和钢-混凝土组合梁斜拉桥，全漂浮结构体系
主跨跨径：938m
桥　　址：湖北省武汉市
建成时间：2021年4月
建设单位：武汉交通工程建设投资集团有限公司
设计单位：中铁大桥勘测设计院集团有限公司、
　　　　　湖北省交通规划设计院股份有限公司
施工单位：中铁大桥局集团有限公司

**Name:** Qingshan Bridge over Yangtze River
**Type:** Double-tower double cable-plane steel box girder and steel-concrete composite girder cable-stayed bridge, full-floating structural system
**Main Span:** 938m
**Location:** Wuhan City, Hubei Province
**Completion:** April, 2021
**Owner(s):** Wuhan Communications Investment Group Co., Ltd.
**Designer(s):** China Railway Major Bridge Reconnaissance & Design Institute Co., Ltd. and Hubei Communications Planning and Design Institute Co., Ltd.
**Contractor(s):** China Railway Major Bridge Engineering Group Co., Ltd.

青山长江大桥位于湖北省武汉市境内，是连接洪山区与黄陂区的过江通道，北起汉施互通，上跨长江水道及天兴洲，南至化工互通，总长7.548km，桥宽48m，桥面为双向八车道高速公路，设计速度120km/h。

大桥自北向南由北岸引桥、北汊副航道桥、南汊主航道桥、南岸引桥组成，线路呈正北至正南布置。主航道桥采用双塔双索面钢箱梁和钢-混凝土组合梁斜拉桥，全漂浮结构体系，跨径布置为100m+102m+148m+938m+148m+102m+100m，全长1638m；主跨主梁采用整体式钢箱梁，边跨主梁采用钢-混凝土组合梁；塔柱采用A形混凝土结构，南塔高271.5m，北塔高279.5m；全桥采用双索面扇形布置，共布置拉索126对，采用高强平行钢丝拉索。

建设过程中，针对该桥"大跨、重载、超宽"的工程特点及水文、地质条件，主桥南主墩钻孔灌注桩采用"吹填筑岛+旋挖钻机"方案施工，南主墩承台采用锁口钢管桩围堰方案施工；北主墩基础采用双壁钢套箱围堰平台一体法施工；针对超高A形塔无下横梁的特点，设置了13道临时横撑，以确保塔柱受力及线形符合要求；结合大桥全漂浮体系特点，采用顶推辅助合龙方案进行合龙施工。

Qingshan Bridge over Yangtze River is located in Wuhan City, Hubei Province. It is a river-crossing passage connecting Hongshan District and Huangpi District. The bridge starts from Hanshi Interchange in the north, crosses the Yangtze River Waterway and Tianxingzhou, and reaches Huagong Interchange in the south. The total length of the bridge is 7.548km, and the bridge width is 48m. The bridge deck is a two-way eight-lane expressway with a design speed of 120km/h.

From north to south, the bridge is composed of the North Bank Approach Bridge, the North Lane Secondary Channel Bridge, the South Lane Main Channel Bridge, and the South Bank Approach Bridge. The line is arranged in a north-to-south direction. The main channel bridge is a double-tower double-cable plane steel box girder and steel-concrete composite girder cable-stayed bridge, and a full-floating structural system. The span arrangement is 100m+102m+148m+938m+148m+102m+100m, with a total length of 1638m. The main span main beam adopts an integral steel box girder, and the side span main beam adopts a steel-concrete combined beam; the bridge tower adopts an A-shaped concrete structure, with a height of 271.5m in the south tower

and 279.5m in the north tower. The whole bridge has a fan-shaped arrangement of double cable planes, with a total of 126 pairs of cables, using high-strength parallel wire cables.

During the construction process, according to the engineering characteristics of "large span, heavy load and ultra-wide" and the hydrological and geological conditions of the bridge, the bored piles of the south main pier were constructed by the scheme of "blowing and filling island + rotary drilling rig". The bearing platform of the south main pier was constructed by the locking steel-pipe-pile cofferdam scheme. The foundation of the north main pier is constructed by the integrated method of a double-walled steel cofferdam platform. Given the characteristics of the ultra-tall A-shaped tower without lower cross-beams, 13 temporary cross-braces are set up to ensure the loading condition and a linear shape of the tower columns. Combined with the characteristics of the full-floating structural system of the bridge, the closure operation was carried out by incremental launching construction technology.

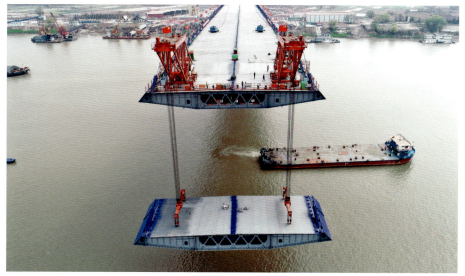

# 武穴长江大桥
## Wuxue Bridge over Yangtze River

| | |
|---|---|
| 桥　名：武穴长江大桥 | **Name:** Wuxue Bridge over Yangtze River |
| 桥　型：双塔双索面钢-混凝土混合箱梁斜拉桥，半漂浮结构体系 | **Type:** Double-tower double-cable plane steel concrete mixed box girder cable-stayed bridge, semi-floating structural system |
| 主跨跨径：808m | **Main Span:** 808m |
| 桥　址：湖北省黄冈市、黄石市 | **Location:** Huanggang City, Huangshi City, Hubei Province |
| 建成时间：2021年9月 | **Completion:** September, 2021 |
| 建设单位：湖北交通投资集团有限公司 | **Owner(s):** Hubei Communications Investment Group Co., Ltd. |
| 设计单位：湖北省交通规划设计院股份有限公司、中交第一公路勘察设计研究院有限公司 | **Designer(s):** Hubei Communications Planning and Design Institute Co., Ltd. and CCCC First Highway Consultants Co., Ltd. |
| 施工单位：湖北省路桥集团有限公司、中国铁建大桥工程局集团有限公司 | **Contractor(s):** Hubei Road and Bridge Group Co., Ltd. and China Railway Construction Bridge Engineering Bureau Group Co., Ltd. |

武穴长江大桥位于湖北省境内，是连接黄冈市与黄石市的过江通道。桥面为双向六车道高速公路，设计速度100km/h。

大桥由主桥、两岸引桥互通组成，主桥线路呈东北至西南方向布置。主桥全长1403m，为双塔双索面钢-混凝土混合箱梁斜拉桥，半漂浮结构体系，跨径布置为80m+290m+808m+75m+75m+75m；北边跨和中跨采用钢箱梁结构，南边跨采用预应力混凝土结构；北主塔采用钻石形混凝土塔，高269m；南主塔为A字形，高233m；共使用208根斜拉索，按扇形布置；北塔基础采用群桩基础，梅花状布置钻孔灌注桩；南塔基础采用群桩基础，行列式布置钻孔灌注桩。

建设过程中，为提高桥面系抗疲劳性能，U肋与顶板焊接设计要求全熔透，采用多头门式焊机+双向反变形胎架；混凝土箱梁采用长节段跳仓支架现浇施工，每个施工段分若干节浇筑；针对主墩大直径钻孔灌注桩、中风化砂岩夹页岩强度高和强风化斜坡岩漏水严重的施工特点，开发了大直径斜坡钻孔系统，确保了施工效率和成孔质量。主墩基础采用哑铃形双壁钢套箱围堰施工，总用钢量达2700t，整体下水的浮运安全风险、定位精度要求高，通过综合设置助浮系统、布设牵引限位装置、建立灵活升降体系等措施，成功实现了超高大型钢围堰下水浮运及定位下沉施工。

Wuxue Bridge over Yangtze River is located in Hubei Province and is a river-crossing passage connecting Huanggang City and Huangshi City. The bridge deck is a two-way six-lane highway with a design speed of 100km/h.

The bridge is composed of the main bridge and the interconnection of the two sides of the strait, and the main bridge line is arranged in a northeast-to-southwest direction. It is a double-tower double-cable plane steel concrete mixed box girder cable-stayed bridge. The total length is 1403m with a span arrangement of 80m+290m+808m+75m+75m+75m. The north span and middle span adopt a steel box girder structure, and the south span adopts a prestressed concrete structure. The north main tower adopts a diamond-shaped concrete tower with a height of 269m. The south main tower is A-shaped and 233m high. A total of 208 cable-stayed cables are used, arranged in a fan shape. The foundation of the north tower adopts a group pile foundation, and the bored pile is arranged in a plum blossom shape. The foundation of the south tower adopts a group pile foundation, and the bored piles are arranged in a columnar manner.

During the construction process, to improve the fatigue resistance of the bridge deck system, the U-rib and roof plate welding design requires full penetration. Therefore a multi-head portal welding machine with a two-way reverse pin jig was adopted. The concrete box girder adopts cast-in-situ construction of long-segment jumping brackets, and each construction section is poured in several sections. Considering the construction characteristics, including large diameter bored piles in the main tower, the high strength of moderately weathered sandstone intercalated with shale, and serious water leakage in strongly weathered slope rock, a large-diameter slope rock drilling system was developed to ensure the construction efficiency and hole formation quality. The main pier foundation adopts dumbbell-type double-walled steel casing cofferdam construction, with a total steel consumption of 2700t. The overall floating transportation safety risk and positioning accuracy requirements are high, and the ultra-high large steel cofferdam floating transportation and positioning sinking construction have been successfully realized by comprehensively setting up the floating system, laying the traction limit device, establishing a flexible lifting system and other measures.

# 赤壁长江公路大桥
## Chibi Highway Bridge over Yangtze River

赤壁长江公路大桥，连接湖北省洪湖市和赤壁市，位于长江水道之上，是《国家公路网规划》中公路跨江控制性工程。线路总长11.200km，双向六车道高速公路，设计速度100km/h。

大桥主桥为双塔双索面组合梁斜拉桥，半漂浮结构体系，跨径布置为90m+240m+720m+240m+90m；主梁采用双边箱式钢-混凝土组合梁结构；塔柱为H形钢筋混凝土结构，北塔高217.33m，南塔高223m；全桥斜拉索呈扇形，共116根，空间双索面布置；基础采用钻孔灌注桩，采用围堰法施工。

建设过程中，塔根主梁架设采用浮吊架设，其余标准主梁节段采用Tot全回转桥面起重机；标准节段采用两节段架设循环工序，在2个节段钢梁架设后进行桥面板湿接缝施工，节约了湿接时间，提高了工效；南桥塔墩施工采用围堰单元块制造、在墩位钻孔平台散拼、与桩基同步施工的技术，克服了度汛工期紧、下放精度要求高、封底质量控制难等一系列难题。

| 桥　名： | 赤壁长江公路大桥 |
| --- | --- |
| 桥　型： | 双塔双索面组合梁斜拉桥，半漂浮结构体系 |
| 主跨跨径： | 720m |
| 桥　址： | 湖北省洪湖市、赤壁市 |
| 建成时间： | 2021 年 7 月 |
| 建设单位： | 湖北交通投资集团有限公司 |
| 设计单位： | 中铁大桥勘测设计院集团有限公司 |
| 施工单位： | 中铁大桥局集团有限公司 |

**Name:** Chibi Highway Bridge over Yangtze River
**Type:** Double-tower double-cable plane composite girder cable-stayed bridge, semi-floating structural system
**Main Span:** 720m
**Location:** Honghu City, Chibi City, Hubei Province
**Completion:** July, 2021
**Owner(s):** Hubei Communications Investment Group Co., Ltd.
**Designer(s):** China Railway Major Bridge Reconnaissance & Design Institute Co., Ltd.
**Contractor(s):** China Railway Major Bridge Engineering Group Co., Ltd.

Chibi Highway Bridge over Yangtze River, connecting Honghu City and Chibi City in Hubei Province, is located on the Yangtze River Waterway as a highway cross-river control project in the *National Highway Network Planning*. The bridge is 11.200km long. It has a two-way six-lane expressway whose design speed is 100km/h.

The main Dridge of Chibi Highway Bridge over Yangtze River is a double-tower double-cable plane composite girder cable-stayed bridge with a semi-floating structural system. Its span arrangement is 90m+240m+720m+240m+90m. The girder adopts a bilateral box-type steel-concrete composite beam structure. The tower is an H-shaped reinforced concrete structure, while the north tower is 217.33m high and the south tower is 223m high.116 cables are fan-shaped and arranged in a double-cable plane. The foundation adopts bored piles and was constructed with the cofferdam method.

During the construction process, the main girder of the tower is erected by floating crane, and the rest of the standard main girder sections adopt Tot full-swing bridge deck crane. The standard section adopts the two-segment erection cycle process, and the bridge deck wet joint construction was carried out after the steel beam of the 2 segments was erected, which saves the wet joint time and improves the working efficiency. The construction of the south tower pier adopts the technology of cofferdam unit block manufacturing, scattering and assembling the drilling platform at the pier position, and synchronous with the pile foundation construction. In these processes, a series of problems were overcome, such as tight construction time during the flood season, high decentralization accuracy requirements, and the requirement for precise quality control of the back cover.

# 京港高铁鳊鱼洲长江大桥
## Bianyu Island Bridge over Yangtze River on Beijing-Hong Kong High-speed Railway

| | |
|---|---|
| 桥　　名：京港高铁鳊鱼洲长江大桥 | **Name:** Bianyu Island Bridge over Yangtze River on Beijing-Hong Kong High-speed Railway |
| 桥　　型：双塔双索面混合梁斜拉桥，半漂浮结构体系 | **Type:** Double-tower and double-cable-plane hybrid girder cable-stayed bridge, semi-floating structural system |
| 主跨跨径：672m | **Main Span:** 672m |
| 桥　　址：湖北省黄冈市、江西省九江市 | **Location:** Huanggang City, Hubei Province, Jiujiang City, Jiangxi Province |
| 建成时间：2021年12月 | **Completion:** December, 2021 |
| 建设单位：武九铁路客运专线湖北有限责任公司 | **Owner(s):** Wuhan-Jiujiang Railway Passenger Line Hubei Co., Ltd. |
| 设计单位：中铁大桥勘测设计院集团有限公司 | **Designer(s):** China Railway Major Bridge Reconnaissance & Design Institute Co., Ltd. |
| 施工单位：中铁大桥局集团有限公司、中铁十一局集团有限公司、中铁九桥工程有限公司等 | **Contractor(s):** China Railway Major Bridge Engineering Group Co., Ltd., China Railway 11th Bureau Group Co.,Ltd., China Railway Jiujiang Bridge Engineering Co., Ltd., etc. |

　　京港高铁鳊鱼洲长江大桥位于连接湖北省黄冈市与江西省九江市的安九高速铁路过江通道，桥梁全长4.260km，桥面为双向四线Ⅰ级铁路，其中上游侧高速铁路设计速度为350km/h，下游侧预留客货双线设计速度200km/h。

　　大桥由南汊航道桥、北汊航道桥、鳊鱼洲简支梁、跨大堤及道路连续梁和简支梁引桥组成。南汊主航道桥为双塔双索面混合梁交叉索斜拉桥，半漂浮结构体系，采用2×50m+224m+672m+174m+3×50m跨径布置；主梁主跨及辅助跨采用单箱三室钢箱梁，边跨及次边跨采用预应力混凝土箱梁；塔柱为H形混凝土结构；斜拉索呈扇形布置；桥塔基础采用钻孔灌注桩，桩基平面按行列式布置。

　　南汊主航道桥为典型的大跨、长联、高墩结构等，通过钢箱混合梁技术与交叉索技术集成创新，解决了跨中区域竖向刚度小、车体竖向加速度超标及轨道高低长波不平顺控制的技术难题；使用索塔大节段式钢锚箱与十字形内腔混凝土组合新结构，该结构大幅缩短了锚固区高度，优化了锚固区结构受力，简化了施工，有效缩短了工期，方便了维养；建设过程中，针对北汊航道桥基岩岩溶地质条件，采用"旋挖钻和旋转钻"接力复合成孔工艺克服了钻孔桩施工难题。

Bianyu Island Bridge over Yangtze River on Beijing-Hong Kong High-speed Railway is located in the Anqing-Jiujiang High-speed Railway crossing channel connecting Huanggang City, Hubei Province and Jiujiang City, Jiangxi Province. The total length of the bridge is 4.260km. The bridge deck is a two-way four-lane I -level railway. The design speed of the upstream high-speed railway is 350km/h, and the design speed of the passenger and freight double line reserved on the downstream side is 200km/h.

The bridge consists of South-branch Main Channel Bridge, the North-branch Main Channel Bridge, Bianyu Island Simple Branch Girder, Cross Embankment and Road Continuous Girder and Simple Supported Girder Approach Bridge. The South-branch Main Channel Bridge is a double-tower cable-stayed bridge, a semi-floating structural system with a 2×50m+224m+672m+174m+3×50m span arrangement. The main span and auxiliary span of the main beam are single-box three-chamber steel box girders. The side span and secondary side span adopt prestressed concrete box girders. The tower columns are H-shaped concrete structures. The cable-stayed cable is arranged in a fan shape, double-cable plane. The foundation of the bridge tower adopts bored piles, and the pile foundation plane is arranged in a determinant pattern.

The South-branch Main Channel Bridge is a typical large-span, long-linked, high-pier structure. Through the integration and innovation of steel box hybrid beam technology and cross cable technology, the technical problems of small vertical stiffness in the cross-middle area, excessive vertical acceleration of the car body and uneven control of track height and low long wave are solved. The new structure of Sota large-section steel anchor box and cross-shaped inner cavity concrete is used, which greatly shortens the height of the anchoring area, optimizes the structural force of the anchorage area, simplifies the construction, effectively shortens the construction period, and facilitates maintenance. During the construction process, according to the karst geological conditions of the bedrock of the North-branch Main Channel Bridge, a "rotary digging and rotary drilling" relay process was used to overcome the construction problem of bored piles.

# 白居寺长江大桥

## Baijusi Bridge over Yangtze River

桥　　名：白居寺长江大桥
桥　　型：双塔双索面钢桁梁斜拉桥，半漂浮结构体系
主跨跨径：660m
桥　　址：重庆市
建成时间：2022年1月
建设单位：重庆中交二航长江大桥建设发展有限公司
设计单位：重庆市市政设计研究院有限公司
　　　　　林同棪国际工程咨询（中国）有限公司
施工单位：中交第二航务工程局有限公司等

白居寺长江大桥位于重庆市境内长江水道之上，连接大渡口区和巴南区，是重庆市"七横线"和重庆轨道交通18号线跨越长江的通道。该桥为公轨两用钢桁梁斜拉桥，线路全长3.687km，上层为双向八车道城市主干道，设计速度为60km/h，下层为双向二线城市轨道交通，设计速度为100km/h。

大桥由主桥、左右引桥及两岸立交组成，主桥路段呈西南至东北方向布置。主桥为双塔双索面钢桁梁斜拉桥，半漂浮结构体系，跨径布置为107m+255m+660m+255m+107m；主塔采用多曲面水滴形混凝土结构，塔高236m；每座桥塔共计20对斜拉索，扇形布置，最大索长350m。

施工过程采用了BIM技术、高塔高掺量泵送混凝土技术、超长间隔期大体积混凝土施工技术等，克服了钢筋配料、线形控制、模板加工、高塔混凝土泵送、大体积混凝土防裂等难题。

Baijusi Bridge over Yangtze River is located on the Yangtze River Waterway in Chongqing, connecting Dadukou District and Ba'nan District, and is the passage of Chongqing's "Seven Horizontal Line" and Chongqing Rail Transit Line 18 which across the Yangtze River. The bridge is a dual-deck steel truss girder cable-stayed bridge with a total length of 3.687km, the upper deck is a two-way eight-lane urban arterial road with a design speed of 60km/h, and the lower deck is a two-way dual-line urban rail transit with a design speed of 100km/h.

The bridge is composed of the main bridge, the left and right approach bridges, and the interchange on both sides. The main bridge section is arranged in a southwest-to-northeast direction. It is a double-tower and double-cable plane steel truss girder cable-stayed bridge, a semi-floating system with a span arrangement of 107m+255m+660m+255m+107m. The main tower adopts a multi-curved drop-shaped concrete structure with a height of 236m. Each tower has a total of 20 pairs of cable-stayed cables, fan-shaped with a maximum cable length of 350m.

The construction process adopts BIM technology, high-volume concrete pumping technology of high towers, and large-volume concrete construction technology with ultra-long intervals. These technologies overcame the problems of steel bar batching, linear control, formwork processing, high tower concrete pumping, and large-volume concrete crack.

**Name:** Baijusi Bridge ove Yangtze River
**Type:** Double-tower and double-cable plane steel truss girder cable-stayed bridge, semi-floating structural system
**Main Span:** 660m
**Location:** Chongqing City
**Completion:** January, 2022
**Owner(s):** Chongqing CCCC Second Navigation Yangtze River Bridge Construction and Development Co., Ltd.
**Designer(s):** Chongqing Municipal Research Institue of Design, T.Y. Lin International Engineering Consulting (China) Co., Ltd.
**Contractor(s):** CCCC Second Harbor Engineering Co., Ltd.,etc.

中国桥梁　BRIDGES IN CHINA　2013—2023

# Chapter 4

## 第四篇

# 拱式桥

## Arch Bridges

# 引言

拱式桥最早以石拱桥的形式出现在古埃及和古希腊，以及后来的古罗马。我国古代石拱桥曾经创造过几百年的辉煌，其中最具代表性的就是公元605年李春设计建造的河北赵县赵州桥（或称安济桥），其开创了空腹式拱桥这一桥型，减轻了桥梁重量，增大了跨度，有利于泄洪，37.5m拱桥跨度的世界纪录一直保持到13世纪末，享誉世界。从14世纪到18世纪，石拱桥的跨度仅仅增长到54m。1779年，第一座铸铁拱桥诞生以后，拱桥跨度有了较快的增长，到1886年，锻铁拱桥最大跨度已经达到172.5m，是第一座铸铁拱桥跨度的3.5倍。从1874年第一座钢拱桥建成到1977年美国新河谷大桥建成的100多年里，拱式桥的跨度增长出现了飞跃，美国工程师们五次创造了拱式桥跨度的世界纪录，并将最大跨度定格在518m，是第一座钢拱桥跨度的3倍。

拱式桥是我国最常见的桥型之一，20世纪80年代改革开放之后，更是兴建了许多形式多样、功能各异、跨度很大的拱式桥。2000年建成的146m跨度的山西新丹河大桥，是世界上跨度最大的石拱桥。1997年建成的420m跨度的万州长江大桥，创造了混凝土拱桥的世界纪录；这一纪录被2016年建成的445m跨度的沪昆高铁北盘江特大桥打破；2023年又将建成600m跨度的天峨龙滩特大桥。2003年建成的550m跨度的上海卢浦大桥，打破了封存26年的拱式桥跨度世界纪录；2009年建成的552m跨度的重庆朝天门大桥，再次刷新了这一世界纪录。2013年建成的518m跨度的合江长江一桥，是第一座跨度突破500m的钢管混凝土拱桥；2020年建成的575m跨度的平南三桥，又一次刷新了钢管混凝土拱桥跨度纪录。2022年，在全世界已经建成的76座跨度超过300m的拱式桥中，我国有46座，占61%，我国已经成为名副其实的大跨度拱式桥大国。

近10年来，我国建成了近百座拱式桥，包括混凝土拱桥、钢拱桥和钢管混凝土拱桥等。本画册选取了14座拱桥，包括混凝土拱桥3座、钢拱桥4座、钢管混凝土拱桥6座和钢-混凝土组合拱桥1座。相比《中国桥梁 2003—2013》，所选拱式桥的跨度有所增长，钢管混凝土拱桥的跨度增长到575m，混凝土拱桥跨度达到了600m。钢管混凝土拱桥和钢管混凝土劲性骨架混凝土拱桥，是我国以苏联钢管混凝土拱桥和意大利型钢劲性骨架米兰法架拱技术为基础发展起来的，形成具有自主知识产权的核心技术，包括塔架斜拉扣索悬臂拼装的智能化索力控制、时间控制膨胀的无收缩管内混凝土材料和真空辅助多级连续泵送混凝土灌注等创新技术。钢管混凝土拱桥和钢管混凝土劲性骨架混凝土拱桥正展现出比钢拱桥更加突出的施工优点和耐久特性。

# INTRODUCTION

Arch bridges first appeared as stone arches in ancient Egypt and Greece and later in ancient Rome. The construction of ancient masonry arch bridges in China extends over hundreds of years and is marked with works of brilliance. The most representative Chinese creation is the Zhaozhou Bridge (or Anji Bridge) in Zhaoxian County, Hebei Province, which was built by Li Chun in AD 605. It created a spandrel arch bridge, which reduced weight, increased span, and minimized impact on flood discharge. The 37.5m span of the Zhaozhou Bridge held the world record span for arch bridges until the end of the 13th century. From this time until the 18th century, the span of masonry arch bridges grew only to 54m. In 1779, after the birth of the first cast iron arch bridge, arch spans increased rapidly. By 1886, the longest span of wrought iron arches had increased by a factor of 3.5 to reach 172.5m. The first steel arch bridge was built in 1874. Following this, American engineers set the world record for arch bridges five times, culminating in the 518m span of the New River Gorge Bridge in 1977. This represents an increase in span by a factor of 3 in just over 100 years.

Arch bridges are one of the most common types in China. After the reform and opening up in the 1980's, many arch bridges with various forms, different functions and long spans were built. The New Dan River Bridge in Shanxi Province with a span of 146m, built in 2000, is the largest masonry arch bridge in the world. The Wanzhou Bridge over Yangtze River with a span of 420m built in 1997 set a world record for concrete arch bridges. This record was broken in 2016 by the 445m span of the Shanghai-Kunming High-speed Railway Bridge over Beipan River. In 2023, the Tian'e Longtan Bridge in Guangxi will be completed. Its span of 600m will set a new world record. The 550m span of the Lupu Bridge in Shanghai, completed in 2003, broke the world record for the arch bridge span that had previously been held for 26 years. The Chaotianmen Bridge in Chongqing with a span of 552m, completed in 2009, broke the world record again. The First Hejiang Bridge over Yangtze River, with a span of 518m and completed in 2013, is the first concrete-filled steel tubular arch bridge with a span of more than 500m. Third Pingnan Bridge, with a span of 575m and completed in 2020, has once again set a record for the span of concrete-filled steel tubular arch bridges. By 2022, among the 76 arch bridges with a span of more than 300m built in the world, there are 46 in China, which accounts for 61%. China has become a veritable large-span arch bridge country.

In the past 10 years, nearly 100 arch bridges have been built in China, including concrete arches, steel arches and concrete-filled steel tubular arches. The fourteeen arch bridges that have been selected for this album include three concrete arch bridges, four steel arch bridges, six concrete-filled steel tubular arch bridges and one steel-concrete composite arch bridge. Compared to the previous edition of this album, the span of the arch bridges included has increased. The span of concrete-filled steel tubular arch bridges has increased to 575m, creating a new world record for the span of this type of bridge. The span of concrete arch bridges has reached 600m, which has broken the world record for the span held for the past three years. The span of arch bridges is continuing to grow. The concrete-filled steel tubular arch bridge and the concrete-filled steel tubular stiff skeleton arch bridges are core technologies with independent intellectual property rights developed by China on the basis of earlier work from the former Soviet Union and the Italian Milan steel stiff skeleton arch technology. The innovative technologies, including intelligent cable force control during cantilever assembly using cable-stayed buckles, non-shrinkage in-tube concrete materials with time-controlled expansion and vacuum-assisted multi-stage continuous pumping and pouring, are showing greater advantages for construction and higher durability than steel arch bridges.

# 云桂铁路南盘江特大桥
## Yunnan-Guangxi Railway Bridge over Nanpan River

云桂铁路南盘江特大桥，位于云南省红河哈尼族彝族自治州弥勒市与文山壮族苗族自治州丘北县交界处，横跨南盘江，是国家铁路网中"八纵八横"的快速客运通道——云桂铁路的重点工程。大桥全长852.43m，桥面宽13.4m，双线高速铁路，设计速度250km/h。

南盘江特大桥的主桥为上承式钢筋混凝土拱桥，主跨跨径416m，矢跨比1/4.2，是目前世界上跨径最大的客货共线铁路混凝土拱桥；钢筋混凝土拱圈采用等高、中段等宽、近拱脚段变宽的单箱三室结构，内设钢管混凝土桁式劲性骨架，钢管弦杆内灌注C80混凝土，拱脚与拱座固结；拱上建筑采用全空腹式构造，中间为多跨预应力混凝土连续梁，两端分别连接预应力混凝土刚构和T构过渡跨，腹孔墩为钢筋混凝土双柱式框架结构。拱圈劲性骨架采用缆索吊装、斜拉扣索悬臂拼装施工方法。

南盘江特大桥采用的桥面综合静态竖向变形的12.5m弦平均曲率、横向变形的拱上相邻跨折角+曲线半径的结构变形控制技术，大幅减小了拱圈结构尺寸；采用扣索拉力的主动调整技术，增加了劲性骨架节段长度，有效控制了骨架拼装和拱圈混凝土浇筑过程中已建结构的受力和变形，缩短了工期，提高了经济性；对拱圈顶底板、分块浇筑拱座施加横向预应力，配合混凝土级配优化和外加剂添加，有效避免了大体积混凝土施工质量问题。

Yunnan-Guangxi Railway Bridge over Nanpan River is located at the junction of Mile City in Honghe Hani and Yi Autonomous Prefecture and Qiubei County in Wenshan Zhuang and Miao Autonomous Prefecture, Yunnan Province. It spans the Nanpan River and is the key project of the "eight vertical and eight horizontal" rapid passenger transport channel, Yunnan-Guangxi Railway, in the national railway network. The bridge is 852.43m long and 13.4m wide. It's a double-track high-speed railway bridge with a design speed of 250km/h.

The main bridge is a deck-type reinforced concrete arch bridge with a main span of 416m and a rise-span ratio of 1/4.2. It is the largest span concrete arch bridge for passenger and freight railway in the world. The reinforced concrete arch has a single box with three cells. The height of the arch is constant, and the width is constant in the middle and then gradually increases to the arch feet. The arch has a stiff skeleton of concrete-filled steel tube truss with chords filled with C80 concrete. The arch feet are fixed with arch seats. The arch spandrel is open. The middle spans of the deck are multi-span prestressed concrete continuous girders, and both ends are prestressed concrete rigid frames and T-frame transition spans. The piers for spandrel are reinforced concrete double-column frames. The arch stiff skeletons are erected by cable hoisting and stayed buckle cable technology.

The structural design adopts a comprehensive static deformation control to reduce the arch size, including the mean curvature of vertical displacement in 12.5m chord length, and for lateral deformation, the deformation angle difference between adjacent deck spans and the deflection radius. The tensile force of the buckle is actively adjusted to increase the length of the stiff skeleton segment, which effectively controls the stress and deformation of the installed structure during the pouring process, shortens the construction period and improves the economy. The transverse prestressing is applied to the top and bottom slabs of arch ribs and the arch seats casted in stages, and the concrete gradation optimization and admixture addition are combined to effectively avoid the construction quality problem of mass concrete.

---

桥　　名：云桂铁路南盘江特大桥
桥　　型：上承式钢筋混凝土拱桥
主跨跨径：416m
桥　　址：云南省红河哈尼族彝族自治州弥勒市、文山壮族苗族自治州丘北县
建成时间：2016年12月
建设单位：云桂铁路云南有限责任公司
设计单位：中铁二院工程集团有限责任公司
施工单位：中铁十八局集团有限公司

**Name:** Yunnan-Guangxi Railway Bridge over Nanpan River
**Type:** Deck-type reinforced concrete arch bridge
**Main Span:** 416m
**Location:** Mile City, Honghe Hani and Yi Autonomous Prefecture, Qiubei County, Wenshan Zhuang and Miao Autonomous Prefecture, Yunnan Province
**Completion:** December, 2016
**Owner(s):** Yungui Railway Yunnan Co., Ltd.
**Designer(s):** China Railway Eryuan Engineering Group Co., Ltd.
**Contractor(s):** China Railway 18th Bureau Group Co., Ltd.

CHAPTER 4     ARCH BRIDGES     拱式桥     第四篇

# 沪昆高铁北盘江特大桥
## Shanghai-Kunming High-speed Railway Bridge over Beipan River

| | |
|---|---|
| 桥　　名： | 沪昆高铁北盘江特大桥 |
| 桥　　型： | 上承式钢筋混凝土拱桥 |
| 主跨跨径： | 445m |
| 桥　　址： | 贵州省安顺市关岭布依族苗族自治县、黔西南布依族苗族自治州晴隆县 |
| 建成时间： | 2016年12月 |
| 建设单位： | 沪昆铁路客运专线贵州有限公司 |
| 设计单位： | 中铁二院工程集团有限责任公司 |
| 施工单位： | 中铁广州工程局集团有限公司 |

**Name:** Shanghai-Kunming High-speed Railway Bridge over Beipan River
**Type:** Deck-type reinforced concrete arch bridge
**Main Span:** 445m
**Location:** Guanling Buyi and Miao Autonomous County, Anshun City, Qinglong County, Qianxinan Buyi and Miao Autonomous Prefecture, Guizhou Province
**Completion:** December, 2016
**Owner(s):** Shanghai-Kunming Railway Passenger Dedicated Line Guizhou Co., Ltd.
**Designer(s):** China Railway Eryuan Engineering Group Co., Ltd.
**Contractor(s):** China Railway Guangzhou Engineering Group Co., Ltd.

沪昆高铁北盘江特大桥，位于贵州省安顺市关岭布依族苗族自治县与黔西南布依族苗族自治州晴隆县交界处，一跨跨越北盘江，是沪昆客运专线铁路贵州西段的重点工程。大桥全长721.25m，桥面宽13.4m，为设计车速350km/h的双线高速铁路桥。

沪昆高铁北盘江特大桥主桥为上承式钢筋混凝土拱桥，主跨跨径445m，矢跨比1/4.45，是目前世界上最大跨径高速铁路混凝土拱桥。主桥钢筋混凝土拱圈采用等高、中段等宽、近拱脚段变宽的单箱三室结构，内设钢管混凝土空间桁式劲性骨架，钢管弦杆内灌注C80混凝土，拱脚与拱座固结；拱上建筑采用全空腹式构造，中间为预应力混凝土连续梁、两端各连预应力混凝土T构过渡跨，腹孔墩为钢筋混凝土双柱式框架结构。拱圈劲性骨架采用缆索吊装、斜拉扣挂悬臂拼装施工方法。

北盘江特大桥的桥面系结构采用了多跨连续梁接T构的全连续长联结构体系，一联长度达到599.6m，在拱跨范围内无缝，提高了列车高速行驶的安全性和舒适性；针对高速铁路特大跨径混凝土拱桥的特点，提出了结构变形高精度分析方法和整体位移控制标准；研发了导风屏障、桥面变形实时智能监测等装置，建立了智能化运行保障系统。

Shanghai-Kunming High-speed Railway Bridge over Beipan River is located at the junction of Guanling Buyi and Miao Autonomous County in Anshun City and Qinglong County in Qianxinan Buyi and Miao Autonomous Prefecture, Guizhou Province. It spans the Beipan River and is the key project of the western section of the Shanghai-Kunming Passenger Dedicated Railway in Guizhou Province. The bridge is 721.25m long and 13.4m wide. It is a double-track high-speed railway bridge with a design speed of 350km / h.

The main bridge is a deck-type reinforced concrete arch bridge with a main span of 445m and a rise-span ratio of 1/4.45. It is the largest span concrete arch bridge for high-speed railway in the world. The reinforced concrete arch has a single box with three cells. The height of the arch is constant and the width is constant in the middle and then gradually increases to the arch feet. The arch has a stiff skeleton of concrete-filled steel tube truss with chords filled with C80 concrete. The arch feet are fixed with arch seats. The arch spandrel is open. The middle spans of the bridge deck are prestressed concrete continuous girders, and both ends are prestressed concrete T-frame transition spans. The piers for spandrel are reinforced concrete double-column frames. The stiff skeletons of arches are erected by cable hoisting and stayed buckle cable technology.

The bridge deck is a long multi-span continuous beam with a length of 599.6m and no seam is set in the arch span to improve the safety and comfort of high-speed train. According to the characteristics of large-span concrete arch bridge of high-speed railway, the high precision analysis method of structural deformation and the overall displacement control standard are put forward. A wind barrier system and a real-time intelligent monitoring device for bridge deck deformation are developed, and an intelligent operation guarantee system is established.

# 梅山红桥
## Meishan Red Bridge

梅山红桥，也称梅山春晓大桥，位于浙江省宁波市，是连接宁波梅山岛与北仑区的特大型跨海桥梁工程。大桥全长1971m，桥面宽33m，主桥采用双层桥面结构，上层为双向六车道一级公路，下层为非机动车道和人行道，是世界首座下层纵移开启式双层桥梁。

梅山红桥的主桥为中承式钢桁组合系杆拱桥，跨径布置为80m+336m+80m，矢跨比为1/5，拱、梁及系杆组合结构，外部全支座支承；钢桁拱由两片平行桁拱与米字形横向风撑组成，上下弦杆和直腹杆为箱形断面，斜腹杆按拉、压受力分别采用H形或箱形截面。主梁采用双层桥面结构，上层为钢箱系梁、横梁及小纵梁与混凝土桥面板的组合梁，钢桁拱的水平推力由拉索系杆和钢箱系梁共同承担；下层为三段式钢桥面结构，两个边段与上层钢桁连接，中段由钢桁下挂于上层。边跨采用支架拼装施工方法，中跨采用缆索吊装、斜拉扣索悬臂拼装及先拱后梁的施工方法。

梅山红桥研制的多点悬挂导向、楔块刚性锁定及重载同步传动的下层桥面纵移开启式系统，解决了桥上车辆与桥下大型船舶全天候通行需求；采用"吊扣合一固塔少扣索"主动控制技术和异性钢桁整体竖转和定点起吊等技术，实现了超高、超重异性构件高效高精度安装；利用中跨钢桁拱的承载能力，仅由2对辅助扣索完成悬臂拼装；将3D激光扫描技术用于钢桁节段多环口模拟预拼装，实现了环缝拼接和节段预拼偏差的数字化校正。

Meishan Red Bridge, also known as Meishan Chunxiao Bridge, is located in Ningbo City, Zhejiang Province. It is a super-large sea-crossing bridge project connecting Ningbo Meishan Island and Beilun District. The bridge has a total length of 1971m and a bridge deck width of 33m. The main bridge has a double-deck. The upper deck is a two-way six-lane first-class highway, and the lower deck is non-motor lanes and sidewalks. It is the world's first double-deck bridge that can be longitudinally opened at the lower-deck.

The main bridge is a half-through steel truss composite tied arch bridge with a span arrangemet of 80m+336m+80m and a rise-span ratio of 1/5. The bridge is fully supported by external bearings. The arch is a steel truss composed of two parallel truss arches and pozidriv-shaped braces. The upper and lower chords and straight webs are box sections, and the diagonal webs are H-shaped or box sections according to tension and compression. Main girder is double deck structure. The upper deck consists of steel box tie beams, cross beams, small longitudinal beams and concrete slabs. The horizontal thrust is balanced by the tension force in tie cables and steel box tie beams. The lower deck is a three-segment steel structure, two side segments are connected with the upper steel truss, and the middle segment is suspended by the steel truss. The side spans are assembled on brackets, and the middle span is installed through cable hoisting and stayed buckle cable technology, and arch first and deck later.

The lower deck longitudinal open system adopts several innovative techniques such as multi-point suspension guide, wedge rigid locking and heavy load synchronous transmission, which meets the all-weather traffic demand of vehicles on the bridge and large ships under the bridge. The high-efficiency and high-precision installation of super-high and super-heavy anisotropic components is realized by using the active control technology of fewer buckles combined with hangers and buckles and the technology of integral vertical rotation and fixed-point lifting of anisotropic steel trusses. Using the bearing capacity of the mid-span steel truss arch, the cantilever assembly is completed by only 2 pairs of auxiliary buckles. The 3D laser scanning technology is used to simulate the pre-assembly of multi-rings of steel truss segments, and the digital calibration of assembly deviation is implemented.

桥　名：梅山红桥
桥　型：中承式钢桁组合系杆拱桥
主跨径：336m
桥　址：浙江省宁波市
建成时间：2017 年 9 月
建设单位：宁波梅山岛开发投资有限公司
设计单位：上海市政工程设计研究总院（集团）有限公司
施工单位：四川公路桥梁建设集团有限公司、
　　　　　中铁山桥集团有限公司

**Name:** Meishan Red Bridge
**Type:** Half-through steel truss composite tied arch bridge
**Main Span:** 336m
**Location:** Ningbo City, Zhejiang Province
**Completion:** September, 2017
**Owner(s):** Ningbo Meishan Island Development Investment Co., Ltd.
**Designer(s):** Shanghai Municipal Engineering Design Institute (Group) Co., Ltd.
**Contractor(s):** Sichuan Road and Bridge（Group）Co., Ltd. and China Railway Shanhaiguan Bridge Group Co., Ltd.

# 官塘大桥

## Guantang Bridge

官塘大桥，位于广西壮族自治区柳州市，是连接市中心东北方向城中区与鱼峰区的主干路。大桥全长1155.5m，桥面宽39.5m，双向六车道城市主干路，两侧设人行道，设计车速80km/h。

官塘大桥主桥为中承式钢箱拱桥，主跨跨径457m，矢跨比为1/4.5；横向采用内倾式双拱肋结构，其间设多道等宽变高一字形钢箱横撑；拱肋采用等宽变高单箱室的钢结构，钢箱拱肋的顶、底板及腹板均采用变厚度设计，纵向设置板式加劲肋，拱脚与拱座固结；桥面结构采用单箱单室扁平全焊钢箱梁，两侧均采用横向双吊杆构造，上端锚具、下端销铰式锚固体系。钢箱拱采用少支架拼装和整体提升安装的施工方法。

官塘大桥采用的拱肋切四角内倾提篮式、变高一字箱形横撑及弧形底面等纵横呼应的细节设计，减小了风阻，提升了箱形拱的景观和视觉效果；提出的边拱段少支架拼装、中拱段低位支架拼接+大节段整体提升安装的施工工艺，实现了长度262m、质量5885t拱段的68m提升；研发的钢筋混凝土咬合桩+钢管内撑的基坑支护技术、外围高压旋喷桩+基底注浆的基坑止水技术，解决了临江溶蚀透水性地质中拱座超大深基坑的开挖难题。

Guantang Bridge, located in Liuzhou City, Guangxi Zhuang Autonomous Region, is the main road connecting Chengzhong District and Yufeng District to the northeast of the city center. The bridge has a total length of 1155.5m, a bridge deck width of 39.5m, a two-way six-lane urban trunk road with sidewalks on both sides, and a design speed of 80km/h.

The main bridge is a half-through steel box arch bridge with a main span of 457m and a rise-span ratio of 1/4.5. The bridge has double inward-inclined arch ribs and multiple linear shaped steel box bracings with equal width and variable height are set between ribs. Each of the arch ribs has steel single box sections with equal width and variable height. The steel box arch ribs have variable thickness top, bottom plates and webs and longitudinally stiffened by plates. The arch feet are fixed with arch seats. The bridge deck is a flat single-box single-cell fully welded steel box girder. The transverse double hangers are arranged on both sides of the box girder, and the hangers adopt an upper anchor and lower pin-hinged anchorage system. The steel box arch adopts the construction method of less bracket assembly and integral lifting.

The design of structural details of Guantang Bridge such as basket-type arch ribs, variable height one-line box braces and curved bottom of ribs, reduces the air drag and improves the landscape and visual effect. The construction technology of side arch segments assembled by less scaffolds, middle arch segments assembled on low brackets and large segments integral lifting is put forward, which realizes 68m lifting of arch segments with 262m length and 5885t weight. The foundation pit support technology of using reinforcement concrete interlocking piles and steel pipe internal supports, and water stopping technology of foundation pit of using external high-pressure rotating piles and grouting basement are adopted to solve the excavation problem of super large deep foundation pit of the abutment in riverside dissolution permeable geology.

| | |
|---|---|
| 桥　名： | 官塘大桥 |
| 桥　型： | 中承式钢箱拱桥 |
| 主跨跨径： | 457m |
| 桥　址： | 广西壮族自治区柳州市 |
| 建成时间： | 2018年11月 |
| 建设单位： | 柳州市城市投资建设发展有限公司 |
| 设计单位： | 四川省公路规划勘察设计研究院有限公司 |
| 施工单位： | 中铁上海工程局集团有限公司 |

**Name:** Guantang Bridge
**Type:** Half-through steel box arch bridge
**Main Span:** 457m
**Location:** Liuzhou City, Guangxi Zhuang Autonomous Region
**Completion:** November, 2018
**Owner(s):** Liuzhou Investment Construction Development Co., Ltd.
**Designer(s):** Sichuan Highway Planning, Survey, Design and Research Institute Ltd.
**Contractor(s):** Shanghai Civil Engineering Co., Ltd. of CREC

# 大小井特大桥
## Daxiaojing Bridge

大小井特大桥，位于贵州省黔南布依族苗族自治州罗甸县，是平塘至罗甸高速公路关键工程，也是黔南地区横向运输大通道重要工程。大桥全长1500m，桥面宽24.5m，双向四车道高速公路，设计车速为80km/h。

大小井特大桥主桥为上承式钢管混凝土拱桥，主跨跨径450m，矢跨比1/4.5；横向采用平行双拱肋结构，其间设多道钢管横向联系；拱肋为等宽变高桁式钢管混凝土结构，每个拱肋由4根直径1360mm的钢管混凝土弦杆、钢管腹杆及横连杆组成，拱肋横截面设竖向V形剪力撑，拱脚与拱座固结；拱上建筑采用全空腹式构造，腹孔墩为两根4肢钢管组合柱+空心钢盖梁的框架结构，桥面系结构为双钢梁-混凝土桥面板组合梁。钢管拱肋采用缆索吊装、斜拉扣索悬臂拼装施工方法。

大小井特大桥提出的拱肋竖向V形剪力撑，保证了截面抗扭刚度，降低了施工难度，减少了材料用量；采用平缀4肢管式组合柱设计，提高了柱身稳定性，减轻了自重，降低了风荷载影响；预制桥面板的预留暗槽构造，简化了与钢梁连接施工；综合应用传感监测、动态控制及云数据等技术，实现了塔架偏移、扣索拉力、锚碇滑移等数据实时自测、采集及控制预报。

Daxiaojing Bridge is located in Luodian County, Qiannan Buyi and Miao Autonomous Prefecture, Guizhou Province. It is a key project of Pingtang-Luodian Expressway and an important project of the transverse transport corridor in Qiannan area. The bridge is 1500m in length and 24.5m in width. It is a two-way four-lane highway with a design speed of 80km/h.

The main bridge is a deck-type concrete-filled steel tubular arch bridge with a main span of 450m and a rise-span ratio of 1/4.5. The main span has a double parallel arch rib and multiple steel pipes connected ribs. Each rib is a truss with equal width and variable height and composed of 4 concrete-filled steel tube chords with a diameter of 1360mm, steel tube web members and transverse connections. The vertical V-shaped shear-braces are set between the arch ribs, and the arch feet and the arch seats are fixed. The piers for the spandrel arch are frame structures with two 4-limb steel tube composite columns and hollow steel cap beams. The bridge deck is composite of double steel girders and concrete slabs. The steel tube arch ribs are erected by cable hoisting and stayed buckle cable technology.

The vertical V-shaped shear-braces enhance the torsional stiffnesses of the sections and reduce the construction difficulty and material consumption. The design of a 4-limb steel tube composite column improves stability and reduces the weight and wind load. The precast deck slabs have reserved moderate grooves to simplify connection construction with steel girders. Through the comprehensive applications of sensor monitoring, dynamic control and cloud data technologies, the construction data such as the tower offsets, cable tension forces and anchorage slips are real-time self-tested, collected and forecasted.

| | |
|---|---|
| 桥　　名： | 大小井特大桥 |
| 桥　　型： | 上承式钢管混凝土拱桥 |
| 主跨跨径： | 450m |
| 桥　　址： | 贵州省黔南布依族苗族自治州罗甸县 |
| 建成时间： | 2019年8月 |
| 建设单位： | 贵州省公路开发有限责任公司 |
| 设计单位： | 中交第二公路勘察设计研究院有限公司 |
| 施工单位： | 贵州桥梁建设集团有限责任公司、贵州路桥集团有限公司 |

**Name:** Daxiaojing Bridge
**Type:** Deck-type concrete-filled steel tubular arch bridge
**Main Span:** 450m
**Location:** Luodian County, Qiannan Buyi and Miao Autonomous Prefecture, Guizhou Province
**Completion:** August, 2019
**Owner(s):** Guizhou Highway Development Co., Ltd.
**Designer(s):** CCCC Second Highway Consultants Co., Ltd.
**Contractor(s):** Guizhou Bridge Construction Group Co., Ltd. and Guizhou Road & Bridge Group Co., Ltd.

CHAPTER 4　　ARCH BRIDGES　　拱式桥　　第四篇

# 秭归长江大桥
## Zigui Bridge over Yangtze River

| | |
|---|---|
| 桥　名： | 秭归长江大桥 |
| 桥　型： | 中承式钢桁拱桥 |
| 主跨跨径： | 531.2m |
| 桥　址： | 湖北省宜昌市秭归县 |
| 建成时间： | 2019年9月 |
| 建设单位： | 湖北秭兴长江大桥建设开发有限公司 |
| 设计单位： | 湖北省交通规划设计院股份有限公司 |
| 施工单位： | 中铁大桥局第七工程有限公司 |

**Name:** Zigui Bridge over Yangtze River
**Type:** Half-through steel truss arch bridge
**Main Span:** 531.2m
**Location:** Zigui County, Yichang City, Hubei Province
**Completion:** September, 2019
**Owner(s):** Hubei Zixing Yangtze River Bridge Construction and Development Co., Ltd.
**Designer(s):** Hubei Communications Planning and Design Institute Co., Ltd.
**Contractor(s):** The 7th Engineering Co., Ltd., MBEC

秭归长江大桥，位于湖北省宜昌市境内，跨越长江连接秭归县郭家坝镇及归州镇两岸，是三峡工程后续规划工作中湖北省投资最大的项目。大桥主桥全长883.2m，桥面宽32.3m，双向四车道一级公路，两侧设人行道，设计车速60km/h。

秭归长江大桥主桥采用中承式钢桁拱桥，主跨跨径531.2m，矢跨比为1/4；钢桁拱由横向两片平行拱桁经平、横联形成空间变截面桁架结构，拱脚由承压式连接构造与拱座固结；桥面结构采用钢梁－混凝土桥面板的组合梁，拱上墩为钢双柱式框架结构，吊杆采用钢绞线整体挤压成型锚具拉索。钢桁拱采用缆索吊装、斜拉扣索悬臂拼装施工方法。

秭归长江大桥研发了承压板与预应力钢棒组合的拱脚连接构造，实现了拱脚全截面受压；桥面结构采用半漂浮式减隔震约束体系，兼顾了拱上长柱稳定和短柱受力要求，限制了桥面纵向位移，减少了结构罕遇地震响应；采用300MPa高应力幅、高耐久钢绞线拉索体系，提高了短吊杆的抗疲劳性能和使用寿命；采用卸载溶蚀顺向边坡岩层的精细化勘察和综合加固技术、大跨度重载缆索吊机及智能监控技术、复杂风场环境下钢桁拱架设技术、拱上钢立柱立式预拼装技术等，保证了大桥施工安全和工程质量。

Zigui Bridge over Yangtze River is located in Yichang City, Hubei Province. It connects Guojiaba Town and Guizhou Town in Zigui County across the Yangtze River. It is the largest investment project in Hubei Province in the follow-up planning of the Three Gorges Project. The main bridge is 883.2m in length and 32.3m in width. It is a two-way four-lane first-class highway with sidewalks on both sides. The design speed is 60km/h.

The main bridge is a half-through steel truss arch bridge with a main span of 531.2m and a rise-span ratio of 1/4. The arch is a spatial variable cross-section truss composed of two parallel arch trusses connecting in parallel and transverse. The arch feet are fixed with the arch seats through the compression connections. The deck is the steel-concrete composite beam, the spandrel piers are steel double-column frames. The suspenders adopt steel strand integral extrusion forming anchorage cables. The steel truss arches are erected by cable hoisting and stayed buckle cable technology.

The arch foot connections of the combination of bearing plate and prestressed steel bars are developed to achieve the full section compression of arch feet. A semi-floating seismic isolation constraint system is applied in the deck, which considers the stability of long columns on arch and the stress requirements of short columns, and limits the longitudinal displacement of the deck and reduces the rare earthquake response of the structure. The 300MPa high-stress amplitude and high durability steel strand cable system are adopted to improve the fatigue resistance and service life of the short hangers. The construction safety and engineering quality of the bridge are ensured by adopting a fine survey and comprehensive reinforcement technology of unloading dissolution consequent rock slope, large-span heavy-duty cable crane and intelligent monitoring technology, steel truss arch erection technology under complex wind field environment, and vertical pre-assembly technology of steel column on arch.

# 成贵铁路鸭池河特大桥
## Chengdu-Guiyang Railway Bridge over Yachi River

| | |
|---|---|
| 桥　　名：成贵铁路鸭池河特大桥 | Name: Chengdu-Guiyang Railway Bridge over Yachi River |
| 桥　　型：中承式钢-混凝土组合拱桥 | Type: Half-through steel-concrete composite arch bridge |
| 主跨跨径：436m | Main Span: 436m |
| 桥　　址：贵州省清镇市、黔西市 | Location: Qingzhen City and Qianxi City, Guizhou Province |
| 建成时间：2019年12月 | Completion: December, 2019 |
| 建设单位：成贵铁路有限责任公司 | Owner(s): Chenggui Railway Co., Ltd. |
| 设计单位：中铁大桥勘测设计院集团有限公司 | Designer(s): China Railway Major Bridge Reconnaissance & Design Institute Co., Ltd. |
| 施工单位：中铁大桥局集团第五工程有限公司 | Contractor(s): The 5th Engineering Co., Ltd., MBEC |

　　成贵铁路鸭池河特大桥，位于贵州省清镇市与黔西市交界鸭池河，是成贵铁路跨越鸭池河的特大桥梁。大桥全长971m，桥面宽22m/15.2m，为设计车速250km/h的双线高速铁路桥。

　　成贵铁路鸭池河特大桥主桥为中承式钢-混凝土组合拱桥，主跨跨径436m，矢跨比1/3.8，是目前世界上跨径最大的中承式钢-混凝土组合拱桥。主桥横向采用各内倾4.62°的双拱肋结构，拱肋的边段为劲性骨架混凝土箱形结构，次中段的上下弦杆及中段的上弦杆采用钢桁-混凝土组合截面结构，拱肋间横向采用钢桁撑和钢箱K形撑等构造，拱脚与拱座固结；主桥桥面结构采用中段等高度单箱三室预应力混凝土连续梁，两端连接预应力混凝土T构过渡跨，连续梁由吊杆悬吊锚固于拱肋并由双柱式框架支承于拱肋。钢桁拱肋采用缆索吊装、斜拉扣索悬臂拼装施工方法。

　　成贵铁路鸭池河特大桥的拱肋采用三种钢桁-混凝土组合结构，降低了铁路大跨混凝土拱桥的自重，方便施工，提高了经济性；在跨度400m级的高速铁路拱桥中取消轨道纵向温度调节器并采用阻尼式半漂浮结构体系，提高了行车舒适度；采用吊杆吊架系统和吊杆张拉控制技术分段浇筑连续梁，降低了施工风险，提高了桥面线形精度；研发了大吨位横移式缆载吊机、钢桁拱肋外包混凝土施工等技术，提高了施工速度和质量。

Chengdu-Guiyang Railway Bridge over Yachi River is located at the junction of Qingzhen City and Qianxi City, Guizhou Province. It is a super-large bridge across the Yachi River on the Chengdu-Guiyang Railway. The bridge has a total length of 971m and a deck width of 22m/15.2 m. It is a double-track high-speed railway bridge with a design speed of 250km/h.

The main bridge is a half-through steel-concrete composite arch bridge with a main span of 436m and a rise-span ratio of 1/3.8. It is currently the largest span half-through steel-concrete composite arch bridge in the world. The arch has a double rib with an inward inclination of 4.62°. The side segments of the ribs are concrete box structures with stiff skeletons, and the other segments are steel truss-concrete composite structures. The steel truss braces and steel box K-shaped braces are set between the ribs. The arch feet are fixed with abutment. The bridge deck includes a single-box three-cell prestressed concrete continuous beam with middle section equal height and prestressed concrete T-frame transition spans connected at both ends. The continuous deck are suspended by suspenders anchored on arch ribs and supported by double column frames on arch ribs. The steel truss arch ribs are erected by cable hoisting and stayed buckle cable technology.

There are three kinds of steel truss-concrete composite structures in the arch ribs, which reduce the dead weight, facilitate construction and improve economy. The track longitudinal temperature regulators are abolished in the 400m span high-speed railway arch bridge and the damping semi-floating structure is applied to improve the driving comfort. The segmental casting of continuous decks adopts an innovative technique of using suspender hangers and hanger tension control to reduce the construction risk and improve the deck alignment accuracy. The construction technologies of large tonnage horizontal moving cable cranes and steel truss arch rib concrete encasement are developed to improve the construction speed and quality.

# 平南三桥
## Third Pingnan Bridge

平南三桥位于广西壮族自治区贵港市平南县,是荔浦至玉林高速公路平南北互通连接线跨越浔江的特大桥。大桥主桥全长1035m,桥面宽36.5m,双向四车道一级公路,两侧设非机动车道和人行道,设计车速为60km/h。

平南三桥主桥为中承式钢管混凝土拱桥,主跨跨径575m,矢跨比1/4,为已建世界上最大跨径的拱桥。主桥横向采用双拱肋结构,其间设多道风撑和横向联系;拱肋为桁式钢管混凝土结构,每个拱肋由4根直径1400mm的钢管混凝土弦杆、钢管腹杆及横连杆组成,拱脚与拱座固结;桥面结构采用钢梁-混凝土桥面板组合梁,由吊杆、拱肋横撑及端墩支承。拱肋采用缆索吊装、斜拉扣索悬臂拼装施工方法。

平南三桥的拱座基础采用"圆形地下连续墙+卵石层注浆加固"方案,避免了粉质黏土、强透水卵石及含溶洞岩层等不利地质条件影响;扣索采用一次张拉不调索力技术,提高了拱段拼装速度;运用了真空辅助四级连续泵送灌注拱肋钢管C70自密实无收缩混凝土技术及密实度超声定量分析法,使钢管混凝土质量得到提升;采用了卫星定位、智能张拉、索力优化等技术及电气化自动控制方法,使拱肋合龙精度在3mm以内、施工塔架顶部偏位小于20mm。

Third Pingnan Bridge is located in Pingnan County, Guigang City, Guangxi Zhuang Autonomous Region. It is a super-large bridge across Xun River on the Pingnan North Interchange Connection Line of Lipu-Yulin Highway. The main bridge is 1035m in length and 36.5m in width. It is a two-way four-lane first-class highway with non-motor lanes and sidewalks on both sides. The design speed is 60km/h.

The main bridge is a half-through concrete-filled steel tubular arch bridge. The main span is 575m and the rise-span ratio is 1/4. It is currently the largest span arch bridge in the world. The main bridge adopts double arch ribs which include multiple wind bracings and transverse connections. Each rib is a truss and composed of four concrete-filled steel tube chords with a diameter of 1400mm, steel tube webs and lateral connections. The arch feet and the arch seats are fixed. The deck adopts composite beams of steel girders and concrete slabs, supported by suspenders, lateral braces and bearings on side piers. The arch ribs are erected by cable hoisting and stayed buckle cable technology.

The abutment foundations adopt a scheme of circular underground continuous wall and pebble layer grouting strengthening to avoid the influence of unfavorable geological conditions such as silty clay, strongly permeable pebble and karst cave rock formation. The technology of one-time cable tensioning without adjusting is adopted to improve the assembling speed of arch segments. The steel tubular chords are filled with C70 self-compacting non-shrinkage concrete and vacuum-assisted four-

stage pumping and pouring technology is used to improve the quality of filled concrete. The technologies of satellite positioning, intelligent tensioning, cable force optimization and electrified automatic control methods are adopted. The closure accuracy of arch ribs is within 3mm and the top deviation of the construction tower is less than 20mm.

**Name:** Third Pingnan Bridge
**Type:** Half-through concrete filled steel tubular arch bridge
**Main Span:** 575m
**Location:** Pingnan County, Guigang City, Guangxi Zhuang Autonomous Region
**Completion:** December, 2020
**Owner(s):** Guangxi Communications Investment Group Co., Ltd.
**Designer(s):** Sichuan Highway Planning, Survey, Design and Research Institute Ltd. and Guangxi Communications Design Group Co., Ltd.
**Contractor(s):** Guangxi Road and Bridge Engineering Group Co., Ltd.

# 仁沐新高速犍为岷江特大桥

## Qianwei Bridge over Min River on Renshou-Muchuan-Xinshi Highway

仁沐新高速犍为岷江特大桥，位于四川省乐山市犍为县，跨越岷江、马边河，是仁沐新高速的重要工程之一。大桥全长2782.8m，桥面宽31.8m，双向四车道高速公路，两侧设人行道，设计速度80km/h。

仁沐新高速犍为岷江特大桥的主桥为中承式钢管混凝土拱桥，主跨跨径457.6m，矢跨比1/4；采用桁式钢管混凝土双拱肋结构，肋间设置一字形、三角形及K形钢管横撑；每个拱肋有4根直径为1320mm的钢管混凝土弦杆，与钢管腹杆及横连杆组成桁式结构，拱脚与拱座固结；桥面结构采用双主梁的钢梁-混凝土桥面板组合梁，由吊杆和双柱式钢管框架墩支承，吊杆采用钢绞线整体挤压成型锚具拉索。钢桁拱肋采用缆索吊装、斜拉扣索悬臂拼装施工方法。

仁沐新高速犍为岷江特大桥的设计采用了钢管混凝土的统一理论、节点承载力和疲劳计算方法，计入了腹杆对桁拱抗弯刚度的影响；拱肋采用全钢管桁架、腹杆竖向与径向布置，桥面结构轻型化并与拱形成限位联合作用等；提出的四边拱形咬合桩围堰的基坑围护技术，在无内支撑条件下进行深基坑快速施工。

Qianwei Bridge over Min River on Renshou-Muchuan-Xinshi Highway is located in Qianwei County, Leshan City, Sichuan Province. It spans Min River and Mabian River and is one of the important projects of Renshou-Muchuan-Xinshi Highway. The bridge has a total length of 2782.8m, a deck width of 31.8m, a two-way four-lane highway with sidewalks on both sides, and a design speed of 80km/h.

The main bridge is a half-through concrete-filled steel tubular arch bridge with a main span of 457.6m and a rise-span ratio of 1/4. The bridge has a double concrete-filled steel tube arch rib, and the braces of I-shaped, triangular and K-shaped steel tubes are set between the ribs. Each arch rib is a truss composed of 4 concrete-filled steel tube chords with a diameter of 1320mm, steel tube web members and horizontal connections. The arch feet and the arch seats are fixed. The bridge deck is a steel beam-concrete deck composite beam with double main girders, supported by hangers and double-column steel pipe frame piers. The suspenders adopt strand integral extrusion forming anchorage cables. The steel truss arch

| | |
|---|---|
| **Name:** | Qianwei Bridge over Min River on Renshou-Muchuan-Xinshi Highway |
| **Type:** | Half-through concrete-filled steel tubular arch bridge |
| **Main Span:** | 457.6m |
| **Location:** | Qianwei County, Leshan City, Sichuan Province |
| **Completion:** | January, 2021 |
| **Owner(s):** | Shudao Investment Group Co., Ltd. |
| **Designer(s):** | Sichuan Highway Planning, Survey, Design and Research Institute Ltd. |
| **Contractor(s):** | Sichuan Road & Bridge (Group) Co., Ltd. |

ribs are erected by cable hoisting and stayed buckle cable technology.

The unified theory of concrete-filled steel tube, joint bearing capacity and fatigue calculation are considered in the design. The influence of web members on the bending stiffness of truss arch is also considered. The arch rib adopts full steel pipe truss, the web members are arranged vertically and radially, and the bridge deck structure is lightweight and forms displacement combined actions with the arch. The foundation pit support technology of a four-sided arched interlocking pile cofferdam is proposed to carry out rapid construction of a deep foundation pit without internal support.

# 藏木雅鲁藏布江大桥
## Zangmu Bridge over Yarlung Zangbo River

| | |
|---|---|
| 桥　名: 藏木雅鲁藏布江大桥 | **Name:** Zangmu Bridge over Yarlung Zangbo River |
| 桥　型: 中承式钢管混凝土拱桥 | **Type:** Half-through concrete-filled steel tubular arch bridge |
| 主跨跨径: 430m | **Main Span:** 430m |
| 桥　址: 西藏自治区山南市加查县 | **Location:** Jiacha County, Shannan City, Tibet Autonomous Region |
| 建成时间: 2021年6月 | **Completion:** June, 2021 |
| 建设单位: 西藏铁路建设有限公司 | **Owner(s):** Tibet Railway Construction Co., Ltd. |
| 设计单位: 中铁二院工程集团有限责任公司 | **Designer(s):** China Railway Eryuan Engineering Group Co., Ltd. |
| 施工单位: 中铁广州工程局集团有限公司 | **Contractor(s):** China Railway Guangzhou Engineering Group Co., Ltd. |

藏木雅鲁藏布江大桥，位于西藏自治区山南市加查县境内，横跨水深达 66m 的雅鲁藏布江，是川藏铁路拉萨至林芝段重点工程。大桥全长 525.1m，桥面宽 18m，为设计车速 160km/h 的双线铁路桥。

　　藏木雅鲁藏布江大桥为中承式钢管混凝土拱桥，主跨跨径 430m，矢跨比 1/3.84，是目前最大跨度铁路钢管混凝土拱桥。大桥横向采用各内倾 4.6° 的双拱肋结构，其间设多道一字形、米字形等钢管横撑；拱肋为采用耐候钢的桁式钢管混凝土结构，每个拱肋由 4 根直径为 1600~1800mm 的渐变钢管混凝土弦杆、箱形和 H 形截面腹杆及横连杆组成，拱脚与拱座固结；桥面结构为单箱双室预应力混凝土连续箱梁，由吊杆和边墩支承。钢管拱肋采用缆索吊装、斜拉扣索悬臂拼装施工方法。

　　藏木雅鲁藏布江大桥首次在拱肋等钢结构中采用耐候钢材料，避免了雪域高原地区的涂装维护工作；拱肋钢管采用变管径设计，降低了钢材用量和拱肋自重；提出的大型钢构件空中姿态调整技术，降低了高原峡谷强风环境下拱肋拼装施工风险；研发了历程可控、分时收缩补偿的混凝土材料，在海拔 3350m 的高原一次灌注钢管拱超千方混凝土，避免了昼夜温差大导致的混凝土冻胀等问题；采用大吨位保温抗风吊索挂篮，完成了强风、大温差环境下桥面混凝土箱梁浇筑。

Zangmu Bridge over Yarlung Zangbo River is located in Jiacha County, Shannan City, Tibet Autonomous Region. It spans the Yarlung Zangbo River with a depth of 66 m. It is a key project of the Lhasa-Nyingchi section of the Sichuan-Tibet Railway. The bridge has a total length of 525.1m and a deck width of 18m. It is a double-track railway bridge with a design speed of 160km/h.

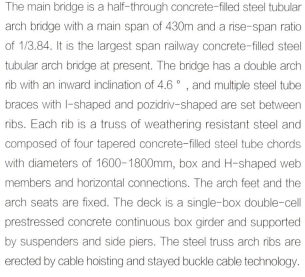

The main bridge is a half-through concrete-filled steel tubular arch bridge with a main span of 430m and a rise-span ratio of 1/3.84. It is the largest span railway concrete-filled steel tubular arch bridge at present. The bridge has a double arch rib with an inward inclination of 4.6°, and multiple steel tube braces with I-shaped and pozidriv-shaped are set between ribs. Each rib is a truss of weathering resistant steel and composed of four tapered concrete-filled steel tube chords with diameters of 1600-1800mm, box and H-shaped web members and horizontal connections. The arch feet and the arch seats are fixed. The deck is a single-box double-cell prestressed concrete continuous box girder and supported by suspenders and side piers. The steel truss arch ribs are erected by cable hoisting and stayed buckle cable technology.

Weathering resistant steel is innovatively adopted in arches to avoid painting and maintenance in the snowy plateau area. The steel tubes of arch ribs are designed with variable diameters to reduce the amount of steel and the dead weights of arch ribs. The proposed posture adjustment technology of large steel components reduces the risk of arch rib hoisting in strong wind environment of plateau canyon. Concrete with the controllable process and time-division shrinkage compensation is developed, and more than one thousand cubic meters of concrete is poured into the steel tube arch at one time at an altitude of 3350m, which avoids the problem of concrete frost heave caused by the temperature difference between day and night. To ensure the concrete casting quality of deck box girders under a strong wind and large temperature difference environment, the cable hanging baskets for large tonnage with heat preservation and wind resistance is utilized.

# 合江长江三桥
## Third Hejiang Bridge over Yangtze River

桥　　名：合江长江三桥
桥　　型：中承式钢管混凝土系杆拱桥
主跨跨径：507m
桥　　址：四川省泸州市合江县
建成时间：2021年6月
建设单位：泸州市交通运输局
设计单位：四川省公路规划勘察设计研究院有限公司
施工单位：中交第二公路工程局有限公司

合江长江三桥位于四川省泸州市合江县，是省道438线跨越长江、连接泸渝高速公路与国道353线的重要桥梁。大桥全长1440m，桥面宽27m，双向四车道一级公路，两侧设人行道，设计速度60km/h。

合江长江三桥主桥为中承式钢管混凝土系杆拱桥，主跨跨径507m，矢跨比1/4。主桥桥面以上采用桁式钢管混凝土双拱肋结构，肋间设置三角形钢管横撑，每个拱肋由4根直径为1300mm的钢管混凝土弦杆、钢管腹杆及横连杆组成；桥面以下为钢桁骨架外包混凝土的箱肋结构，肋间设置钢管混凝土横撑，拱脚与拱座固结；桥面结构采用钢梁与钢-混凝土组合桥面板组合梁，由吊杆、钢管混凝土立柱支承；系杆采用环氧喷涂钢绞线成品索，搁置于桥面结构。钢桁拱肋采用缆索吊装、斜拉扣索悬臂拼装施工方法。

合江长江三桥采用的钢梁与钢-混凝土组合桥面板组合梁，避免了采用钢桥面加劲构造的疲劳问题，方便了混凝土桥面板施工，提高了经济性；拱段采用整体制造、运输及安装的一体化技术，将每个拱段的现场安装和高空作业时间缩短一半以上；充分利用墩柱及基础的承载力，减少了系杆张拉次数2/3以上；通过数十次试验，研制了满足力学和大高差泵送工作性能的C70高强混凝土。

**Name:** Third Hejiang Bridge over Yangtze River
**Type:** Half-through concrete-filled steel tubular tied arch bridge
**Main Span:** 507m
**Location:** Hejiang County, Luzhou City, Sichuan Province
**Completion:** June, 2021
**Owner(s):** The Bureau of Communications and Transportation in Luzhou
**Designer(s):** Sichuan Highway Planning, Survey, Design and Research Institute Ltd.
**Contractor(s):** CCCC Second Highway Engineering Co., Ltd.

Third Hejiang Bridge over Yangtze River is located in Hejiang County, Luzhou City, Sichuan Province. It is an important bridge for provincial highway 438 crossing the Yangtze River and connecting Luzhou-Chongqing Expressway with national highway 353. The bridge has a total length of 1440m, a deck width of 27m, a two-way four-lane first-class highway with sidewalks on both sides, and a design speed of 60km/h.

The main bridge is a half-through concrete-filled steel tubular tied arch bridge with a main span of 507m and a rise-span ratio of 1/4. The arch above the deck is a truss with a double concrete-filled steel tube arch rib and the triangular steel tube braces are set between the ribs. Each rib is composed of four concrete-filled steel tube chords with a diameter of 1300mm, steel tube web members and transverse connections. The arch ribs below the deck are concrete-encased structures with steel truss skeletons. The arch feet are fixed with arch seats. The bridge deck is composite of steel girders and steel-concrete composite slabs, and supported by suspenders and concrete-filled steel tube columns. The tie bars are finished products of epoxy-coating strands and are placed on the deck. The steel truss arch ribs are erected by cable hoisting and stayed buckle cable technology.

The bridge deck is a composite girder of steel girders and steel-concrete composite slabs, which avoids fatigue problem of steel deck stiffeners, facilitates concrete deck construction and improves the economy. The integrated technology of manufacturing, transportation and installation shortens the on-site installation time and high-place work time of each arch segment by more than half. The bearing capacity of piers and foundations are fully utilized to reduce the tie bar tension times by more than 2/3. Through dozens of tests, high strength C70 concrete is developed to meet the mechanical requirements and the performance of large height difference pumping.

# 明珠湾大桥
## Pearl Bay Bridge

明珠湾大桥位于广东省广州市，北起南沙新港大道，跨越龙穴南水道，南至万新大道，是粤港澳大湾区的重要连接通道。大桥全长2640m，桥面宽43.2m，主桥采用双层桥面结构，上层为双向八车道城市主干道，两侧设人行道，设计车速为60km/h；下层两侧预留四个公交车专用道，中间为管线走廊。

明珠湾大桥主桥为中承式钢桁组合拱桥，跨径布置为96m+164m+436m+164m+96m+60m，钢桁拱矢跨比1/4.45，是目前世界上最大跨径的城市双层桥面中承式钢桁组合拱桥；横向采用三片式钢桁拱与钢桁梁组合构造，由多道平、竖联形成外部无推力的五跨连续空间桁架结构，主跨钢桁梁横向设3根吊杆。钢桁拱杆件均采用箱形截面，上、下弦杆由渐变截面段和等截面段组成；钢桁梁的上、下弦杆采用箱形和H形截面，上、下层钢桥面板均采用正交异性结构，钢桁梁采用双曲面球型减隔震支座。大桥采用塔架斜拉扣索拱、梁同步悬臂拼装施工方法。

明珠湾大桥利用拱-梁组合结构的受力特点，主动调节钢桁梁长度来改变结构内力分布，优化了拱和梁的受力状态；采用塔架斜拉扣索拱、梁同步悬臂拼装施工方法，在超大悬臂下经历多次体系转换后快速完成了全桥施工；从设计到建造全过程采用BIM技术，配置多向变位智能检查车及3D激光扫描设备，实现了桥梁数字化管理。

桥　　名：明珠湾大桥
桥　　型：中承式钢桁组合拱桥
主跨跨径：436m
桥　　址：广东省广州市
建成时间：2021年6月
建设单位：广州市南沙区建设中心
设计单位：广州市市政工程设计研究总院有限公司
施工单位：中国铁建大桥工程局集团有限公司

**Name:** Pearl Bay Bridge
**Type:** Half-through steel truss composite arch bridge
**Main Span:** 436m
**Location:** Guangzhou City, Guangdong Province
**Completion:** June, 2021
**Owner(s):** Guangzhou Nansha District Construction Center
**Designer(s):** Guangzhou Municipal Engineering Design & Research Institute Co., Ltd.
**Contractor(s):** China Railway Construction Bridge Engineering Bureau Group Co., Ltd.

Pearl Bay Bridge is located in Guangzhou City, Guangdong Province. It starts from Nansha Xingang Avenue in the north, crosses Longxue South Waterway, and ends at Wanxin Avenue in the south. It is an important connecting channel for the Guangdong-Hong Kong-Macao Greater Bay Area. The total length of the bridge is 2640m, and the width of the bridge deck is 43.2m. The main bridge has a double deck. The upper deck is a two-way eight-lane urban main road with sidewalks on both sides and the design speed is 60km/h. Four bus lanes are reserved on both sides of the lower deck with pipeline corridors in the middle.

The main bridge is a half-through steel truss composite arch bridge with a span arrangement of 96m+164m+436m+164m+96m+60m and a rise-span ratio of 1/4.45. It is currently the world's largest span urban double-deck half-through steel truss composite arch bridge. The bridge has a three-piece steel truss arch and steel truss girder, which are combined to form a five-span continuous truss without external thrust by multiple horizontal and vertical connections. Three hangers are set transversely for the steel truss beam of main span. The steel truss arch members have box sections, and the upper and lower chords are composed of gradient section segments and constant section segments, and the chords of the steel truss girders have box-shaped and H-shaped sections. The upper and lower bridge decks adopt orthotropic steel structures, and the steel truss girder adopts hyperboloid spherical seismic isolation bearings. The arch and deck are installed synchronously through cable hoisting and stayed buckle cable technology.

According to the structural characteristics of the arch-beam composite bridge, the internal force distribution is actively adjusted by means of changing the length of the steel truss beam to optimize the stress state in the arch and beam. The construction method of synchronous cantilever assembly of pylon cable arch and beam is adopted, and the whole bridge construction is completed quickly after many system transformations under the super-large cantilever stages. BIM technology is adopted in the whole process from design to operation. The bridge is equipped with a multi-directional displacement intelligent inspection vehicle and 3D laser scanning equipment for digital management.

# 德余高速乌江特大桥
## Dejiang-Yuqing Expressway Bridge over Wu River

| | |
|---|---|
| 桥　名： | 德余高速乌江特大桥 |
| 桥　型： | 上承式钢管混凝土拱桥 |
| 主跨跨径： | 504m |
| 桥　址： | 贵州省铜仁市思南县、石阡县 |
| 建成时间： | 2023年12月 |
| 建设单位： | 贵州中交德余高速公路有限公司 |
| 设计单位： | 中交公路规划设计院有限公司 |
| 施工单位： | 中交一公局第四工程有限公司 |

**Name:** Dejiang-Yuqing Expressway Bridge over Wu River
**Type:** Deck-type concrete-filled steel tubular arch bridge
**Main Span:** 504m
**Location:** Sinan County, Shiqian County, Tongren City, Guizhou Province
**Completion:** December, 2023
**Owner(s):** Guizhou Zhongjiao Deyu Expressway Co., Ltd.
**Designer(s):** CCCC Highway Consultants Co., Ltd.
**Contractor(s):** The Fourth Engineering Co., Ltd. of CCCC First Highway Engineering Co., Ltd.

德余高速乌江特大桥，位于贵州省铜仁市思南县、石阡县交界处，是德江至余庆高速公路全线的重要工程。大桥全长1834m，桥面宽25.5m，双向四车道高速公路，设计车速80km/h。

德余高速乌江特大桥主桥为上承式钢管混凝土拱桥，拱、柱、梁全刚结式结构体系，主跨跨径504m，矢跨比约1/5.3，为目前世界最大跨径上承式钢管混凝土拱桥。主桥横向采用双拱肋结构，其间设多道K形风撑；拱肋为等宽变高的桁式钢管混凝土结构，每个拱肋由4根直径1400mm钢管混凝土弦杆、箱形或H形钢腹杆及横连杆组成，拱脚与拱座固结；拱上建筑采用全空腹式结构，桥面系结构为分离双槽形钢梁-粗骨料UHPC桥面板的连续组合梁，腹孔墩采用钢箱截面双柱式框架结构。拱肋采用缆索吊装、斜拉扣索悬臂拼装施工方法。

德余高速乌江特大桥采用的拱、柱、梁全刚结式结构体系，提高了结构整体受力性能，减少了养护工作量；钢构件和桥面板采用工厂化预制、大件化水运及现场拼装；大部分拱段整体水运，现场组拼场地需求小；采用节点板栓接替代圆管相贯线焊接，改善了节点抗疲劳性能，加快了拼接速度；采用UHPC桥面板降低自重约5000t，增强了抗裂性；基于数字预拼装模型的姿态控制技术，配合三维激光扫描仪等设备，提高了拱段定位和拼装精度；提出的拱段拼接变形复位法，使拱肋杆件栓接顺利进行。

Dejiang-Yuqing Expressway Bridge over Wu River is located at the junction of Sinan County and Shiqian County in Tongren City, Guizhou Province. It is an important project of Dejiang-Yuqing Expressway. The bridge has a total length of 1834m, a bridge deck width of 25.5m, a two-way four-lane highway, and a design speed of 80 km/h.

The main bridge is a deck-type concrete-filled steel tubular arch bridge with a main span of 504m and a rise-span ratio of about 1/5.3. It is currently the world's largest span deck-type concrete-filled steel tubular arch bridge. The arch, column and deck are all rigidly connected. The main span has a double arch rib with multiple K-shaped bracings. Each arch rib is a truss with equal width and variable height, and composed of four concrete-filled steel tube chords with a diameter of 1400mm, box-shaped or H-shaped steel web members and transverse connections. The arch feet are fixed with arch seats. The arch spandrel is open. The deck is a continuous beam composited by double-channel steel beams and CA-UHPC slabs. The piers for spandrel are double column frames with steel box section. The arch ribs are erected by cable hoisting and stayed buckle cable technology.

The fully rigid structure system of arches, columns and girders is utilized in large span arch bridges, which improves the structural performance and reduces maintenances. Steel components and deck slabs are factory prefabricated, water transported in large component and on-site erected. Most of arch segments are integrally water transported and the on-site field is less needed. The bolting of joint plates replaces the welding of the crossing curve of cylinder pipes to improve the fatigue resistance at joints and accelerate splicing. UHPC is used in the deck to reduce the weight of about 5000t and enhance the crack resistance. The attitude control technology based on digital pre-assembly models, combined with 3D laser scanner and other equipment, improves the positioning and assembly accuracy of arch sections. A deformation reset method of arch segment splicing is proposed to make the bolt connection of arch rib smoothly.

# 天峨龙滩特大桥
## Tian'e Longtan Bridge

**桥　　名**：天峨龙滩特大桥
**桥　　型**：上承式钢筋混凝土拱桥
**主跨跨径**：600m
**桥　　址**：广西壮族自治区河池市天峨县
**建成时间**：2023年12月
**建设单位**：广西交通投资集团有限公司
**设计单位**：广西交通设计集团有限公司
**施工单位**：广西路桥工程集团有限公司

天峨龙滩特大桥位于广西壮族自治区河池市天峨县内，跨越龙滩库区，桥址在龙滩水电站上游6km处，是南丹至天峨下老高速公路的重要工程。大桥全长2488.55m，桥面宽24.5m，双向四车道高速公路，设计速度为100km/h。

天峨龙滩特大桥主桥为上承式钢筋混凝土拱桥，主跨跨径600m，矢跨比1/4.8，为在建的世界最大跨径拱桥。主桥采用分离式平行双等宽变高箱肋拱，拱肋之间设多道箱形截面横向联系，拱肋内设置了由钢管混凝土弦杆与钢腹杆组成的桁式劲性骨架，拱脚与拱座固结；拱上建筑采用全空腹式构造，中间为多跨预应力混凝土先简支后连续T梁，两端均连接预应力混凝土连续刚构过渡跨，腹孔墩采用实心和空心钢筋混凝土结构。拱肋劲性骨架采用缆索吊装、斜拉扣索悬臂拼装施工方法。

天峨龙滩特大桥提出的增强劲性骨架、横强纵弱普通钢筋的设计原则，使拱肋混凝土的应力水平与跨径400m级拱桥持平，非线性安全系数达到2.4以上；对劲性骨架外包混凝土施工设计了3环、6段、8工作面、19次浇筑的加载程序，使混凝土瞬时拉应力不超出2MPa，施工全过程的弹性稳定安全系数大于4；对拱肋劲性骨架采用大节段预制、快速连接及扣索一次控制张拉等技术，优化了骨架拼装过程、拼接质量及成型线形。

Tian'e Longtan Bridge is located in Tian'e County, Hechi City, Guangxi Zhuang Autonomous Region, across the Longtan reservoir area. The bridge site is 6km upstream of the Longtan Hydropower Station. It is an important project of Nandan-Tian'e Xialao Expressway. The bridge has a total length of 2488.55m and a bridge deck width of 24.5m. It is a two-way four-lane highway with a design speed of 100km/h.

The main bridge is a deck-type reinforced concrete arch bridge with a main span of 600m and a rise-span ratio of 1/4.8, which is the world's largest span arch bridge under construction. The main arch is composed of two parallel equal width and variable height box ribs and multiple box-shaped lateral connections between the ribs. There are stiff skeleton frames made up of concrete-filled steel tubular chords and steel truss webs casted in each arch rib. And the arch feet and the arch seats are fixed. The arch has open spandrel which includes multi-span prestressed concrete simple supported to continuous T-girders in the middle and both ends are connected to transition spans of prestressed concrete continuous rigid frame bridges. The piers for spandrel spans adopt reinforcement concrete structures with solid or hollow sections. The stiff skeletons in arch ribs are erected by cable hoisting and stayed buckle cable technology.

The design principles of enhancing a stiff skeleton and using strong transverse and weak longitudinal reinforcement are utilized, thus the concrete stress degree of the arch ribs is equivalent to that of the 400m-span arch bridges, and the nonlinear safety factor reached above 2.4. The arch rib concrete encasement is cast by 3 rings, 6 sections, 8 working faces and 19 times of pouring, so the instantaneous tensile stress of concrete never exceeds 2MPa and the elastic stability factor in the construction process is greater than 4. The arch stiff skeletons are prefabricated in large size, connected rapidly on site and locked by one-time tensioning stayed buckle cable, such innovative techniques optimize the assembly process and improve the construction quality and alignment.

**Name:** Tian'e Longtan Bridge
**Type:** Deck-type reinforced concrete arch bridge
**Main Span:** 600m
**Location:** Tian'e County, Hechi City, Guangxi Zhuang Autonomous Region
**Completion:** December, 2023
**Owner(s):** Guangxi Communications Investment Group Co., Ltd.
**Designer(s):** Guangxi Communications Design Group Co., Ltd.
**Contractor(s):** Guangxi Road and Bridge Engineering Group Co., Ltd.

中国桥梁　BRIDGES IN CHINA　2013—2023

# Chapter 5

## 第五篇

# 梁式桥

## Girder Bridges

# 引言

梁式桥是最古老的桥型，从远古时代的伐木为桥和垒石成桥起就有了梁式桥，使用天然材料的木梁桥和石梁桥的跨径很小。钢和混凝土两种人工合成材料的出现，促进了梁式桥跨径的增大。大跨径钢梁桥始于1840年用锻铁建造的英国威尔士布列坦尼亚桥，其跨径达到了146m，直到第二次世界大战后才被德国杜易兹桥超越；此后，德国和南斯拉夫将钢梁桥的跨径提升到了250m；1974年建成的跨径300m的巴西里约热内卢-尼特罗伊大桥，几乎达到了钢梁桥跨径的极限，保持世界纪录至今。大跨径混凝土梁桥的跨径增长稍晚于钢梁桥，并主要得益于预应力混凝土技术的发展，20世纪60年代，预应力混凝土梁桥的跨径分别突破100m、150m和200m大关；70年代，跨径纪录达到264m；90年代，新跨径纪录又有270m的虎门大桥辅航道桥、298m的挪威拉脱圣德桥和301m的挪威斯托尔马桥。2006年建成的重庆石板坡长江大桥复线桥，采用钢-混凝土混合梁，以330m跨径创造了新的梁式桥世界纪录，并一直保持至今。

随着梁式桥跨径的增大，预应力混凝土连续刚构桥中间墩顶主梁承受的弯矩成了跨径增大的最大挑战。虎门大桥辅航道桥是首个遇此挑战的预应力混凝土连续刚构桥，1997年建成时创下270m跨径和4000MN·m墩顶负弯矩的世界纪录。由于梁式桥依靠自身的截面高度抵抗荷载，致使大跨径梁式桥的恒载占比在总荷载的80%以上，解决这个挑战性问题最有效的方法是减轻自重和辅助抗弯。前者主要包括采用轻骨料混凝土、空腹式连续刚构、钢-混凝土混合梁；用钢桁架腹板、波形钢腹板或碟形腹板代替混凝土腹板，以减轻腹板重量；采用钢或碟形腹板混凝土箱梁可以减小混凝土收缩和徐变，以避免腹板开裂，提高结构耐久性；后者采用索辅梁桥（俗称矮塔斜拉桥），通过体外预应力索巨大的偏心距辅助体内预应力筋抗弯。我国近10年建成的跨径200m以上预应力混凝土梁式桥30多座，1/3以上采用了索辅梁桥，最大跨径达到了270m，双主跨达到了235m。

近10年来，我国建成了几百座梁式桥以及数以千计的非通航孔和引桥，包括钢或混凝土梁式桥、钢与混凝土组合或混合梁桥和索辅梁桥等。本画册选取了17座梁式桥，包括2座预应力混凝土梁桥、6座钢-混凝土组合或混合梁桥和9座索辅梁桥。相比《中国桥梁 2003—2013》，虽然入选梁式桥的跨径没有继续增大，但大跨径梁式桥的数量增多了。从近10年建成的大跨径梁式桥来看，跨径200m以上的梁式桥基本没有采用传统的预应力混凝土梁式桥，而是采用索辅梁桥以及具备水路运输通道的钢-混凝土混合梁桥或空腹式预应力混凝土连续刚构桥，填补了传统梁式桥到斜拉桥或拱式桥之间的桥型空白，跨径为100~200m的波形钢腹板桥梁也日渐增多。非传统梁式桥的数量不断增长、技术更趋成熟，因其具有经济性、耐久性和可持续性的特点，而成为大跨径预应力混凝土梁式桥的合理选择。

# INTRODUCTION

Girder bridges are the oldest bridge type. This type of bridge was used in ancient times when logs and stone piling were used to build bridges. Only very short spans could be built using this method. The appearance of two kinds of synthetic materials, steel and concrete, enabled the span of girder bridges to increase. Long-span steel girder bridges began with the Britannia Bridge in Wales, UK, which was built with forged iron in 1840. Its span reached 146m, a record that was not surpassed until the Second World War with the construction of the Deutzer Bridge in Germany. Since then, Germany and the Yugoslavia increased the span of steel girder bridges to 250m. The 300m-span Rio-Niterói Bridge in Brazil, completed in 1974, is likely to be close to the limit for the span of steel girder bridges since it still holds the world record to this day. Large increases in span came later for concrete girder bridges, since these arose mainly from the development of prestressed concrete technology. In the 1960s, the spans of prestressed concrete girder bridges gradually broke through 100m, 150m and 200m. In the 1970s, the record span reached 264m. In the 1990s, new span records included the 270m span of the auxiliary channel bridge of Humen Bridge, the 298m span of the Raftsundet Bridge in Norway and the 301m span of the Stolma Bridge in Norway. The steel-concrete hybrid girder of the Shibanpo Parallel Bridge over Yangtze River in Chongqing, set the current world record for girder bridges with a span of 330m.

With regard to prestressed concrete continuous bridge with integral piers, the main challenge as spans increase is the negative bending moment of the main girder over the central piers. This was the case for the auxiliary channel bridge of Humen Bridge. When it was completed in 1997, it set a world record of 270m span and 4,000 MN·m negative moment in the girder over the pier. Because girder bridges rely on their own section height to resist loads, the dead load of long-span girder bridges accounts for more than 80% of the total load. The most effective way to solve this challenging problem is to reduce the self weight and to get partial support from other structural members. The former method, i.e., to reduce the self weight, mainly includes using lightweight aggregate concrete, using open spandrel continuous rigid frame, using steel-concrete hybrid girders, and reducing the weight of webs by replacing traditional solid concrete webs with steel truss webs, corrugated steel webs or X type concrete webs. Steel or X type webs can reduce concrete shrinkage and creep, completely prevent web cracking, and improve structural durability. The most commonly used method to get partial support by other members is the extradosed girder bridge (also known as the low pylon cable-stayed bridge), which assists the bending resistance of internal prestressing tendons through the larger eccentricity of external prestressing tendons. More than 30 prestressed concrete girder bridges with main span more than 200m have been built in China in the past 10 years. More than one third of them are extradosed girder bridges, in which the maximum main span has reached 270m, and the maximum double main span has reached 235m.

In the past 10 years, hundreds of girder bridges and thousands of non-navigational spans and approach bridges have been built in China, including steel girders, concrete girders, steel-concrete composite or hybrid girders, and extradosed grider bridges. This album selectes 17 girder bridges, including 2 prestressed concrete girder bridges, 6 steel-concrete composite or hybrid girder bridges and 9 extradosed girder bridges. Compared with the selected bridges in the previous edition, although the spans of the selected bridges in this album have not continued to grow, the number of long-span girder bridges has increased. The long-span girder bridges built in the past decade show that the traditional prestressed concrete girder bridges are mostly not used for spans over 200m. Rather, extradosed girder bridges, steel-concrete hybrid girder bridges, or open spandrel prestressed concrete continuous bridges with integral piers are used, filling the bridge type gap between traditional girder bridges and cable-stayed or arch bridges. The number of corrugated steel web bridges in the span range from 100m to 200m is also increasing. The number of unconventional girder bridges are increasing continuously, and the technology is becoming more mature, which makes them reasonable choices for large-span prestressed concrete girder bridges that provide economy, durability and sustainability.

# 天津吉兆桥
## Tianjin Jizhao Bridge

天津吉兆桥是天津海河中游后5km提升改造的第一座跨河桥梁，位于城市副中心，连接东丽区和津南区，起于雪莲南路与海河东路相交路口，止于吉兆路与柳盛道相交路口，全长907m，桥宽40m，双向六车道。

天津吉兆桥主桥为三跨变截面钢-混凝土组合桁架梁桥，跨径布置为55m+90m+55m，梁高1.8~6.69m。横向共由9榀桁架组成，每榀桁架顺桥向为直线，桁架横向中心间距为4.6m，桁架节点标准间距为4m。在下弦杆内，主桥中墩两侧各12.5m范围浇筑微膨胀混凝土。采用280mm混凝土桥面板，局部加腋厚度为350mm。北引桥采用3×25m三跨连续等截面预应力混凝土箱梁桥，南引桥采用20m+21m+31m+18m四跨连续等截面预应力混凝土箱梁桥，梁高均为1.80m。主桥下部均采用群桩基础。

天津吉兆桥工程针对连续组合桁架桥负弯矩区混凝土桥面板易开裂、支点附近下弦杆受压稳定、高烈度地震区桥梁抗震等问题，采用"抗拔不抗剪T形连接件"连接钢主梁和混凝土桥面板，并采用部分组合技术、双重组合技术以及系列施工工艺，隔断钢主梁和混凝土桥面板之间的剪力传递，以解决连续组合桁架桥负弯矩区桥面板易开裂、下弦杆易失稳等问题；采用由铅芯橡胶减隔震支座+剪切型软钢耗能阻挡装置组成的混合耗能减隔震系统，更好地解决了高烈度地震区桥梁抗震问题。

Tianjin Jizhao Bridge is the first river crossing bridge in the upgraded zone five kilometers after the middle reaches of Hai River in Tianjin. It is located in the sub center of the city, connecting Dongli District and Jinnan District. It starts at the intersection of Xuelian South Road and Haihe East Road, and ends at the intersection of Jizhao Road and Liusheng Road. It is 907m long, 40m wide, and has six lanes in dual directions.

The main bridge of Tianjin Jizhao Bridge is a three-span steel-concrete composite truss girder bridge with variable section, with the span arrangement of 55m+90m+55m and the girder height of 1.8-6.69m. It is composed of 9 trusses in the transverse direction. Each truss is straight along the bridge direction. The transverse spacing of the truss is 4.6m, and the standard spacing between diagonal elements is 4m. In the lower chord, micro expansion concrete is poured within 12.5m on both sides of the middle piers. Concrete bridge deck which is 280mm thick is adopted, and the thickness of local haunched part is 350mm. The north approach bridge is a 3×25m three-span continuous prestressed concrete box girder with constant cross-section. The south approach bridge is a 20m+21m+31m+18m four-span continuous prestressed concrete box girder with constant cross-section. The girder height of the two approach bridge is 1.80m. Pile group foundation is adopted for the substructure of the main bridge.

Aiming at the problems of the concrete deck slab in the negative bending moment area of the continuous composite truss bridge which is vulnerable to crack, the stability of the lower chord near the support and the seismic resistance of the bridge in the high seismic intensity area, Tianjin Jizhao Bridge uses the "uplift-restricted and slip-permitted T-shaped connectors" to connect the steel girder and the concrete bridge deck, and uses partial composite technology, dual composite technology, and series of construction technology to prevent the shear transfer between the steel girder and the concrete bridge deck, in order to solve the problems of potential cracking of concrete deck slab and buckling of lower chord in negative bending moment area. A hybrid energy dissipation isolation system consisting of lead rubber bearing and shear type mild steel energy dissipation barrier device is adopted to better solve the seismic problem of bridges in high seismic intensity areas.

桥　　名：天津吉兆桥
桥　　型：钢-混凝土组合桁架梁桥
主跨跨径：90m
桥　　址：天津市
建成时间：2013年11月
建设单位：天津市海河建设发展投资有限公司
设计单位：天津城建设计院有限公司
施工单位：天津城建集团有限公司

**Name:** Tianjin Jizhao Bridge
**Type:** Steel-concrete composite truss girder bridge
**Main Span:** 90m
**Location:** Tianjin City
**Completion:** November, 2013
**Owner(s):** Tianjin Haihe Construction Development & Investment Co., Ltd.
**Designer(s):** Tianjin Urban Construction Design Institute Co., Ltd.
**Contractor(s):** Tianjin Urban Construction Group Co., Ltd.

# 六盘水至盘县高速公路北盘江特大桥
## Liupanshui–Panxian Expressway Bridge over Beipan River

六盘水至盘县高速公路北盘江特大桥位于贵州省西部的六盘水市水城区发耳镇和营盘乡交会处，跨越北盘江大峡谷，是六盘水至盘县高速公路项目的控制性工程。桥梁全长1261m，最大墩高170m，单幅桥宽10.5m，双向四车道，设计速度80km/h。

该桥为世界上首座空腹（斜腿）式预应力混凝土连续刚构桥。全桥共五跨，主跨290m，跨径布置为82.5m+220m+290m+220m+82.5m。主梁采用直腹板单箱单室截面，箱梁底板宽6.5m。两边墩墩顶为相当于150m跨径的传统箱梁截面T形刚构（即墩顶两侧对称双悬臂各75m），墩顶梁高10m，跨中梁高4.5m。中间两墩顶为290m跨径带斜腿的T形刚构，墩顶建筑高35m，跨中梁高4.5m。斜腿部分采用等截面箱形截面，梁高7.5m。上弦采用单箱单室截面，梁高由5m通过三个节段过渡到7m。斜腿部分下弦箱梁与上弦箱梁在相交处形成竖向的单箱双室截面。全桥采用三向预应力，按照全预应力混凝土梁桥设计。

该桥刚度大、自重轻，结构具有梁拱组合的力学特征，跨越能力、抗变形能力强。大桥采用交叉锚固的新型布束形式，改善了结构的受力性能，减少了超长预应力索的预应力损失。大桥下弦采用斜爬挂篮结合临时扣挂系统悬浇，上弦采用支架结合移动模架滞后下弦节段现浇的施工方法，形成上下弦异步平行施工工艺。该桥的成功建设为山区桥梁的设计提供了新的大跨径梁式桥形式。

桥　　名：六盘水至盘县高速公路北盘江特大桥  
桥　　型：空腹式预应力混凝土连续刚构桥  
主跨跨径：290m  
桥　　址：贵州省六盘水市  
建成时间：2013年8月  
建设单位：贵州高速公路集团有限公司  
设计单位：中交第二公路勘察设计研究院有限公司  
施工单位：贵州路桥集团有限公司、中交第二航务工程局有限公司

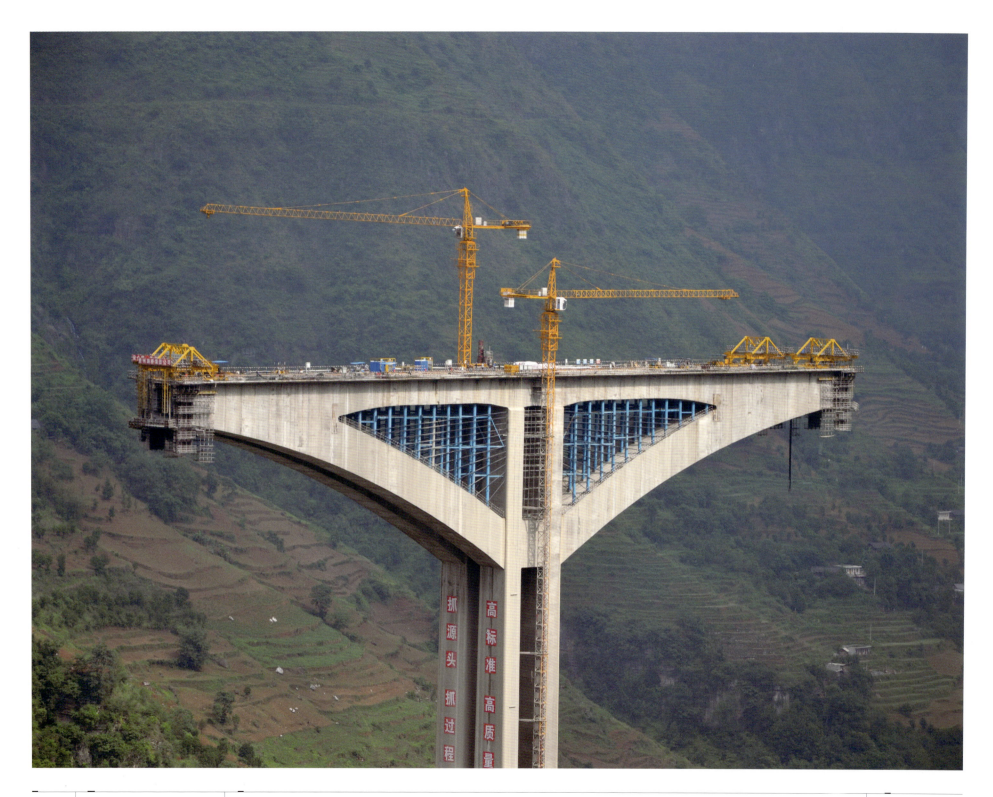

Liupanshui-Panxian Expressway Bridge over Beipan River is located at the junction of Fa'er Town and Yingpan Town of Shuicheng District, Liupanshui City, west of Guizhou Province. The bridge is across the Beipan River Grand Canyon. The bridge is a control project of Liupanshui to Panxian Expressway, which has a total length of 1261m and maximum pier height of 170m. The bridge has four lanes in dual directions with two parallel bridges of 10.5m wide each. The design speed of the bridge is 80km/h.

The bridge is the first open spandrel (inclined lower chord) prestressed concrete continuous bridge with integral piers in the world. The bridge has five spans with the main span of 290m. The span arrangement of the bridge is 82.5m+220m+290m+220m+82.5m. The straight web single cell box section is adopted for the deck, and the width of the bottom of the box section is 6.5m. The superstructure on both side piers is like a 150m-span T-shaped rigid frame with traditional box section (that is, 75m symmetrical balanced cantilevers on both sides of the pier top). The height of the girder on the pier top is 10m, while the height of the girder at mid span is 4.5m. The superstructure on the middle piers is 290m-span T-shaped rigid frame with open spandrel. The building height of the superstructure on the pier top is 35m, and the height of girder at the mid span is 4.5m. Constant box section with a height of 7.5m is adopted for the inclined lower chord. The upper chord adopts single cell box section, and the height of girder varies from 5m to 7m through three sections. At the intersection of the lower and upper chord of the superstructure, a vertical double cell single box section is formed. The bridge is designed as a fully prestressed concrete girder bridge with three-dimensional prestressing.

The bridge has large stiffness and light deadweight. The structure has combined the mechanical characteristics of girder bridge and arch bridge, and has strong spanning ability and deformation resistance. A new way of cross anchorage for the prestressing tendons is adopted, which improves the mechanical performance of the structure and reduces the prestress loss of the super long prestressing tendons. The balanced cantilever

construction method using inclined climbing hanging basket combined with temporary cable system is adopted for the lower chord of the bridge, while the scaffolding construction method combined with mobile formwork is adopted for the upper chord of the bridge. The construction of the upper chord is one segment behind the construction of the lower chord, forming the asynchronous parallel construction process. The successful construction of the bridge provides a new form of long-span girder bridge design in mountainous areas.

**Name:** Liupanshui-Panxian Expressway Bridge over Beipan River
**Type:** Open spandrel prestressed concrete continuous bridge with integral piers
**Main Span:** 290m
**Location:** Liupanshui City, Guizhou Province
**Completion:** August, 2013
**Owner(s):** Guizhou Expressway Group Co., Ltd.
**Designer(s):** CCCC Second Highway Consultants Co., Ltd.
**Contractor(s):** Guizhou Road & Bridge Group Co., Ltd. and CCCC Second Harbor Engineering Co., Ltd.

# 扶典口西江特大桥 1 号主桥
## Fudiankou No. 1 Main Bridge over Xi River

桥　　名：扶典口西江特大桥 1 号主桥
桥　　型：预应力混凝土索辅梁桥
主跨跨径：270m
桥　　址：广西壮族自治区梧州市
建成时间：2018 年 10 月
建设单位：广西交通投资集团有限公司
设计单位：广西交通设计集团有限公司
施工单位：广西路桥工程集团有限公司

扶典口西江特大桥 1 号主桥位于广西壮族自治区东部的梧州市环城高速公路 K29 处，自北向南跨越西江，是梧州市环城高速公路控制性工程。桥梁为双向六车道，设计速度为 100km/h，主桥设计宽度为 28.5m。

该桥是预应力混凝土索辅梁桥。全桥共三跨，主跨 270m，边跨 145m，主梁为单箱三室截面，顶板宽 28.5m，底板宽 19.5m，跨中梁高 4.5m，墩顶梁高 11.0m，梁高及底板厚度均以 1.8 次抛物线变化，箱梁采用三向预应力体系。索塔高度为 44m，单索面布置 21 对拉索，全桥共计 84 根拉索。

该桥充分利用高速公路中央分隔带宽度设置索塔及拉索锚固区，桥梁横断面布置紧凑且功能完善。结构空间受力特征显著。大桥拉索采用可更换抗滑钢绞线拉索，经过优化主梁梁高、索塔高度、无索区长度、拉索区长度及间距、拉索角度，选择合理索梁活载比等措施，达到兼顾安全、美观、经济、适用的目的。

Fudiankou No. 1 Main Bridge over Xi River is located at Ring Expressway K29 of Wuzhou City, east of Guangxi Zhuang Autonomous Region. It crosses the Xi River from the north to the south. It is a control project of the Wuzhou City Ring Expressway. The bridge has six lanes in dual directions. The design speed is 100km/h, and the width of the main bridge is 28.5m.

The bridge is an extradosed prestressed concrete girder bridge. The whole bridge has three spans. The main span is 270m and the side spans are 145m. The main girder is of three-cell single box section. The width of the top of the deck is 28.5m, while the width of the bottom of the deck is 19.5m. The height of the girder at the mid-span and the pier top is 4.5m and 11.0m respectively. The height of the girder and the thickness of the bottom slab vary according to the 1.8 order parabola. The box girder adopts three-dimensional prestressing system. The height of the pylon is 44m. 21 pairs of cables are arranged on a single cable plane, and there are 84 cables in the whole bridge.

The bridge makes full use of the gap between the two parallel bridges to set the pylon and the anchorage zone, making the cross section of the bridge compact and functional. The design of the main girder makes the structural spatial stress characteristics of the bridge significant. The cable used for the bridge adopts replaceable anti-sliding steel strands. By optimizing the height of main girder, the height of cable pylon, the length of non-cable zone, the length and spacing of cable zone, the angle of cable and the reasonable live load ratio of cable and girder, the purposes of safety, aesthetics, economy and applicability are achieved.

**Name:** Fudiankou No. 1 Main Bridge over Xi River
**Type:** Extradosed prestressed concrete girder bridge
**Main Span:** 270m
**Location:** Wuzhou City, Guangxi Zhuang Autonomous Region
**Completion:** October, 2018
**Owner(s):** Guangxi Communications Investment Group Co., Ltd.
**Designer(s):** Guangxi Communications Design Group Co., Ltd.
**Contractor(s):** Guangxi Road and Bridge Engineering Group Co., Ltd.

# 鱼山大桥
Yushan Bridge

鱼山大桥位于浙江省舟山市岱山县，连接岱山岛和舟山绿色石化基地。大桥始于岱山县双合村后沙洋山嘴，沿西北方向往海里延伸，在花鼓山南侧转向西南，跨越2000t级航道后转向西北，在大鱼山东面约2km处，跨过规划的围垦区海堤，终点与舟山绿色石化基地内规划道路相接。大桥全长7781.75m，由通航孔桥、岱山侧非通航孔桥、鱼山侧非通航孔桥三部分组成。双向四车道，桥宽15.6m，设计速度为80km/h。

鱼山大桥通航孔桥为连续梁与连续刚构组合体系，跨径布置为70m+140m+180m+260m+180m+140m+70m，其中260m主跨为钢-混凝土混合梁连续刚构桥，中部85m采用钢箱梁，其余位置均采用预制节段悬臂拼装施工的预应力混凝土箱形梁，两者间通过5m的钢-混凝土结合段连接。箱梁截面为单箱单室直腹板截面，箱梁预制节段共238片，下部结构采用群桩基础。

鱼山大桥通航孔桥采用12台桥面起重机同时进行6个T形刚构的悬臂拼装，边跨及次边跨依次完成合龙后，吊装钢箱梁实现中跨合龙。其中，180m的次中跨孔为截至2022年我国悬臂拼装施工最大跨径预应力混凝土桥梁。

鱼山大桥非通航孔桥有70m和50m两种跨径，均是预制节段施工预应力混凝土箱梁桥，采用等高度单箱单室斜腹板箱形截面。70m跨径采用平衡悬臂节段拼装施工，50m跨径采用预制节段逐跨拼装施工。70m跨径的箱梁预制节段共1349片，50m跨径的箱梁预制节段共783片。下部结构采用单桩基础。

桥　　名：鱼山大桥
桥　　型：钢-混凝土混合梁连续刚构桥
主跨跨径：260m
桥　　址：浙江省舟山市
建成时间：2018年12月
建设单位：浙江省舟山北向大通道有限公司
设计单位：浙江省交通规划设计研究院有限公司
（现更名为浙江数智交院科技股份有限公司）
施工单位：浙江省交通工程建设集团有限公司
（现更名为浙江交工集团股份有限公司）、
中交第二航务工程局有限公司

Yushan Bridge is located at Daishan County, Zhoushan City, Zhejiang Province, connecting Daishan Island and Zhoushan Green Petrochemical Base. The bridge, starting from Houshayang Mountain Pass, Shuanghe Village, Daishan County, extends to the sea along the northwest and turns southwest at the south side of Huagu Mountain. It turns northwest after crossing the 2000t waterway, crossing the planned reclamation area seawall about 2km east of Dayu Mountain, and ends at the planned road in Zhoushan Green Petrochemical Base. The total length of the bridge is 7781.75m, consisting of the navigable bridge, the non-navigable bridge on Daishan side and the non-navigable bridge on Yushan side. The bridge has four lanes in dual directions with the width of 15.6m. The design speed of the bridge is 80km/h.

The navigable part of Yushan Bridge is the combination of continuous prestressed concrete girder bridge and continuous prestressed concrete girder bridge with integral piers. The span arrangement is 70m+140m+180m+260m+180m+140m+70m. The 260m-long main span is a steel-concrete hybrid girder including a 85m long steel box girder in the middle. The rest of the main span is prestressed concrete box girder built by precast segmental balanced cantilever method. The two parts are connected by a 5m-long steel-concrete joint section. Straight web single cell box section is adopted for the deck. There are 238 precast segments of the box girder. Pile group foundation is adopted for the substructure.

Twelve deck cranes are used for cantilever assembly of six T-shaped frames at the same time in the navigable part of Yushan Bridge. After the closure of the side spans and the secondary side spans are completed in turn, the steel box girder is lifted to achieve the closure of the middle span. Among them, the 180m-long secondary middle span is the longest precast prestressed concrete bridge constructed by balanced cantilever method in China up to 2022.

The non-navigable bridge of Yushan Bridge has two types of span arrangement: 70m and 50m, both of which are precast segmental prestressed concrete box girders, and adopt inclined web single cell box section with constant height. The construction method of the 70m span is balanced cantilever, while the 50m span is span by span. There are a total of 1349 precast segments for 70m span and 783 precast segments for 50m span. Single pile foundation is used for the substructure.

**Name:** Yushan Bridge
**Type:** Steel-concrete hybrid continuous bridge with integral piers
**Main Span:** 260m
**Location:** Zhoushan City, Zhejiang Province
**Completion:** December, 2018
**Owner(s):** Zhejiang Zhoushan North Passage Co., Ltd.
**Designer(s):** Zhejiang Institute of Communications Co.,Ltd.
**Contractor(s):** Zhejiang Communications Construction Group Co., Ltd. and CCCC Second Harbor Engineering Co., Ltd.

# 三江口大桥
## Sanjiangkou Bridge

三江口大桥位于福州市南台岛东端北侧，横跨闽江，南岸起点为仓山区环岛路，北岸终点与机场高速二期相接，是连接马尾区与仓山区的重要交通枢纽，也是南台岛向宁德、浙江方向辐射的重要通道。桥梁全长1684m，双向八车道，单幅桥宽20.25m，设计速度为80km/h。

三江口大桥跨江段为空腹式钢-混凝土混合梁连续梁桥，主桥跨径布置为71m+83m+123.5m+240m+123.5m+83m+71m，联长795m，主跨中部设置96m长的钢箱梁，其余均为单箱双室直腹板截面预应力混凝土箱梁桥，主桥墩顶段均采用空腹式预应力混凝土箱梁结构。主墩处上部结构建筑高度为20m，其中上弦处梁高3.8m，下弦处竖向高度为4.5m，跨中钢箱梁梁高3.8m。三江口大桥首次在钢-混凝土混合梁桥中采用墩顶空腹式结构，在平原水道上采用空腹式连续梁桥。

全桥除钢箱梁区段外均按照全预应力混凝土桥梁设计，采用三向预应力。钢-混凝土结合段采用填充混凝土后承压板式构造，通过配置体外预应力钢束进一步使两者传力平顺。

为降低桥梁的地震响应，14号、15号主墩布置摩擦摆球型支座，其他桥墩均布置摩擦摆柱面支座。

| 桥　　名： | 三江口大桥 |
|---|---|
| 桥　　型： | 空腹式钢-混凝土混合梁连续梁桥 |
| 主跨跨径： | 240m |
| 桥　　址： | 福建省福州市 |
| 建成时间： | 2019年1月 |
| 建设单位： | 福州市城乡建总集团有限公司 |
| 设计单位： | 中交第二公路勘察设计研究院有限公司 |
| 施工单位： | 中交第二航务工程局有限公司 |

Sanjiangkou Bridge is located on the north side of the east end of Nantai Island, Fuzhou City, across the Min River. The starting point of the south bank is Huandao Road, Cangshan District, and the terminal point of the north bank is connected with the Phase II of the Airport Expressway. It is an important transportation hub connecting Mawei District and Cangshan District, and also an important way for Nantai Island to radiate towards Ningde City and Zhejiang Province. The bridge has a total length of 1684m, and eight lanes in dual directions with two parallel bridges of 20.25m wide each. The design speed of the bridge is 80km/h.

The river-crossing part of Sanjiangkon Bridge is a steel-concrete hybrid girder continuous bridge with open spandrel on all pier top. The span arrangement of the main bridge is 71m+83m+123.5m+240m+123.5m+83m+71m, with a continuous length of 795m between expansion joints. A 96m-long steel box girder is designed in the middle of the main span. The rest is prestressed concrete box girder with straight web and two-cell single box section. The top sections on the main piers are all open spandrel prestressed concrete box girders. The superstructure of the main pier is 20m high. The height of the upper chord beam is 3.8m, while the vertical height of the lower chord beam is 4.5m. The height of the steel box girder in the middle is 3.8m. For the first time, the open spandrel prestressed concrete structure is adopted for the steel-concrete hybrid girder bridge, as well as used on the plain waterway.

Except for the steel girder section, the whole bridge is designed as fully prestressed concrete bridge with three-dimensional prestressing. The steel-concrete joint section is constructed with concrete filling back bearing plate, and the external prestressing tendon are used to further make the force transmission smooth.

In order to reduce the seismic response of the bridge, friction pendulum ball bearings are arranged for 14[#] and 15[#] main piers, and friction pendulum cylinder bearings are arranged for the other piers.

**Name:** Sanjiangkou Bridge
**Type:** Open spandrel steel-concrete hybrid girder continuous bridge
**Main Span:** 240m
**Location:** Fuzhou City, Fujian Province
**Completion:** January, 2019
**Owner(s):** Fuzhou Urban Rural Construction Group Co., Ltd.
**Designer(s):** CCCC Second Highway Consultants Co., Ltd.
**Contractor(s):** CCCC Second Harbor Engineering Co., Ltd.

# 运宝黄河大桥

Yunbao Bridge over Yellow River

桥　名：运宝黄河大桥
桥　型：波形钢腹板索辅梁桥
主跨跨径：220m
桥　址：山西省运城市芮城县和河南省灵宝市交会处
建成时间：2019 年 8 月
建设单位：山西路桥建设集团有限公司
设计单位：山西省交通规划勘察设计院有限公司
施工单位：中交第二航务工程局有限公司

**Name:** Yunbao Bridge over Yellow River
**Type:** Extradosed prestressed concrete girder bridge with corrugated steel webs
**Main Span:** 220m
**Location:** the junction of Ruicheng County, Yuncheng City, Shanxi Province and Lingbao City, Henan Province
**Completion:** August, 2019
**Owner(s):** Shanxi Road & Bridge Construction Group Co.,Ltd.
**Designer(s):** Shanxi Province Communications Planning Surveying and Designing Institute Co., Ltd.
**Contractor(s):** CCCC Second Harbor Engineering Co., Ltd.

　　运宝黄河大桥位于山西省运城市芮城县和河南省灵宝市交会处，跨越黄河水道，是国家高速公路网中南北纵线呼和浩特—北海高速公路的重要组成部分。桥梁全长 1690m，桥宽 34m，桥面为双向六车道高速公路，设计速度为 80km/h。

　　运宝黄河大桥主桥为三塔四跨单索面波形钢腹板索辅梁桥，跨径布置为 110m+2×220m+110m，边中跨比为 0.55，塔墩梁固结体系。主桥主梁为整体式断面，采用变高度单箱五室波形钢腹板-混凝土腹板混合截面，中间 2 道腹板为混凝土腹板，其余 4 道腹板为波形钢腹板。主梁根部梁高 7m，跨中梁高 3m，梁高按 1.8 次抛物线变化。主桥拉索为中央单索面布置，锚固于中间箱室 2 道混凝土腹板之间，横向双排索面，每个索面共 13 对拉索，锚固点纵向间距为 4.8m，横向间距为 1.0m。

　　运宝黄河大桥主梁设置 4 道波形钢腹板，降低了上部结构自重，具有较好的抗震性能；避免腹板的开裂，提高了腹板抗剪性能和结构耐久性。主梁中间 2 道腹板设置为混凝土腹板，拉索锚固在中间箱室 2 道混凝土腹板之间，改善了拉索锚固条件，增强了锚固处主梁截面的整体性，提高了腹板纵向刚度，使拉索水平分力更均匀地作用于主梁截面。桥墩纵向采用双薄壁实心墩，纵向刚度小，减小了地震效应。

enhances the integrity of the main girder section at the anchorage, improves the longitudinal stiffness of the webs, and makes the longitudinal component of the cable force more evenly act on the section of the main girder. The piers adopt double thin-walled solid shafts in the longitudinal direction and thus have small longitudinal stiffness and reduce the seismic effect.

Yunbao Bridge over Yellow River is located at the junction of Ruicheng County, Yuncheng City, Shanxi Province and Lingbao City, Henan Province. It crosses the Yellow River Waterway and is an important part of the Hohhot-Beihai Expressway on the north-south vertical line of the national expressway network. The total length of the bridge is 1690m, and the bridge width is 34m. The bridge deck has six lanes in dual directions with a design speed of 80km/h.

The main bridge of Yunbao Bridge over Yellow River is a three-pylon four-span single-plane extradosed prestressed concrete girder bridge with corrugated steel webs. The span arrangement of the main bridge is 110m + 2×220m+110m and the side-to-middle span ratio is 0.55. The pylon, girder and piers are fixed together. The main girder of the main bridge uses five-cell single box section with variable height and mixed webs: four of the six webs are corrugated steel webs and the other two webs in the middle are concrete. The height of the deck at the support is 7m, while that at the mid-span is 3m, varying according to the 1.8 order parabola. The cables of the main bridge are arranged in the central single cable plane with two cable arrays, which is anchored between the two concrete webs of the middle cell of the box section. There are 13 pairs of cables in each cable plane. The longitudinal spacing of the anchorages is 4.8m, and the transverse spacing is 1.0m.

The main girder of Yunbao Bridge over Yellow River adopts four corrugated steel webs, which reduces the dead weight of the superstructure, and thus makes the bridge have good seismic performance. It also avoids web cracking, and improves the shear performance and durability of the web. The middle two webs of the main girder are designed as concrete webs, between which the cables are anchored in the middle box. This anchorage arrangement improves the cable anchorage condition,

# 浩吉铁路汉江特大桥
## Haoji Railway Bridge over Han River

浩吉铁路汉江特大桥途经湖北省襄阳市樊城区和襄城区，跨越汉江，是浩吉铁路全线的重难点及控制性工程之一。主桥全长626.8m，线路等级为Ⅰ级，有砟轨道，正线数目为双线，线距为4.0m，设计速度为120km/h，主桥桥墩高19m，河流与线路大里程夹角为99°。

浩吉铁路汉江特大桥主桥为五跨预应力混凝土索辅梁桥，跨径布置为72m+116m+248m+116m+72m。大桥结构采用塔梁固结、墩与塔梁分离的体系。主梁采用单箱双室截面，中支点梁高13.0m，中跨跨中及边支点梁高6.0m，梁底为圆曲线变化。箱梁顶板宽11.6m，中支点桥塔处局部两侧各加宽2.8m，在桥塔外侧布置人行道，在拉索位置人行道外侧桥面加宽1.1m。箱梁底板宽10.2m，主梁设纵向、横向和竖向预应力。桥塔采用双柱型桥塔，梁顶面以上高57m。拉索横向为双索面布置，立面为半扇形布置。每个索塔设9对拉索，塔上索距为1.5m，梁上索距为9.0m。

浩吉铁路汉江特大桥主桥采用索辅梁桥方案，梁高仅13.0m，为跨径的1/19.1，能有效满足通航净空要求，梁部为混凝土结构，经济指标良好。采用悬臂浇筑施工对通航无影响，且具有外形简洁、流畅的优点。主桥索塔采用液压爬模法施工。主梁采用挂篮悬臂浇筑法，边直段及零号块采用支架现浇施工，先进行边跨合龙，后进行中跨合龙。

Haoji Railway Bridge over Han River passes through Fancheng District and Xiangcheng District of Xiangyang City, Hubei Province. The bridge crosses the Han River and is one of the key and difficult structures and control projects of the whole line of Haolebaoji-Ji'an Railway. The total length of the main bridge is 626.8m. The track grade is grade Ⅰ, using ballast track with double tracks in dual directions. The spacing between the two tracks is 4.0m. The design speed is 120km/h. The height of the main pier is 19m, and the angle between the river and the track line is 99°.

The main bridge of Haoji Railway Bridge over Han River is a five-span extradosed prestressed concrete girder bridge. The span arrangement is 72m+116m+248m+116m+72m. The structural system includes fixing between pylon and girder and they seperate from the piers. The main girder adopts two-cell single box section, with the deck height of 13.0m at the middle supports and of 6.0m at the mid-span and side supports. The bottom of the deck varies according to the circular curve. The top flange of the box girder is 11.6m wide, and the local area at the both sides of the pylons is widened by 2.8m. The sidewalk is arranged outside the pylons, and the bridge deck outside the sidewalk is widened by 1.1m at the cable anchorage position. The width of bottom slab of box girder is 10.2m. Longitudinal, transverse and vertical prestressing are arranged in the main girder. The pylon is double-column type, 57m high above the top of the deck. There are two cable planes transversely, adopting semi-fan-shaped cable arrangement. Each pylon has 9 pairs of cables, with the cable spacing of 1.5m on the pylon and of 9.0m on the deck.

The main bridge of Haoji Railway Bridge over Han River adopts the design of extradosed prestressed concrete girder bridge. The height of the deck is only 13.0m, which is 1/19.1 of the span, effectively meeting the requirement of navigational clearance. The girder is concrete structure with good economic index. The cast-in-situ balanced cantilever construction method has no effect on navigation, and has the advantages of simple and smooth appearance. The main pylons are constructed by hydraulic climbing formwork. The main girder is constructed by cast-in-situ balanced cantilever method with hanging basket. The side section with constant depth and the segment on the main piers are cast on scaffolding. The closure of the side spans and then the middle span are carried out after having finished the cantilever part of the bridge.

**Name:** Haoji Railway Bridge over Han River
**Type:** Extradosed prestressed concrete girder bridge
**Main Span:** 248m
**Location:** Xiangyang City, Hubei Province
**Completion:** September, 2019
**Owner(s):** Haoji Railway Co., Ltd.
**Designer(s):** China Railway Siyuan Survey and Design Group Co., Ltd.
**Contractor(s):** China Railway 11th Bureau Group Corporation Limited

# 汉十铁路崔家营汉江特大桥
## Cuijiaying Bridge over Han River on Wuhan-Shiyan Railway

| | |
|---|---|
| 桥　名：汉十铁路崔家营汉江特大桥 | **Name:** Cuijiaying Bridge over Han River on Wuhan-Shiyan Railway |
| 桥　型：预应力混凝土拱辅梁桥 | **Type:** Partially arch-supported prestressed concrete girder bridge |
| 主跨跨径：300m | **Main Span:** 300m |
| 桥　址：湖北省襄阳市 | **Location:** Xiangyang City, Hubei Province |
| 建成时间：2019年11月 | **Completion:** November, 2019 |
| 建设单位：湖北汉十城际铁路有限责任公司 | **Owner(s):** Hubei Hanshi Intercity Railway Co., Ltd. |
| 设计单位：中铁第四勘察设计院集团有限公司 | **Designer(s):** China Railway Siyuan Survey and Design Group Co., Ltd. |
| 施工单位：中铁大桥局集团有限公司 | **Contractor(s):** China Railway Major Bridge Engineering Group Co., Ltd. |

汉十铁路崔家营汉江特大桥，是湖北省襄阳市境内连接襄州区和襄城区的过江通道，位于汉江水道之上，是武汉至十堰铁路的控制性工程。大桥全长13.0km，设计速度为350km/h，桥宽14.6m。

汉十铁路崔家营汉江特大桥主桥建成时是世界上最大跨径的预应力混凝土拱辅梁桥，主桥跨径布置为135m+2×300m+135m。主梁为变高度预应力混凝土箱梁，采用单箱双室截面，中支点处梁高16.5m，跨中梁高6.5m。拱肋采用钢管混凝土结构，中跨拱肋高4.85~5.85m，边跨拱肋高2.8m，矢跨比为1/5。拱脚与主梁刚性连接，拱肋与主梁采用柔性吊杆连接。

汉十铁路崔家营汉江特大桥首次采用四联拱加劲的混凝土梁拱组合结构，提高了结构刚度，实现了高速铁路混凝土梁拱桥300m级跨径的技术突破；采用"拱肋低位拼装、大节段垂直提升"的施工方法，实现了300m跨径拱肋既无缆索吊又无扣索塔架施工；使用"大型旋挖钻机+回旋钻机+摩阻杆"成套设备，解决了复杂岩溶地质、超长孔深、超硬岩层大直径钻孔桩施工问题。

Cuijiaying Bridge over Han River on Wuhan-Shiyan Railway is a river crossing channel connecting Xiangzhou District and Xiangcheng District in Xiangyang City, Hubei Province. It is located on the Han River Waterway and is a control project of Wuhan-Shiyan Railway. The bridge is 13.0km long, with the design speed of 350km/h and the width of 14.6m.

The main bridge of Cuijiaying Bridge over Han River on

Wuhan-Shiyan Railway is the largest span of partially arch-supported prestressed concrete girder bridge at the time it was completed in the world. The span arrangement of the main bridge is 135m+2×300m+135m. The deck is a prestressed concrete double-cell single box girder with variable heights. The height of the deck at the central supports is 16.5m, while that at the mid-span is 6.5m. The arch rib is concrete-filled steel tube structure. The arch rib of the middle spans is 4.85m to 5.85m high, while the arch rib of the side spans is 2.8m high. The rise-span ratio is 1/5. The arch foot is rigidly fixed with the main girder, and the arch rib is connected with the main girder by flexible suspenders.

For the first time, the hybrid structure with the concrete girder partially supported by four continuous arches is adopted by the Cuijiaying Bridge over Han River on Wuhan-Shiyan Railway, which improves the structural stiffness and achieves a technical breakthrough in the 300m span level of concrete girder bridges for high-speed railway. The construction method of "low position assembly of arch rib and vertical lifting of large segment" is adopted to achieve the construction of 300m span arch rib without cable cranes or temporary supporting towers. The equipment of "large rotary drilling rig with circle round drilling rig and friction rod" is used to solve the problems of large diameter bored piles in complex karst geology, super deep holes and super hard rock stratum in construction.

# 成功大桥
Chenggong Bridge

| | |
|---|---|
| 桥　　名：成功大桥 | **Name:** Chenggong Bridge |
| 桥　　型：钢-混凝土混合梁连续刚构桥 | **Type:** Steel-concrete hybrid girder continuous bridge with integral piers |
| 主跨跨径：300m | **Main Span:** 300m |
| 桥　　址：福建省泉州市 | **Location:** Quanzhou City, Fujian Province |
| 建成时间：2020年12月 | **Completion:** December, 2020 |
| 建设单位：福建省高速公路集团有限公司 | **Owner(s):** Fujian Expressway Group Co., Ltd. |
| 设计单位：福建省交通规划设计院有限公司 | **Designer(s):** Fujian Provincial Communications Planning & Design Institute Co., Ltd. |
| 施工单位：中交一公局集团有限公司 | **Contractor(s):** CCCC First Highway Engineering Group Co., Ltd. |

成功大桥是福建省泉州市境内连接晋江市和南安市的跨海桥梁，位于安海湾之上，是福州—厦门高速公路、泉州环城高速公路、泉州—厦门—漳州高速公路泉州段的组成部分之一。大桥东起东石镇，西至石井镇。线路全长27.36km，桥梁全长7.5km，主桥面为双向六车道高速公路，设计速度为100km/h。

成功大桥为钢-混凝土混合梁连续刚构桥，跨径布置为135m+300m+135m。中跨钢箱梁长度为103m，其余部分均为预应力混凝土结构，采用悬臂浇筑施工。主跨桥梁全长570m，单幅桥面宽16.25m，上部结构采用C55海工耐久混凝土，钢箱梁采用Q235qD钢板。下部结构主墩采用双薄壁实心墩，钻孔灌注桩群桩基础，桥墩采用C50海工混凝土。

该桥位于中国唯一的沿海高风速带，热带气旋（台风）是影响大桥的主要灾害性天气，除了热带气旋的影响外，建设该桥还需考虑大桥处于海洋环境的耐久性，超过10km跨海距离的长桥结构安全，施工期、运营期的安全问题及景观要求等因素。

Chenggong Bridge is a sea crossing bridge connecting Jinjiang City and Nan'an City in Quanzhou City, Fujian Province. It is located on Anhai Bay and is one of the components of Fuzhou-Xiamen Expressway, Quanzhou City Ring Expressway, Quanzhou Section of Quanzhou-Xiamen-Zhangzhou Expressway. The bridge starts from Dongshi Town in the east and ends at Shijing Town in the west. The road route is 27.36km long, while the bridge is 7.5km long. The main bridge is a six-lane expressway in dual directions with the design speed of 100km/h.

Chenggong Bridge, with the span arrangement of 135m+300m+135m, is a steel-concrete hybrid girder continuous bridge with integral piers. The length of the steel box girder in the middle span is 103m, while the rest of the bridge is prestressed concrete structure, which is constructed by cast-in-situ balanced cantilever method. The length of the main bridge is 570m, with two parallel bridges of 16.25m wide each. The superstructure is made of C55 marine durable concrete, and the steel box girder is made of Q235qD steel plate. Double thin-walled solid pier shafts are adopted for the main piers of the substructure and bored pile group foundation is used. C50 marine concrete is adopted for the piers.

The bridge is located in the only coastal high wind speed zone in China. Tropical cyclones (typhoons) are the main disastrous weather affecting the bridge. In addition to the impact of tropical cyclones, the construction of the bridge should also take into account the durability of the bridge in the marine environment, the structural safety of the long bridge with sea crossing length of more than 10km, the safety requirements during the construction period and the operation period, and the landscape requirements and other factors.

# 喀腊塑克水库特大桥
## Kalasuke Reservoir Bridge

喀腊塑克水库特大桥位于新疆维吾尔自治区阿勒泰地区富蕴县，跨越喀腊塑克水库，是额尔齐斯河干流上的控制性工程，也是"引额供水工程"中重要的水源工程之一。桥梁全长约980m，最高桥墩高43m。

喀腊塑克水库特大桥为预应力混凝土索辅梁桥，主桥跨径布置为140m+270.8m+140m，全桥采用挂篮悬臂浇筑法施工。主梁采用单箱单室直腹板箱形截面，中支点梁高13.5 m，边支点梁高6.5m，梁体下缘按1.8次抛物线变化。桥塔在桥面以上高38m，钻石形结构。拉索采用双索面扇形布置，全桥设置56对共112根拉索，梁上拉索水平间距为6.0m，塔部拉索竖向间距为1.2m。

喀腊塑克水库特大桥主梁刚度大，以梁为主、以索为辅，拉索实质上起体外预应力索的作用。大桥桥塔的建筑高度小，拉索的倾角小，拉索为梁提供较大的轴向力。

**Name:** Kalasuke Reservoir Bridge
**Type:** Extradosed prestressed concrete girder bridge
**Main Span:** 270.8m
**Location:** Altay Prefecture, Xinjiang Uygur Autonomous Region
**Completion:** December, 2020
**Owner(s):** China Railway Urumqi Group Co.,Ltd.
**Designer(s):** China Railway First Survey and Design Institute Group Co.,Ltd.
**Contractor(s):** China Railway 10th Bureau Group No.1 Engineering Co., Ltd.

| 桥　　名： | 喀腊塑克水库特大桥 |
|---|---|
| 桥　　型： | 预应力混凝土索辅梁桥 |
| 主跨跨径： | 270.8m |
| 桥　　址： | 新疆维吾尔自治区阿勒泰地区 |
| 建成时间： | 2020年12月 |
| 建设单位： | 中国铁路乌鲁木齐局集团有限公司 |
| 设计单位： | 中铁第一勘察设计院集团有限公司 |
| 施工单位： | 中铁十局集团第一工程有限公司 |

Kalasuke Reservoir Bridge is located in Fuyun County, Altay Prefecture, Xinjiang Uygur Autonomous Region. It crosses the Kalasuke Reservoir. It is a control project on the mainstream of the Irtysh River. It is also one of the important projects in the water supply project to use the Irtysh River. The total length of the bridge is about 980m, and the highest pier is 43m.

Kalasuke Reservoir Bridge is an extradosed prestressed concrete girder bridge. The main bridge span arrangement is 140m+270.8m+140m. The whole bridge is constructed by cast-in-situ balanced cantilever method with hanging basket. The main girder adopts straight web single cell single box section. The height of the girder at the middle support is 13.5m, while that at the side support is 6.5m. The bottom of the deck varies according to the 1.8 order parabola. The pylon is 38m high above the bridge deck, using a diamond-shaped structure. The cables are arranged in a fan shape with double cable planes. There are 56 pairs of 112 cables in the whole bridge. The longitudinal spacing of the cables on the deck is 6.0m, and the vertical spacing of the cables on the pylon is 1.2m.

The main girder of Kalasuke Reservoir Bridge has large stiffness, which is mainly supplied by girder and supplemented by cables. The cables essentially play the role of external prestressing tendons. The building height of the bridge pylon is low and the inclination angle of the cables is small. The cables provide large axial force for the girder.

# 龙丽温高速洪溪特大桥

## Hongxi Bridge on Longyou-Lishui-Wenzhou Expressway

　　龙丽温高速洪溪特大桥位于浙江省温州市泰顺县洪溪水库下游，地处峡谷地带，是溧阳—宁德高速公路（G4012）浙江省文成至泰顺段的控制性工程。桥梁全长571m，塔顶距谷底282m，桥面距离谷底240.4m，桥梁底以下墩高为126m，双向四车道，单幅桥面宽15.25m，设计速度为80km/h。

　　该桥为双塔双索面预应力混凝土索辅梁桥，桥梁跨径布置为150m+265m+150m，边中跨比为0.566，采用塔墩梁固结体系。主梁采用单箱双室预应力箱梁，箱梁跨中及边跨现浇段梁高4.5m，高跨比为1/58.9，桥塔处根部梁高9.2m，高跨比为1/28.8，梁高按1.8次抛物线变化，主梁设纵、横、竖三向预应力。桥塔采用Y形塔，拉索采用扇形双索面布置，每塔设32根，全桥（双幅）共128根。拉索在塔上连续通过鞍座，两侧对称锚固于主梁翼缘。拉索在主梁上纵向间距为5.0m，塔上竖向间距为1.0m。

　　该桥为峡谷高墩索辅梁桥，塔墩梁固结体系显著提高了桥梁的整体刚度和抗风性能。通过对中跨合龙口预顶可以减小主梁收缩徐变引起的塔底弯矩，改善桥塔受力。有索区节段采用"拉索滞后张拉"施工技术，即在当前节段纵向预应力束张拉完成后即前移挂篮进行下一节段钢筋绑扎，并同步进行当前节段拉索张拉，将流水施工调整为部分平行施工，每个节段工期由15d缩短为12d。

| | |
|---|---|
| 桥　　名： | 龙丽温高速洪溪特大桥 |
| 桥　　型： | 预应力混凝土索辅梁桥 |
| 主跨跨径： | 265m |
| 桥　　址： | 浙江省温州市 |
| 建成时间： | 2020年12月 |
| 建设单位： | 浙江省交通投资集团有限公司 |
| 设计单位： | 浙江数智交院科技股份有限公司 |
| 施工单位： | 浙江交工集团股份有限公司 |

Hongxi Bridge on Longyou-Lishui-Wenzhou Expressway is located at the downstream of Hongxi Reservoir in Taishun County, Wenzhou City, Zhejiang Province. It is a control project of Liyang-Ningde Expressway (G4012) from Wencheng to Taishun in Zhejiang Province. The total length of the bridge is 571m. The distance from the top of the pylon to the bottom of the valley is 282m, while the distance from the bridge deck to the bottom of the valley is 240.4m, and the height of the pier below the bottom of the bridge deck is 126m. The bridge has four lanes in dual directions with two parallel bridge decks and the width of each bridge deck is 15.25m. The design speed is 80km/h.

The Bridge is an extradosed prestressed concrete girder bridge with double pylons and double cable planes. The span arrangement of the bridge is 150m+265m+150m, with the side-to-middle span ratio of 0.566.The bridge adopts fixing system among pylon, girder and pier. The main girder adopts prestressed concrete box girder section with double-cell single box. The height of the bridge deck at mid-span and side-span section built on scaffoldings is 4.5m, with the height-span ratio of 1/58.9, while the height of the bridge deck at the middle supports is 9.2m, with the height-span ratio of 1/28.8. The height of the deck varies according to the 1.8 order parabola. The main girder is prestressed in longitudinal, transverse and vertical directions. The bridge pylon adopts Y-shape transversely, and the cables are arranged in the fan-shape with double cable planes. There are 32 cables on each pylon, with 128 cables in total for the two parallel bridges. The cables continuously deviate at the saddle on the pylon, and are symmetrically anchored at the flange of the main girder on both sides. The longitudinal spacing of the cables on the deck is 5.0m, while the vertical spacing on the pylon is 1.0m.

The bridge is an extradosed prestressed concrete girder bridge with high piers in gorge area. The fixing system among pylon, girder and pier significantly improves the overall stiffness and wind-resistant performance of the bridge. The pre-jacking of the closure section at the mid-span can reduce the bending moment at the pylon bottom caused by the concrete shrinkage and creep of the main girder and improve the state of the force of the bridge pylon. The cable segments use the "lag tensioning" construction method, that is, after the completion of the longitudinal prestressing tendons of the current segment, move forward the hanging basket for the reinforcement assembly of the next segment, and the cables of the current segment are tensioned at the same time. This method adjusts the construction procedure, i.e., to carry out some construction steps simultaneously, reducing the construction period for each segment from 15 days to 12 days.

**Name:** Hongxi Bridge on Longyou-Lishui-Wenzhou Expressway
**Type:** Extradosed prestressed concrete girder bridge
**Main Span:** 265m
**Location:** Wenzhou City, Zhejiang Province
**Completion:** December, 2020
**Owner(s):** Zhejiang Communications Investment Group Co., Ltd.
**Designer(s):** Zhejiang Institute of Communications Co., Ltd.
**Contractor(s):** Zhejiang Communications Construction Group Co., Ltd.

# 剑潭东江特大桥
## Jiantan Bridge over Dong River

桥　　名：剑潭东江特大桥
桥　　型：预应力混凝土索辅梁桥
主跨跨径：260m
桥　　址：广东省惠州市
建成时间：2021年12月
建设单位：中国铁路广州局集团有限公司
设计单位：中铁第四勘察设计院集团有限公司
施工单位：中交第三航务工程局有限公司

**Name:** Jiantan Bridge over Dong River
**Type:** Extradosed prestressed concrete girder bridge
**Main Span:** 260m
**Location:** Huizhou City, Guangdong Province
**Completion:** December, 2021
**Owner(s):** China Railway Guangzhou Group Co., Ltd.
**Designer(s):** China Railway Siyuan Survey and Design Group Co., Ltd.
**Contractor(s):** CCCC Third Harbor Engineering Co., Ltd.

Jiantan Bridge over Dong River is located at the junction of Huicheng District and Boluo County, Huizhou City, Guangdong Province. It crosses the Dong River in Jiantan Section and is a control project of Beijing-Kowloon High-speed Railway (Ganshen Railway Section). The bridge has a total length of 925.74m with a main span of 260m. The width of the bridge is 31m. The four rail lines on the bridge all use ballastless tracks. The design speed is 350km/h.

Jiantan Bridge over Dong River is an extradosed prestressed concrete girder bridge adopting fixing structural system among pylon, girder and pier. The span arrangement of the bridge is 136m+260m+136m. The main girder is a three-cell single box section with variable height. The height of girder at the middle supports is 13m, and the height of girder at the mid-span and the side supports are 6m. The bottom of the girder varies according to a circular curve. The pylon is an inverted Y-shaped single column, 56m high with the height-span ratio of 1/4.6. The bridge has two cable planes in the transverse direction, and each cable plane has 10 pairs of extradosed tendons. The construction of the pylons is carried out together with the construction of the girder. The balanced cantilever method with hanging baskets is adopted for the construction of the main girder.

The bridge has a wide deck, thus the transverse force distribution needs to be paid close attention. The box stiffening scheme of "three full diaphragms+seven cross beams" is adopted in the half span of the bridge. On the one hand, the distortion of the wide deck is reduced, which better meets the requirements of the structural mechanics. On the other hand, the disturbance of too many diaphragms to the cantilever construction is avoided to the greatest extent.

剑潭东江特大桥位于广东省惠州市惠城区与博罗县交会处，在剑潭段跨越东江河道，为京九高速铁路（赣深铁路段）的控制性工程。桥梁全长925.74m，主跨260m，桥面宽度为31m，桥上四线均采用了无砟轨道，设计速度为350km/h。

剑潭东江特大桥为预应力混凝土索辅梁桥，采用塔墩梁固结体系，桥梁的跨径布置为136m+260m+136m，主梁为单箱三室变高度整体箱形截面，中支点梁高13m，跨中及边支点梁高6m，梁底按圆曲线变化。索塔整体上呈独柱式，高56m，高跨比为1/4.6，呈倒Y形。拉索横向为双索面布置，一个索面设置10对拉索。工程整体使用塔梁同步施工方法，主梁采用挂篮悬臂浇筑法对称浇筑施工。

该桥是宽幅主梁，需重点关注横向受力。该桥半跨范围内采用"3道全隔板+7道横梁"的箱内加劲方案，一方面降低了宽幅主梁的畸变效应，满足了结构受力的要求，另一方面也最大限度避免了过多的横隔板对悬臂施工产生干扰。

# 道庆洲大桥
## Daoqingzhou Bridge

道庆洲大桥是福建省首座双层公轨两用桥梁，位于福州市闽江和乌龙江的交汇处，距下游青州闽江大桥约7km，距上游乌龙江大桥约5km，连接福州市仓山区与长乐区。项目全长6.82km，上层为双向六车道一级公路兼城市主干道和人行非机动车混行通道，设计速度为60km/h；下层承载地铁六号线，设计速度为100km/h。

道庆洲大桥全长2268.5m，跨江主桥主跨276m，截至2022年，它是世界上跨径最大的变高度连续钢桁结合梁桥。该桥采用体内、体外预应力钢束混合布置。主桥钢桁梁横向设2片主桁，采用无竖杆三角形桁式，桁宽15m，标准桁高9.5m，主墩处桁高23m。主桥上层公路桥面宽31m，采用"密横梁+混凝土板"结合桥面；下层轨道桥面宽15m，采用"纵横梁+正交异性板"整体钢桥面体系。主墩支座采用竖向承载力为135MN的双曲面球型减震支座。

引桥为标准跨径84m和73m的等高度钢桁结合梁桥。引桥第二、第七联采用变宽度钢桁梁，第五联采用折线钢桁梁。

道庆洲大桥下层的地铁桥面采用无砟轨道结构，减轻了轨道荷载；上层公路桥面系采用体内预应力和体外预应力钢束混合布置，改善了混凝土板受力；在混凝土桥面板和钢梁结合过程中，采取顶、落梁措施，调整和优化了混凝土桥面结构受力。

桥　名：道庆洲大桥
桥　型：连续钢桁结合梁桥
主跨跨径：276m
桥　址：福建省福州市
建成时间：2022年1月
建设单位：福州左海控股集团有限公司
设计单位：中铁大桥勘测设计院集团有限公司
施工单位：中国建筑第六工程局有限公司

**Name:** Daoqingzhou Bridge
**Type:** Continuous steel truss composite girder bridge
**Main Span:** 276m
**Location:** Fuzhou City, Fujian Province
**Completion:** January, 2022
**Owner(s):** Fuzhou Zuohai Holding Group Co., Ltd.
**Designer(s):** China Railway Major Bridge Reconnaissance & Design Institute Co., Ltd.
**Contractor(s):** China Construction Sixth Engineering Bureau Co., Ltd.

Daoqingzhou Bridge is the first double-layer road and rail bridge in Fujian Province. It is located at the intersection of the Min River and the Wulong River in Fuzhou City. It is about 7km from the Qingzhou Min River Bridge at the downstream and 5km from the Wulong River Bridge at the upstream, connecting Cangshan District and Changle District of Fuzhou City. The total length of the project is 6.82km. The upper layer has six lanes of arterial highway in dual directions, which is also main urban road and mixed pedestrian and non-motor vehicle passage. The design speed is 60km/h. The lower layer carries Metro Line 6, the design speed of which is 100km/h.

The total length of Daoqingzhou Bridge is 2268.5m, and the main span of the river crossing main bridge is 276m. It is a continuous steel truss composite girder bridge with variable height, which is the longest span in the world up to 2022. Mixed arrangement of internal and external prestressing tendons is used for the bridge. The steel truss girder of the main bridge has two main trusses at the two sides transversely, which are of the triangle truss type without vertical components. The truss is 15m wide. The standard truss is 9.5m high, and the truss at the main pier is 23m high. The upper highway deck of the main bridge is 31m wide, and the composite bridge deck is composed of "multi-crossbeams+concrete slab". The lower track deck is 15m wide, and the integral steel deck system of "longitudinal and transverse stiffeners and orthotropic steel plate" is adopted. The main pier bearing is a hyperbolic spherical shock absorption bearing with a vertical bearing capacity of 135MN.

The approach bridge is steel truss composite girder bridge with constant height, and the standard spans are 84m and 73m. Continuously widened steel truss girder is adopted in the second and seventh sections of the approach bridge, while discontinuously widened steel truss girder is adopted in the fifth section.

The ballastless track structure is adopted for the subway deck for the lower layer of Daoqingzhou Bridge, which reduces the track load. Mixed arrangement of internal and external prestressing tendons is adopted in the upper highway bridge deck system to improve the stress of concrete slab. In the process of combination of concrete deck slab and steel girder, the measures of jacking and dropping are used to adjust and optimize the stress of the concrete deck.

# 嘉华轨道专用桥
## Jiahua Rail Transit Bridge

嘉华轨道专用桥位于重庆市轨道交通9号线化龙桥站和李家坪站之间，连接渝中区和江北区。桥梁位于嘉华大桥上游约100m处，是轨道交通9号线跨越嘉陵江的关键控制性工程。桥梁全长618.915m，桥宽12.5m。

嘉华轨道专用桥是跨径布置为138m+252m+138m的钢-混凝土混合梁连续刚构桥，主梁为变截面箱梁，主跨跨中92m范围内采用钢箱梁结构，其余均为预应力混凝土结构，钢箱梁两端各有一段长2.5m的钢-混凝土结合段，钢箱梁与钢-混凝土结合段之间采用栓焊连接。箱梁截面均为单箱单室断面，梁底宽7.6m。墩顶梁高15.7m，跨中梁高5m。钢箱梁高度由7.5m变至5.0m。

嘉华轨道专用桥采用大节段钢箱梁整体吊装与安装技术，确保提升平稳，持荷稳定；设置八字形合龙口，将钢箱梁提升至合龙口内测量、配切，消除了结构参数取值误差和温度场影响带来的误差，配切精度高，具有可靠的操作性。

| | |
|---|---|
| 桥　　名： | 嘉华轨道专用桥 |
| 桥　　型： | 钢-混凝土混合梁连续刚构桥 |
| 主跨跨径： | 252m |
| 桥　　址： | 重庆市 |
| 建成时间： | 2022年1月 |
| 建设单位： | 中铁隆工程集团有限公司 |
| 设计单位： | 重庆市轨道交通设计研究院有限责任公司 |
| 施工单位： | 中建三局第三建设工程有限责任公司 |

Jiahua Rail Transit Bridge is located between Hualongqiao Station and Lijiaping Station of Metro Line 9, connecting Yuzhong District and Jiangbei District in Chongqing. The bridge is located about 100 meters upstream of the Jiahua Bridge, and is a key control project for Metro Line 9 to cross the Jialing River. The bridge is 618.915m long and 12.5m wide.

Jiahua Rail Transit Bridge is a steel-concrete hybrid girder continuous bridge with integral piers with the span arrangement of 138m+252m+138m. The girder adopts box girders with variable cross sections. The steel box girder is 92m in the middle of the main span, and the rest of the bridge is prestressed concrete structure. The steel-concrete joint section at both ends of the steel box girder is 2.5m long, and is connected to the steel box girder by bolting and welding. The box girder uses single cell single box section, with the bottom width of the deck is 7.6m. The height of the girder at the pier-top is 15.7m, while that at the mid-span is 5m. The height of the steel box girder varies from 7.5m to 5.0m.

The integral hoisting and installation technology of large-section steel box girder is adopted in Jiahua Rail Transit Bridge to ensure the stable lifting and load holding. By setting the splay closure, the steel box girder is lifted into the closure for measurement and matching cutting, which eliminates the errors caused by structural parameter selection and temperature field influence, and has high matching cutting accuracy and reliable operability.

**Name:** Jiahua Rail Transit Bridge
**Type:** Steel-concrete hybrid girder continuous bridge with integral piers
**Main Span:** 252m
**Location:** Chongqing Municipality
**Completion:** January, 2022
**Owner(s):** Ranken Railway Construction Group Co., Ltd.
**Designer(s):** Chongqing Rail Transit Design and Research Institute Co., Ltd.
**Contractor(s):** The Third Construction Co., Ltd. of China Construction Third Engineering Bureau

# 甘溪特大桥
## Ganxi Bridge

| | |
|---|---|
| 桥　　名： | 甘溪特大桥 |
| 桥　　型： | 空腹式预应力混凝土连续刚构桥 |
| 主跨跨径： | 300m |
| 桥　　址： | 贵州省黔南布依族苗族自治州 |
| 建成时间： | 2022 年 9 月 |
| 建设单位： | 贵州高速公路集团有限公司 |
| 设计单位： | 中交第一公路勘察设计研究院有限公司 |
| 施工单位： | 中交第二公路工程局有限公司 |

**Name:** Ganxi Bridge
**Type:** Open spandrel prestressed concrete continuous bridge with integral piers
**Main Span:** 300m
**Location:** Qiannan Buyi and Miao Autonomous Prefecture, Guizhou Province
**Completion:** September, 2022
**Owner(s):** Guizhou Expressway Group Co., Ltd.
**Designer(s):** CCCC First Highway Consultants Co., Ltd.
**Contractor(s):** CCCC Second Highway Engineering Group Co., Ltd.

甘溪特大桥位于贵州省黔南布依族苗族自治州贵定县，横跨贵州甘溪国家森林公园独木河水库，是贵黄高速的控制性工程，也是贵黄高速全线施工难度最大、安全风险等级最高的控制性桥梁之一。大桥全长1220m，南北岸设置引桥。

甘溪特大桥主桥为空腹式预应力混凝土连续刚构桥，主跨300m。该桥上、下行线双幅布置，净距3.5m。单幅桥梁跨径布置为18×30m（简支变连续T梁桥）+155m+300m+155m（空腹式连续刚构桥）+2×35m（简支变连续T梁桥）。单幅主梁为单箱单室预应力混凝土结构，采用C55混凝土。主墩为矩形双肢柔性薄壁墩，双肢净距7m，过渡墩为空心薄壁墩。基础为群桩基础。

针对空腹式连续刚构桥的墩顶空腹区域施工工序多、工艺复杂、技术难度较大的问题，甘溪特大桥采用了"上弦设置活动立柱支顶配合挂篮悬浇，下弦设置扣索配合挂篮悬浇"的施工方案。

Ganxi Bridge is located in Guiding County, Qiannan Buyi and Miao Autonomous Prefecture, Guizhou Province, across the Dumuhe Reservoir in Ganxi National Forest Park Province, Guizhou Province. It is a control project of Guiyang-Huangping Expressway and one of the control bridges with the largest construction difficulty and the highest safety risk level along the whole expressway. The bridge has a total length of 1220m. Approach bridges are arranged on the north and south banks.

The main bridge of Ganxi Bridge is an open-spandrel prestressed concrete continuous bridge with integral piers. The main span of the bridge is 300m. Parallel bridges are arranged for the dual directions with a gap in between of 3.5m. The span arrangement of the bridge on each side is 18×30m (continuous T-girder bridge constructed by span by span)+155m+300m+155m (open spandrel continuous bridge with integral piers)+2×35m (continuous T-girder bridge constructed by span by span). The main girder of the parallel bridge is prestressed concrete girder with single-cell single box section, using C55 concrete. The main pier is composed of rectangular double flexible thin walls, with a clear distance of 7m between the two walls. The transition pier is hollow thin-walled shaft, and pile group foundation is adopted.

Aiming at too many construction procedures, complex process and significant technical difficulty in the open spandrel area on the pier top of the open spandrel continuous bridge with integral piers, the construction scheme of "setting movable column for the cast-in-situ balanced cantilever method with hanging basket for the upper chord, and using temporary working cables for the cast-in-situ balanced cantilever method with hanging basket for the lower chord" is adopted for Ganxi Bridge.

# 福平铁路乌龙江特大桥
## Fuzhou-Pingtan Railway Bridge over Wulong River

福平铁路乌龙江特大桥位于福州南站东侧,连接清凉山和金牛山,跨越闽江南支乌龙江,为福平铁路全线的重难点控制性工程。主桥总长576m,设计速度为200km/h,铁路为有砟轨道。

乌龙江特大桥主桥为预应力混凝土索辅梁桥,跨径布置为144m+288m+144m,主墩塔、梁、墩固结,边墩设置纵向活动支座。主梁采用直腹板单箱双室截面,拉索锚固于悬臂板。主梁中支点梁高和跨中梁高分别为15.5m和5.5m,箱梁顶板宽13.4m,底板宽11.4m,设置纵向、竖向预应力体系。桥塔采用矩形双柱式钢筋混凝土结构,桥面以上塔高40.0m,桥面以上塔高跨比为1/7.2,桥塔与主梁连接处设置为倒Y形。拉索采用平行双索面扇形布置,每个桥塔设置10对拉索,其梁上索距为8.0m,塔上索距为1.0m,张拉端设置于主梁上。主墩采用双薄壁实心墩,矩形截面,墩高22.5m,顺桥向双壁墩中心距为7m。

该桥主桥以主梁受力为主,拉索桥塔在施工过程中辅助主梁受力,成桥时与主梁共同承担二期恒载和活载,在后期运营阶段可通过对梁的弹性约束有效控制主梁后期徐变下挠,具有较高的经济性。主梁采用挂篮悬臂浇筑法,滞后一个悬臂节段张拉拉索,先进行边跨合龙,后进行中跨合龙,合龙后张拉梁内预应力,对桥面和附属工程进行施工,调整至拉索设计索力。

Fuzhou-Pingtan Railway Bridge over Wulong River is located at the east side of Fuzhou South Railway Station, connecting Qingliang Mountain and Jinniu Mountain. It crosses the Wulong River, the southern branch of the Min River, and is a key and difficult control project for the whole Fuzhou-Pingtan Railway. The total length of the main bridge is 576m, with the design speed of 200km/h, and the railway adopts ballasted track.

The main bridge of Fuzhou-Pingtan Railway Bridge over Wulong River is an extradosed prestressed concrete girder bridge with span arrangement of 144m+288m+144m. The structural system adopts fixing among pylon, girder and main piers, with movable bearings arranged at the side piers. The main girder uses straight web double-cell single-box section, and the cables are anchored on the cantilever flanges of the box section. The height of the girder at the middle supports and the mid-span are 15.5m and 5.5m respectively. The width of the top flange of the box girder is 13.4m and the width of the bottom slab is 11.4m. The longitudinal and vertical prestressing systems are adopted. The pylon is reinforced concrete double column with rectangular section. The pylon above the bridge deck is 40.0m high, with the height-span ratio of the pylon above deck is 1/7.2. The lower part of the pylon connecting the main girder is designed to be inverted Y-shape. The cables are designed in parallel double planes with fan-shaped arrangement, and 10 pairs of cables are arranged on each pylon. The cable spacing on the girder is 8.0m, while the cable spacing on the pylon is 1.0m, and the tensioning end is placed on the main girder. The main pier adopts double thin-wall solid shafts

with rectangular section. The pier height is 22.5m, and the spacing between the center of the two pier shafts along the bridge is 7m.

The loads of the bridge are mainly carried by the main girder. The cables and the pylons assist the main girder during the construction process, and after the bridge is completed, they carry the secondary dead load and live load together with the main girder. In the later operation stage, the elastic constraint to the girder can effectively control the long-term creep deflection of the main girder, which is highly economical. The main girder is constructed by cast-in-situ balanced cantilever method with hanging bracket. The cable is tensioned after the completion of the next cantilever segment. The closure of the side spans is carried out before the closure of the middle span. After closure, the prestressing tendons are tensioned in the girder, and the bridge deck and ancillary works are performed. The cables are then adjusted to the final designing force.

| | |
|---|---|
| 桥　名： | 福平铁路乌龙江特大桥 |
| 桥　型： | 预应力混凝土索辅梁桥 |
| 主跨跨径： | 288m |
| 桥　址： | 福建省福州市 |
| 建成时间： | 2022年12月 |
| 建设单位： | 福建福平铁路有限责任公司（现更名为福建铁路有限公司） |
| 设计单位： | 中铁第四勘察设计院集团有限公司 |
| 施工单位： | 中铁十八局集团有限公司 |

**Name:** Fuzhou–Pingtan Railway Bridge over Wulong River
**Type:** Extradosed prestressed concrete girder bridge
**Main Span:** 288m
**Location:** Fuzhou City, Fujian Province
**Completion:** December, 2022
**Owner(s):** Fujian Railway Co., Ltd.
**Designer(s):** China Railway Siyuan Survey and Design Group Co., Ltd.
**Contractor(s):** China Railway 18th Bureau Group Corporation Limited

# 六律邕江特大桥
## Liulv Bridge over Yong River

桥　名：六律邕江特大桥
桥　型：钢-混凝土混合梁索辅梁桥
主跨跨径：320m
桥　址：广西壮族自治区南宁市
建成时间：2023年12月
建设单位：广西交通投资集团有限公司
设计单位：中铁第一勘察设计院集团有限公司
施工单位：中铁十四局集团第三工程有限公司

六律邕江特大桥位于广西壮族自治区南宁市，是南玉高速铁路全线控制性工程，主桥全长622m，为双线无砟轨道高速铁路，设计速度为350km/h。

六律邕江特大桥主跨320m，是介于斜拉桥和矮塔斜拉桥之间的一种桥型，主梁为钢-混凝土混合梁。主桥跨径布置为41m+109m+320m+109m+41m，边支点及跨中梁高6.0m，中支点梁高14.5m，梁底变化段按二次抛物线变化。中跨钢箱梁长度为83m，混凝土梁与钢箱梁之间采用钢-混凝土结合段连接。主桥桥面以上桥塔高70m，采用52对钢绞线拉索，单个塔柱单侧13根，梁上拉索水平间距为8.0m和11.0m，桥塔上竖向锚固间距为1m。

六律邕江特大桥主跨跨中设置为钢箱梁，可以减轻主跨结构自重，由此大幅度提高了索辅梁桥的跨越能力，同时减小了收缩徐变对结构的影响。桥塔采用爬模法施工，混凝土主梁、钢-混凝土结合段采用造桥机悬臂浇筑法施工，中跨钢箱主梁采用节段拼装法施工。

**Name:** Liulv Bridge over Yong River
**Type:** Partially cable-supported steel-concrete hybrid girder bridge
**Main Span:** 320m
**Location:** Nanning City, Guangxi Zhuang Autonomous Region
**Completion:** December, 2023
**Owner(s):** Guangxi Communications Investment Group Corporation, Ltd.
**Designer(s):** China Railway First Survey and Design Institute Group Co., Ltd.
**Contractor(s):** China Railway 14th Bureau Group No.3 Engineering Co., Ltd.

Liulv Bridge over Yong River is located in Nanning City, Guangxi Zhuang Autonomous Region. It is a control project of the whole line of the Nanning-Yulin High-speed Railway. The main bridge is 622m long and carries high-speed railway in dual directions with ballastless track. The design speed is 350 km/h.

The main span of Liulv Bridge over Yong River is 320m. It is a bridge type between cable-stayed bridge and extradosed prestressed concrete girder bridge. The main girder is steel-concrete hybrid structure. The span arrangement of the main bridge is 41m+109m+320m+109m+41m, the height of the girder at the side support and the mid-span is 6.0m, while the height of the girder at the middle support is 14.5m. The bottom of the concrete deck varies according to the quadratic parabola. The length of steel box girder in the middle span is 83m. The concrete girder and the steel box girder are connected by steel-concrete joint section. The pylon above the bridge deck is 70m high, and 52 pairs of steel strand cables are used, i.e., 13 pairs for each single pylon. The longitudinal spacing of the cables on the girder are 8.0m and 11.0m, and the vertical anchorage spacing on the pylon is 1m.

The middle main of span of Liulv Bridge over Yong River adopts a steel box girder, which can reduce the self weight of the main span structure. As a result, the spanning capacity of the extradosed prestressed concrete girder bridge is greatly improved, and the influence of concrete shrinkage and creep to the structure is reduced. The pylon is constructed by climbing formwork method. The concrete main girder and the steel-concrete joint section are constructed by cast-in-situ balanced cantilever method with a launching movable formwork, while the steel box girder in the middle span is constructed by prefabricated segmental assembly method.

中国桥梁　BRIDGES IN CHINA　2013—2023

# Chapter 6

第六篇

# 城市桥梁

Urban Bridges

# 引言

　　城市桥梁是指城市范围内为行人、公路交通、铁路交通等提供通道的桥梁。古代城市桥梁一般是根据人行需求而建造的，单一功能是供行人过河，兼供人力或兽力车行，以用天然的石材和木材建造的石桥和木桥为主，除了具有桥梁技术属性之外，还有社会属性。近代城市桥梁是因工业革命后人口向城市聚集而催生出的人行桥梁和车行桥梁以及铁路桥梁，如反映时代特征的 18 世纪法国巴黎协和桥和英国科布鲁克代尔桥、19 世纪美国纽约布鲁克林桥和英国伦敦塔桥、20 世纪初澳大利亚悉尼海港大桥和美国旧金山金门大桥等。到 20 世纪初，钢和混凝土已经成为主要结构材料。近代城市桥梁不仅具有桥梁技术和社会属性，而且强调艺术属性。现代城市桥梁的重要特征是多功能、重美学和可持续，杰出代表有西班牙埃拉米罗桥、英国盖茨黑德千禧桥、日本美秀美术馆步行桥、美国旧金山—奥克兰新海湾东桥、丹麦圆环桥等，这些城市桥梁并不是很长，也没有太大的跨径，主要满足城市桥梁的多功能要求，并且重视美学和标志性，长寿命和可持续是现代城市桥梁设计和建造追求的新目标。

　　我国现代城市桥梁建设主要经历了三个发展阶段。中华人民共和国成立后的 30 年里，城市桥梁建设主要解决交通出行基本问题，因此，城市桥梁功能单一，20 世纪 50 年代的武汉长江大桥、60 年代的南京长江大桥、80 年代的重庆长江大桥是这个阶段的杰出代表。改革开放后的 20 年里，随着桥梁技术的发展和经济实力的提升，在注重城市桥梁功能的同时，开始重视美学，诞生了上海恒丰路桥、南浦大桥和杨浦大桥等斜拉桥，广州大桥、哈尔滨松花江大桥和桂林雉山漓江大桥等梁式桥，南宁邕江大桥和武汉晴川桥等拱式桥。进入 21 世纪后，城市桥梁真正走上了多功能、重美学和可持续发展之路，出现桂林解放桥、南昌生米大桥、天津大沽桥和杭州九堡大桥等各式造型优美的拱式桥以及上海卢浦大桥、重庆朝天门大桥和宁波明州大桥等大跨径拱式桥，南京大胜关长江公路大桥、太原祥云桥、宁波外滩大桥和太原北中环桥等塔形别致唯美的斜拉桥，宁波庆丰桥、广州猎德大桥和武汉古田桥等外形柔美的自锚式悬索桥。

　　近 10 年来，我国建成了数以百计的城市桥梁，本画册选取了城市梁式桥 1 座，城市拱式桥 4 座，城市斜拉桥 6 座和城市悬索桥 2 座，共 13 座城市桥梁。

　　在 21 世纪，我国城市桥梁建设经历了历史性的发展，取得了举世瞩目的成就，实现了城市桥梁跨径大超越、创新了城市桥型结构和功能，研发了深水大跨桥梁建设技术，提升了桥梁美学创作理念，延长了城市桥梁使用寿命。同时在美学理念和设计创新上，与世界领先水平还有差距，还需更加关注安全耐久性，一些城市桥梁所暴露出的质量缺陷和安全事故，不同程度地反映出在设计、施工、材料、运维、管理等方面存在缺憾和不足。我国的城市桥梁建设空前繁荣，只要坚持美学创作、技术创新、经济合理和可持续发展，一定能够达到更新、更高的水平。

# INTRODUCTION

The term "urban bridges" refers to those bridges that provide passage for pedestrians, highway traffic, and railway traffic in urban areas. Ancient urban bridges were generally built to enable pedestrians, as well as human or animal powered vehicles to cross rivers. They were generally made of natural stone and wood. In addition to their technical attributes, these ancient bridges have important social attributes. Modern urban bridges are pedestrian bridges, vehicular bridges, and railway bridges built to suit the needs of the growing population of cities after the Industrial Revolution. Early examples include the Concorde Bridge in Paris and the Coalbrookdale Bridge in UK, both built in the 18th century, New Yorks's Brooklyn Bridge in USA and London's Tower Bridge in UK, built in the 19th century, the Sydney Harbour Bridge in Australia and the Golden Gate Bridge in San Francisco of USA, built in the early 20th century. These bridges all contain features representative of their era of construction. By the early 20th century, steel and concrete became the main materials for building urban bridges. Modern urban bridges not only embody technical and social attributes but also signify the artistic attributes. The distinguishing features of contemporary urban bridges are the multi-functionality, the appreciation of aesthetics, and sustainability. Outstanding representatives of contemporary urban bridges include the Alamillo Bridge in Spain, the Gateshead Millennium Bridge in UK, the Miho Museum Footbridge in Japan, the New Oakland Bay East Bridge in San Francisco of USA, and the Infinite Bridge in Denmark. These urban bridges are not very long nor do they have long spans. Rather, they are adapted to the thematic-functionality of urban bridges and can take on significance as landmarks due to their aesthetic characteristics. Long service, the long life and sustainability are the new goals pursued in the design and construction of the contemporary urban bridges.

The construction of contemporary urban bridges in China has gone through three main developmental stages. During the thirty years after the founding of the People's Republic of China, the main object of building urban bridges was to solve the basic transportation problems. Consequently, they had only a single function. Outstanding representatives of this era are the Wuhan Yangtze River Bridge built in the 1950s, the Nanjing Yangtze River Bridge built in the 1960s, and the Chongqing Yangtze River Bridge built in the 1980s. Over the twenty years after the beginning of reform and opening up, both the functional and aesthetic aspects of urban bridges were considered in conjunction with the development of bridge technologies and the country's increase in economic strength. The Shanghai Hengfeng Road Bridge, the Shanghai Nanpu Bridge, and the Shanghai Yangpu Bridge are representative cable-stayed bridges built in this period. The Guangzhou Third Pearl River Bridge, the Harbin Songhua River Bridge, and the Guilin Zhishan Lijiang Bridge are representative girder bridges built in this period. The Nanning Yongjiang Bridge and the Wuhan Qingchuan Bridge are representative arch bridges built in this period. After entering the 21th century, urban bridges entered an era of multi-functionality, in which sustainable development joined with aesthetics and technical function. Various sleek arch bridges, such as the Guilin Jiefang Bridge, the Nanchang Shengmi Bridge, the Tianjin Dagu Bridge and the Hangzhou Jiubao Bridge, various large-span arch bridges, such as the Shanghai Lupu Bridge, the Chongqing Chaotianmen Bridge and the Ningbo Mingzhou Bridge, aesthetic cable-stayed bridges with elaborate towers, such as the Nanjing Dashengguan Bridge over the Yangtze River, the Taiyuan Xiangyun Bridge, the Ningbo Bund Bridge and the Taiyuan North Central Ring Bridge, and graceful self-anchored suspension bridges, such as the Ningbo Qingfeng Bridge, the Guangzhou Liede Bridge and the Wuhan Gutian Bridge over the Han River, were built during this period.

During the past ten years, hundreds of urban bridges have been built in China. Thirteen urban bridges are selected for this bridge album, including one girder bridge, four arch bridges, six cable-stayed bridges, and two suspension bridges.

In the 21th century, the construction of urban bridges in China has experienced historic development and made remarkable achievements attracting worldwide attention, including new span records, innovation of the structural types and functions, research and development in the construction technology of deep-water long-span bridges, improvements in creation and appreciation of aesthetic bridge concepts, and ways of extending the service life of urban bridges. There remains a gap in the aesthetic concept and design innovation compared with the world-class level, and more attention needs to be paid to safety and durability. The quality defects and safety accidents exposed on some urban bridges, to some extent, reflect the defects and shortcomings in the design, construction, materials, operation and maintenance, and management of bridges. Urban bridge construction is unprecedentedly vibrant in China. So long as we persist in aesthetic creation, technical innovation, economic rationality, and sustainable development, the construction of urban bridges in China will certainly reach a new and higher level.

# 兰州深安黄河大桥
## Lanzhou Shen'an Bridge over Yellow River

兰州深安黄河大桥位于兰州市西固区与安宁区之间，南起西固区深沟桥，横跨黄河，连通北岸的安宁区。与黄河南岸的南滨河路、黄河北岸的北滨河路相交。主线道路桥梁全长1.32km，其中主桥长度为272m。

兰州深安黄河大桥主桥采用下承式蝶形钢拱组合梁桥，犹如两片张开的翅膀飞舞于黄河之上，既解决了拱肋的面外稳定问题，又兼顾了城市桥梁景观的需求。桥梁主跨156m，桥宽36.5m，梁高3m，吊索间距8m。拱肋系统由两个外倾主拱肋、两个内倾副拱肋以及主副拱肋之间的横向连杆和位于两副拱顶的横撑等构件组成。主拱外倾角为10°，立面矢高37.669m，采用矩形钢箱截面，高3m，宽2m。副拱肋轴线为空间曲线，立面矢高30m，采用圆形钢管截面，直径1.5m。主梁采用双主梁梁格体系，钢-混凝土组合截面。为改善主梁桥面板受力，主梁内设置水平系杆索。主墩采用V形墩，圆端形承台，桩基础为Φ2.0m钻孔灌注桩。

主桥施工采用步履式梁拱整体顶推技术，钢构梁拱在陆上拼装成型，结合临时加固，由黄河北岸共计顶进313.6m至设计桥位后，落梁成桥。

Lanzhou Shen'an Bridge over Yellow River is located between Xigu District and Anning District of Lanzhou City. It starts from Shengou Bridge in Xigu District in the south, crosses the Yellow River, and connects to Anning District on its north end. It intersects with South Binhe Road on the south bank and North Binhe Road on the north bank of the Yellow River. The total length of the main road line including the bridge is 1.32km, and the length of the main bridge is 272m.

| | |
|---|---|
| 桥　名： | 兰州深安黄河大桥 |
| 桥　型： | 下承式蝶形钢拱组合梁桥 |
| 主跨跨径： | 156m |
| 桥　址： | 甘肃省兰州市 |
| 建成时间： | 2014年9月 |
| 建设单位： | 兰州市城市发展投资有限公司 |
| 设计单位： | 上海市政工程设计研究总院（集团）有限公司 |
| 施工单位： | 宏润建设集团股份有限公司 |

**Name:** Lanzhou Shen'an Bridge over Yellow River
**Type:** Composite girder through arch bridge with butterfly-shaped steel arch rib system
**Main Span:** 156m
**Location:** Lanzhou City, Gansu Province
**Completion:** September, 2014
**Owner(s):** Lanzhou Urban Development Investment Co., Ltd.
**Designer(s):** Shanghai Municipal Engineering Design Institute (Group) Co., Ltd.
**Contractor(s):** Hongrun Construction Group Co., Ltd.

The main bridge of Lanzhou Shen'an Bridge over Yellow River is a composite girder through arch bridge with a butterfly-shaped steel arch rib system. It likes a pair of open wings flying over the Yellow River, which not only solves the problem of the out-of-plane stability of arch ribs but also meets the requirement for urban bridge landscape. The main span of the bridge is 156m. The width and height of the bridge girder is 36.5m and 3m, respectively. The interval space of hangers is 8m. The arch rib system consists of two outward-inclined main arch ribs, two inward-inclined auxiliary arch ribs, transverse links between the main and auxiliary arch ribs, and cross braces between the top of the two auxiliary arch ribs. The main arch leans 10° outward, and adopts a rectangular steel box cross section with a height of 3m and a width of 2m. The elevation rise of the arch is 37.669m. Both auxiliary arch ribs are arranged with spatially-curved axes with a elevation rise of 30m, and adopt a circular steel tube cross section with a diameter of 1.5m. The main girder adopts a grillage system with double beams and a steel-concrete composite section. The horizontal tie cables are installed in the main girder to improve the mechanical performance of the main girder deck slab. The main pier is V-shaped with a round end cap, and the pile foundation adopts $\phi$ 2.0m bored piles.

The construction of the main bridge adopts the walking-type beam-arch integral incremental launching technology. The steel structure comprised of girder and arch system was firstly assembled on land and reinforced temporarily, then was pushed from the north bank of the Yellow River to the designed bridge site by a total distance of 313.6m, and finally was laid down on the piers for completion.

# 重庆双碑嘉陵江大桥
## Chongqing Shuangbei Bridge over Jialing River

重庆双碑嘉陵江大桥是连接重庆市沙坪坝区和江北区的重要过江通道，西接沙坪坝区双碑街道双碑西立交，上跨嘉陵江水道，东至江北区石马河街道大农立交。大桥全长1928m，主桥长645m，东引桥长263.5m，西引桥长1019.5m。桥面按双向六车道城市快速路设计，总宽32.5m，中间有5.5m的拉索分隔带，两侧各有一条2.5m宽的人行道。设计速度为60km/h。

主桥为高低独柱塔混凝土斜拉桥，塔梁墩固结，跨径布置为75m+145m+330m+95m，高塔边跨设置辅助墩，低塔边跨位于曲线上。主梁采用单箱三室预应力混凝土箱梁，顶板宽32.5m，底板宽9.0m，梁高3.6m，两侧悬臂板长4.0m。外腹板向外倾斜角大于60°，以减小底板宽度和自重、形成扁平流线型倒梯形截面，使主梁既轻巧、美观，又具有更好的抗风性能。两个预应力混凝土桥塔，桥面以上均采用独柱结构，桥面以下的塔墩采用沿顺桥向分离的紧贴双肢结构，上塔柱和下塔墩每一肢均采用单室单箱截面。高塔总高172.2m，上塔柱高108.3m，墩高63.9m；低塔总高118.3m，上塔柱高60.3m，墩高58.0m。扇形中央平行双索面的横向间距为1.8m，全桥共176根斜拉索，采用高强低松弛镀锌钢绞线，钢绞线直径15.2mm，抗拉强度1860MPa。

简洁、生动的高低搭配直线造型独柱式桥塔，配合塔顶曲线切角，形似两座尖碑，寓意"双碑"，与地形、地名相融合，体现了重庆的山城特色。

Chongqing Shuangbei Bridge over Jialing River is an important passageway crossing Jialing River connecting Shapingba District and Jiangbei District, Chongqing City. The whole bridge is 1928m long, starting from west at the West Shuangbei Interchange in Shuangbei Subdistrict of Shapingba District, crossing the watercourse of Jialing River, ending eastward at the Danong Interchange in Shimahe Subdistrict of Jiangbei District. It is comprised of a main bridge 645m in length, an eastern approach bridge 263.5m in length, and a western approach bridge 1019.5m in length. The bridge road is designed as an expressway with six lanes in dual directions. The overall width of bridge road is 32.5m, including a 5.5m-wide middle separation zone for cable anchorage and two 2.5m-wide side pedestrian ways. The design speed is 60km/h.

The main bridge is a concrete cable-stayed bridge with a pair of higher and lower single-column pylons. Its pylons and piers are connected to the bridge girder fixedly. Its span arrangement is 75m+145m+330m+95m, with an auxiliary pier in the high-pylon side span and a curved low-pylon side span. Its 3.6m-high PC main girder has a single three-chamber box configuration, with a 32.5m-wide top plate including two 4.0m-long side cantilever plates, and a 9.0m-wide bottom plate. Its side webs of the box girder were designed to incline outward at an angle greater than 60°, to reduce the bottom plate width and the dead load and to form flat streamline-type inverted trapezoidal cross section, which makes the main girder not only light and beautiful

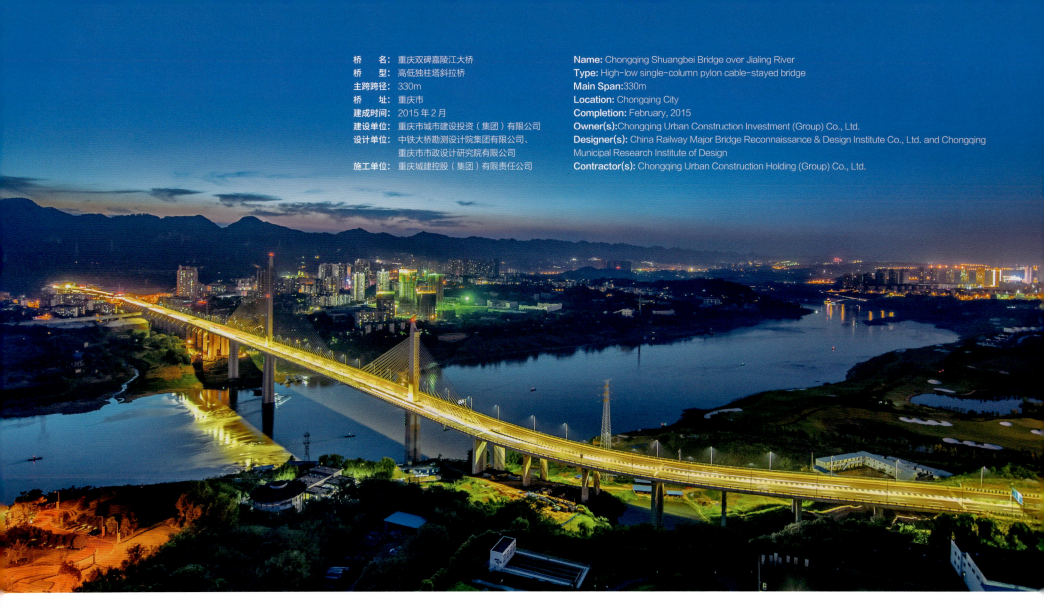

| 桥　名： | 重庆双碑嘉陵江大桥 | **Name:** Chongqing Shuangbei Bridge over Jialing River |
|---|---|---|

桥　名： 重庆双碑嘉陵江大桥
桥　型： 高低独柱塔斜拉桥
主跨跨径： 330m
桥　址： 重庆市
建成时间： 2015年2月
建设单位： 重庆市城市建设投资（集团）有限公司
设计单位： 中铁大桥勘测设计院集团有限公司、
　　　　　重庆市市政设计研究院有限公司
施工单位： 重庆城建控股（集团）有限责任公司

**Name:** Chongqing Shuangbei Bridge over Jialing River
**Type:** High-low single-column pylon cable-stayed bridge
**Main Span:** 330m
**Location:** Chongqing City
**Completion:** February, 2015
**Owner(s):** Chongqing Urban Construction Investment (Group) Co., Ltd.
**Designer(s):** China Railway Major Bridge Reconnaissance & Design Institute Co., Ltd. and Chongqing Municipal Research Institute of Design
**Contractor(s):** Chongqing Urban Construction Holding (Group) Co., Ltd.

but also have better wind-resistant performance. A single-column structure was adopted for the two PC pylons above the bridge deck. An appressed double-column structure was employed for the pylon piers beneath the bridge deck. Each pylon over the bridge deck and the two columns of each pylon pier beneath the bridge deck have a single one-chamber box cross section. The high pylon is 172.2m high in all, with a 108.3m high single-column part above the bridge deck and a 63.9m-high pylon pier beneath the bridge deck. The low pylon is 118.3m high in all, with a 60.3m-high single-column part above the bridge deck and a 58.0m-high pylon pier beneath the bridge deck. The transverse distance between two fan-shaped cable planes located in the middle separation zone are 1.8m. The whole bridge has 176 cables in all, which are made of high strength and low relaxation galvanized steel strands. The diameter and tensile strength of the steel strands are 15.2mm and 1860MPa, respectively.

The high-low pylon collocation in conjunction with the curved chamfer at the top makes the single-column pylons in the style of straight line pithy and vivacious, and like two sharp steles, implying a moral of "dual stelae", which matches with the local landform and geographic name, and epitomizes the mountain City features of Chongqing City.

# 株洲枫溪大桥
## Zhuzhou Fengxi Bridge

　　株洲枫溪大桥是湖南省株洲市跨越湘江的一座特大桥，连接天元区和芦淞区，对进一步完善城市功能，促进枫溪生态新城、航空工业园的开发和建设具有重要意义。

　　主桥为双塔单跨自锚式悬索桥，跨径布置为3×45m+300m+3×45m，主跨采用单箱三室超高性能轻型组合加劲梁，边跨加劲梁及锚跨加劲梁采用混凝土箱梁，矢跨比为1/5。

　　针对钢桥面板疲劳开裂的难题，株洲枫溪大桥首次采用了力学性能优越的超高性能轻型组合加劲梁构想，应用了密配筋超高性能混凝土（STC），通过形成正交异性钢桥面板-STC组合结构提高局部刚度，大大减小了钢桥面应力幅。此外，针对悬索桥主缆防腐问题，株洲枫溪大桥采用了纤维增强复合材料缠包带，其具有抗紫外线、抗盐雾、高弹性等特点，大幅延长了主缆的结构寿命。大桥主跨钢箱梁采用步履式多点连续顶推法进行施工，通过研发集顶升、纵移、横移、回缩、调整于一体的顶推设备，实现了顶推一体化施工，施工灵活，控制精度高。

桥　　名：株洲枫溪大桥
桥　　型：双塔单跨吊自锚式悬索桥
主跨跨径：300m
桥　　址：湖南省株洲市
建成时间：2016年11月
建设单位：株洲市城市建设发展集团有限公司
设计单位：湖南省交通规划勘察设计院有限公司
施工单位：中交第二航务工程局有限公司

**Name:** Zhuzhou Fengxi Bridge
**Type:** Double-pylon single-suspended-span self-anchored suspension bridge
**Main Span:** 300m
**Location:** Zhuzhou City, Hunan Province
**Completion:** November, 2016
**Owner(s):** Zhuzhou Urban Construction Investment Operation Co., Ltd.
**Designer(s):** Hunan Provincial Communications Planning, Survey and Design Institute Co., Ltd.
**Contractor(s):** CCCC Second Harbour Engineering Co., Ltd.

Zhuzhou Fengxi Bridge is a grand bridge across the Xiang River in Zhuzhou City, Hunan Province, connecting Tianyuan District and Lusong District. This bridge is of great significance in further improving the City's functions and promoting the development and construction of Fengxi Ecological New Town and Aviation Industrial Park.

The main bridge is a double-pylon single-span self-anchored suspension bridge, with the span arrangement of 3×45m+300m+3×45m. The main span is made of single-box three-cell ultra-high performance lightweight composite girders, and the girders for side and anchor spans adopt concrete box girders. The rise-span ratio of this bridge is 1/5.

To solve the problem of fatigue cracking of steel bridge decks, Zhuzhou Fengxi Bridge first adopted the concept of ultra-high performance lightweight composite girders with superior mechanical properties and dense reinforced super high performance concrete (STC). The stress amplitude of the steel bridge deck is greatly reduced by improving the local stiffness of the composite girder that combines orthogonal anisotropic steel bridge deck

and STC. In addition, for the corrosion problem of the main cable, the Zhuzhou Fengxi Bridge uses fiber-reinforced wrapping tape, which is ultraviolet ray, salt spray resistant and highly elastic, significantly extending the lifetime of the main cable. The bridge's main span steel box girder was constructed by the walking-type multi-point continuous jacking method. By developing the jacking equipment that integrates jacking, longitudinal movement, transverse movement, retraction and adjustment, the integrated construction of lifting and jacking is achieved, with flexible construction and high control accuracy.

# 泸州沱江六桥
## Sixth Luzhou Bridge over Tuo River

泸州沱江六桥位于四川省泸州市，跨越沱江航道和珍稀鱼类保护区，是连接城北、城西新城的重要通道。该项目路线设计预留了轨道通道，近期为双向八车道，远期为双向六车道+轨道通道。

主桥采用独塔双索面钢-混凝土混合梁斜拉桥方案，跨径布置为55m+200m+58m+50m。桥塔造型顺桥向呈古饮酒器"爵"的外形，横桥向呈"人"字形，神似诗仙李白"把酒邀月"的形态意境，与中国酒城泸州的地域文化相融合。桥塔总高150m，中、下塔柱采用混凝土结构并与混凝土主梁固结，上塔柱采用钢-混凝土组合塔。主梁采用大展翅分离式双扁平箱断面，宽49m，中心处高3.5m。中跨为钢箱梁，长246.5m；边跨为预应力混凝土箱梁，长116.5m。

该桥索塔锚固段设计成分离式混凝土双壁结构，将钢锚箱设于混凝土塔壁之间，采用剪力钉连接形成夹心组合截面；通过纵向钢系梁将两个塔肢连接，由钢系梁承受拉索水平力，钢锚箱与混凝土塔壁共同承受竖向力，保证将索力安全、均匀地传递到中、下塔柱。双索面锚固于中间轨道通道两侧，减小了主梁横向弯矩，使索力更直接地传递至主梁断面。

Sixth Luzhou Bridge over Tuo River is located in Luzhou City, Sichuan Province, spans the navigation channel of Tuo River and the rare fish reserve. It is an important passageway connecting the north and the west new urban area of the City. The bridge route is designed to reserve a railway. It currently has 8 carriage ways in dual directions and will be changed to 6 carriage ways plus railway in the future.

The main bridge is a single-tower double-cable-plane cable-stayed bridge with steel-concrete compounded girder and a span arrangement of 55m+200m+58m+50m. The bridge tower looks like an ancient drinking vessel "Jue" in the front view while exhibits a herringbone in the sideview, being an excellent likeness to a morphological artistic conception of "I raise my cup to invite the moon" by Libai, the Poet Celestial, and also conforms to the local spirits culture of Luzhou, a Chinese liguor City. The total height of the bridge tower is 150m. Its middle and lower columns are made of concrete and consolidated with the concrete main girder, while the upper columns adopt steel-concrete composite structure. The main girder adopts a big-wing section with separated double flat boxes. Its width and central height are respectively 49m and 3.5m. The middle span is made of steel box girder with a length of 246.5m, and the side span is made of prestressed concrete box girder with a length of 116.5m.

The anchorage zone of the bridge tower was designed to have separated double middle concrete walls, and the steel anchor box was installed between the two concrete tower walls and connected to them by shear nails to form a sandwich composite section. The two tower limbs are connected by longitudinal steel tie beams, which undertake the horizontal force of the cables, while the vertical force is undertaken by the steel anchor boxes and the concrete tower walls, ensuring the safe and uniform transmission of the cable force to the middle and lower tower columns. Two cable planes are anchored at the sides of the middle railway to reduce the transverse bending moment of the main girder and to make the transmission of cable force more directly to the main girder section.

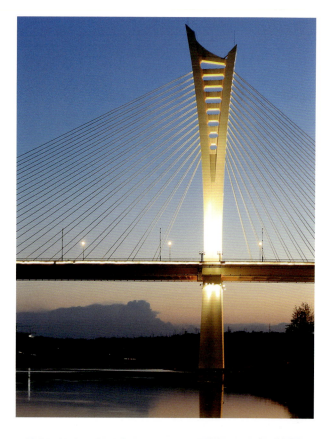

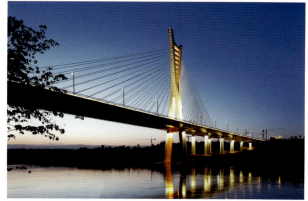

| | |
|---|---|
| 桥　　名： | 泸州沱江六桥 |
| 桥　　型： | 独塔双索面钢-混凝土混合梁斜拉桥 |
| 主跨跨径： | 200m |
| 桥　　址： | 四川省泸州市 |
| 建成时间： | 2018年1月 |
| 建设单位： | 泸州市政府投资建设工程管理中心 |
| 设计单位： | 林同棪国际工程咨询（中国）有限公司 |
| 施工单位： | 四川公路桥梁建设集团有限公司 |

**Name:** Sixth Luzhou Bridge over Tuo River
**Type:** Single-tower double-cable-plane cable-stayed bridge with steel-concrete compounded girder
**Main Span:** 200m
**Location:** Luzhou City, Sichuan Province
**Completion:** January, 2018
**Owner(s):** Luzhou Government Investment Construction Project Management Center
**Designer(s):** T.Y.Lin International Engineering Consulting (China) Co., Ltd.
**Contractor(s):** Sichuan Road and Bridge (Group) Co., Ltd.

# 漳州沙洲岛大桥
## Zhangzhou Shazhou Island Bridge

| 桥　　名： | 漳州沙洲岛大桥 |
| --- | --- |
| 桥　　型： | 独塔扭背索斜拉桥 |
| 主跨跨径： | 200m |
| 桥　　址： | 福建省漳州市 |
| 建成时间： | 2019年2月 |
| 建设单位： | 漳州市路桥经营有限公司 |
| 设计单位： | 中交第二公路勘察设计研究院有限公司 |
| 施工单位： | 中交第二航务工程局有限公司 |

漳州沙洲岛大桥位于漳州市龙海区，跨越九龙江北汊（北溪）、沙洲岛及九龙江南汊（西溪），包括北溪引桥、北溪主桥、沙洲岛互通立交、西溪主桥及西溪引桥，全长3.12km。

西溪主桥为独塔扭背索斜拉桥，跨径布置为88m+200m，其位于边跨的背索锚固于梁的两侧，通过反转拉索在梁端的锚固顺序，与略向边跨倾斜的独柱式桥塔配合，形成一个扭曲的空间索面。桥塔全高134.6m（包括15m高的装饰性塔冠），桥面以上塔高117m，桥面以下塔高17.6m。塔身沿顺桥向向边跨倾斜8°，桥面以上塔柱采用矩形箱形截面，其横桥向高度为5m，顺桥宽度在锚索区为8.2m，锚索区以下部分变化，到桥面处为15.5m。

西溪主桥主梁采用大悬臂翼缘的整体箱式断面，宽51m，中心处高度为4.0m。主跨为钢梁，边跨为混凝土梁。为减小主梁剪力滞效应不利影响，采用了增加纵腹板以减小箱室宽度、运用精细化分析手段优化纵横向钢束布置、提高对混凝土梁现浇支架刚度的要求并在受力分析中精确模拟支架约束条件等多种方法和措施。

**Name:** Zhangzhou Shazhou Island Bridge
**Type:** Single-tower cable-stayed bridge with twisted back-cable net
**Main Span:** 200m
**Location:** Zhangzhou City, Fujian Province
**Completion:** February, 2019
**Owner(s):** Zhangzhou Road and Bridge Management Co., Ltd.
**Designer(s):** CCCC Second Highway Consultants Co., Ltd.
**Contractor(s):** CCCC Second Harbor Engineering Co., Ltd.

Zhangzhou Shazhou Island Bridge is located in Longhai District of Zhangzhou City, and crosses the northern branch of the Jiulong River (Beixi), Shazhou Island, and the southern branch of the Jiulong River (Xixi). It is comprised of the Beixi Approach Bridge, the Beixi Main Bridge, the Shazhou Island Interchange, the Xixi Main Bridge and the Xixi Approach Bridge. The total length is 3.12km.

The Xixi Main Bridge is a single-tower cable-stayed bridge with a twisted back-cable net. Its span arrangement is 88m+200m. Its back cables in the side span are anchored at the two sides of the main girder. Coordinated with the single-column bridge tower slightly inclined to the side span, the back cables constitute a spatial cable net with a twisted shape by reversing the anchoring sequence of the stay cables on the girder. The total height of the bridge tower is 134.6m (including a 15m-high decorative tower crown), with a 117m-high upper part above the bridge deck and a 17.6m-high lower part beneath the bridge deck. The tower inclines towards the shoreside by 8°. The tower column above the bridge deck adopts a rectangular box section, with a constant height (5m) in the transverse direction of bridge, and a varying width in longitudinal direction of the bridge, which is 8.2m wide in the anchorage zone, and then varies below until 15.5m at the bridge deck level.

The main girder of the Xixi Main Bridge adopts a monolithic box section with large cantilever flanges. It has a width of 51m and a central height of 4.0m. The main span is of steel girder and the side span is of concrete girder. To reduce the adverse influence of shear lag effect of the main girder, a variety of methods and measures are employed, such as adding longitudinal webs to reduce the width of the box chamber, optimizing the arrangement of vertical and horizontal steel bundles by refined analysis, increasing the stiffness requirement of support frame used for casting concrete in place and accurately simulating the constraint conditions of support frame in mechanical analysis.

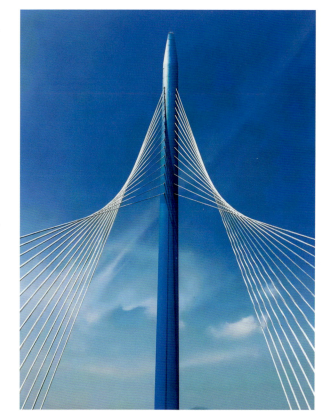

# 北京新首钢大桥
## Beijing New Shougang Bridge

桥　　名：北京新首钢大桥
桥　　型：斜拉刚构组合桥
主跨跨径：280m
桥　　址：北京市
建成时间：2019年9月
建设单位：北京市公联公路联络线有限责任公司
设计单位：北京戈建建筑设计顾问有限责任公司、北京市市政工程设计研究总院有限公司
施工单位：北京城建集团有限责任公司

**Name:** Beijing New Shougang Bridge
**Type:** Cable-stayed rigid-frame composite bridge
**Main Span:** 280m
**Location:** Beijing City
**Completion:** September, 2019
**Owner(s):** Beijing Gonglian Highway Connection Line Co., Ltd.
**Designer(s):** Nicolas Godelet Architects & Engineers and Beijing General Municipal Engineering Design & Research Institute Co., Ltd.
**Contractor(s):** Beijing Urban Construction Group Co., Ltd.

北京新首钢大桥位于北京长安街西延长线上，横跨永定河，东起石景山区古城大街，横穿首钢工业园区，西连门头沟区石担路。全桥总长1353.8m，设双向八车道，设计速度为70km/h。主桥为五跨双塔双索面斜拉刚构组合桥，中线与河道中线斜交角为57.4°，全长639m，主跨280m。两座外倾拱形钢桥塔呈三维空间扭曲构造形态，一高一矮矗立在大桥两端，通过斜拉索拉起全桥30000多吨钢箱梁，从远处看，好像两个面对面坐在地上的人，脚抵着脚，手拽着钢索，各自向后拉伸，寓意"合力之门"。

高塔桥面以上高约114m，与主梁和桥墩固结；矮塔桥面以上高66m，与主梁固结，在梁底设单向活动支座。斜拉索采用竖琴式渐变索距布置，塔上索间距为2.90~7.26m，梁上索间距为3.76~14.4m。主梁采用分离式变截面全焊接钢箱，中间设横梁，横梁间距为3m，中跨主梁宽度从54.9m到47m再到53.7m逐渐变化。

北京新首钢大桥桥型新颖、独特，自然和谐，既简洁优雅，又富于变化，从整体到细节充分体现艺术性、技术性、舒适性和人性化，把艺术、工程、结构和技术融于一身，成为京西发展的一个新地标。

Beijing New Shougang Bridge, crossing the Yongding River, is located on the westward extended line of Chang'an Street in Beijing, which starts from east at the Gucheng Avenue in Shijingshan District, goes through Shougang Industrial Park, ends westward at Shidan Road in Mentougou District. The whole bridge has an overall length of 1353.8m, and 8 driving lanes in dual directions. The design speed is 70km/h. The main bridge is a cable-stayed rigid-frame composite bridge with double inclined towers and double cable-planes and five spans. The oblique crossing angle between the center lines of the bridge and the river is 57.4°. The overall length of the main bridge is 639m and the main span length is 280m. Two arched steel towers incline to their each side spans and possess a three-dimensional twisted spatial structural configuration. They stand, one tall and one short, at the two ends of the main span of the bridge, and pull up the steel box deck over 30000t via stay cables. Viewing from afar, they seem to be two persons siting on the ground front to front and feet against feet, pulling back the steel cables with hands. This vivid scenery gives out an allusion of a "gate of combined strength".

The tall tower is about 114m high above the bridge deck, and is rigidly fixed with the main girder and the bridge pier. The short tower is 66m high above the bridge deck and is rigidly fixed with the main girder, but connected to the bridge pier through one-way movable supports. The cables are arranged in a way of harp with gradually-changed spaces. The cable space changes from 2.90m to 7.26m on the towers and from 3.76m to 14.4m on the main girder. The main girder uses separated fully-welded steel boxes with varying cross sections. Transverse diaphragms are set inside the main girder at an interval space of 3m. The width of the main girder in the central span varies gradually from 54.9m to 47m to 53.7m.

Beijing New Shougang Bridge possesses a neoteric and unique type, which is of natural harmony. It is concise and elegant as well as rich in variation and is characterized by artistry, technical nature, comfort and humanization from the whole to the details. As a combination of art, engineering, structure and technology, this bridge becomes a new landmark reflecting the development of the west Beijing.

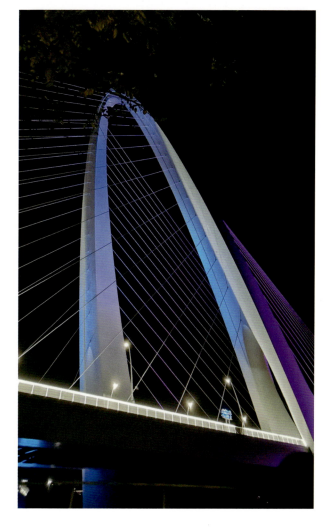

# 厦门山海健康步道和美桥
## Xiamen Hemei Bridge of Shanhai Fitness Trail

厦门山海健康步道和美桥位于海沧大桥桥头，横跨交通繁忙、具有14个车道的仙岳路，两头分别连着仙岳山和狐尾山，是一座单侧悬挂曲线形钢箱梁悬索桥。该桥全长234.7m，主跨216.7m，是截至2022年世界上同类型桥梁结构中跨度最大的桥梁，在设计和建造上极具挑战性。

桥面钢箱梁采用不对称截面，宽5m，高1.2m，通过由3段全封闭主缆和34根不锈钢绞线吊索组成的缆索体系悬挂在外倾V形桥塔顶部。主缆直径140mm，总长270m，吊索直径30mm或45mm。桥塔总高52.3m，位于主跨跨中、曲线形桥面外侧，通过根部直径600mm的实心钢铸球铰和4根背索固定到地面。在桥面南端设有一个V形墩，形成一个约9m跨度的过渡孔，用于跨越设置在山坡上约6.0m宽的步道。此外，在主梁外侧安装了导流板以改善桥梁的空气动力性能，在钢箱梁内部安装了19个调谐质量阻尼器(TMD)，在桥塔箱形塔柱内安装了2个阻尼器，以减少3个临界固有频率的人致振动影响，防止有可能出现的涡激共振。

厦门山海健康步道和美桥以其对称的外观、外倾V形桥塔、等间距（6m）有序排列的吊索以及弯曲有度的纤细桥面等特点，展现了一个"张开双臂热情洋溢地拥抱路过行人、欢迎远方来客，使其宾至如归"的城市形象。

Xiamen Hemei Bridge of Shanhai Fitness Trail is located near the end of Haicang Bridge, and crosses the Xianyue Road which has 14 carriageways bearing heavy traffic. This bridge is a unilateral-suspended curred box girder suspension bridge connecting Xianyue Hill and Huwei Hill. With an overall length of 234.7m and a main span length of 216.7m, it has the largest main span in the same type bridges in the world by 2022, and is very challenging in design and construction.

The bridge deck adopts steel box girder with an asymmetric cross section 5m in width and 1.2m in height, and is suspended on the two-column tops of an outward-inclined V-shaped bridge pylon through a suspending cable system comprised of three-segment fully-closed main cables and 34 suspenders of stainless steel wires. The diameter and whole length of the main cables is 140mm and 270m, respectively, while the diameters of the suspending ropes are 30mm or 45mm. The total height of the bridge pylon is 52.3m and is located on the outside the curved bridge deck at the mid-span of the main span, and fixed to the ground via a cast solid steel spherical joint with a diameter of 600mm at its root and 4 back cables. On the south side of the bridge, there is a V-shaped pier to support the bridge deck, forming a 9m-long transitional span to cross a 6.0m wide footpath on the hillside. Furthermore, a deflector is installed on the outside of the curved main girder to improve its aerodynamic performance. To reduce the pedestrian-induced vibrations of 3 critical inherent frequencies and prevent vortex-induced vibrations, 19 TMDs are installed inside the steel box girder and 2 dampers are installed in the box columns of the bridge pylon.

Xiamen Hemei Bridge of Shanhai Fitness Trail possesses a symmetric appearance, an outward-inclined V-shaped pylon, steel-wire suspenders orderly arranged at a constant interval space(6m) as well as a moderately curved slender bridge deck. These features exhibit a city image with an open arms, effusively embracing passing pedestrians and welcoming guests from afar, making them feel at home.

桥　　名：厦门山海健康步道和美桥
桥　　型：单侧悬挂曲线形钢箱梁悬索桥
主跨跨径：216.7m
桥　　址：福建省厦门市
建成时间：2020 年 9 月
建设单位：厦门市市政建设开发有限公司（现更名为厦门市市政城市开发建设有限公司）
设计单位：Dissing + Weitling Architecture、SBP 施莱希工程设计咨询有限公司、
　　　　　厦门市市政工程设计院有限公司
施工单位：江苏省交通工程集团有限公司

**Name:** Xiamen Hemei Bridge of Shanhai Fitness Trail
**Type:** Unilateral-suspended curred box girder suspension bridge
**Main Span:** 216.7m
**Location:** Xiamen City, Fujian Province
**Completion:** September, 2020
**Owner(s):** Xiamen Municipal Construction and Development Co., Ltd.
**Designer(s):** Dissing + Weitling Architecture, Schlaich Bergermann Partner and Xiamen Municipal Engineering Design Institute Co., Ltd.
**Contractor(s):** Jiangsu Provincial Transportation Engineering Group Co., Ltd.

# 宁波中兴大桥
## Ningbo Zhongxing Bridge

| | |
|---|---|
| 桥　名： | 宁波中兴大桥 |
| 桥　型： | 钢-混凝土混合梁矮塔斜拉桥 |
| 主跨跨径： | 400m |
| 桥　址： | 浙江省宁波市 |
| 建成时间： | 2020年9月 |
| 建设单位： | 宁波宏嘉建设有限公司 |
| 设计单位： | 上海市政工程设计研究总院（集团）有限公司 |
| 施工单位： | 宏润建设集团股份有限公司 |

**Name:** Ningbo Zhongxing Bridge
**Type:** Steel-concrete hybrid girder extradosed cable-stayed bridge
**Main Span:** 400m
**Location:** Ningbo City, Zhejiang Province
**Completion:** September, 2020
**Owner(s):** Ningbo Hongjia Construction Co., Ltd.
**Designer(s):** Shanghai Municipal Engineering Design Institute (Group) Co., Ltd.
**Contractor(s):** Hongrun Construction Group Co., Ltd.

　　宁波中兴大桥是宁波市跨越甬江的特大型桥梁，全长约1.7km。主桥一跨过江，为主跨400m单索面矮塔斜拉桥，是截至2022年世界上最大跨度的矮塔斜拉桥。

　　主桥跨径布置为64m+86m+400m+86m+64m，桥宽29m。主梁中跨468m区段及部分边跨采用钢箱梁，其余区段采用钢-混凝土组合箱梁，跨中梁高4.5m，支点梁高10.5m。大桥上层为机动车道，采用双向六车道标准，下层人行道及非机动车道悬臂布置于主梁下缘，单侧宽5.5m，解决了甬江两岸慢行系统沟通难题。受限于机场航空限高，主塔采用钢结构V形塔，横桥向宽3.6m，纵桥向宽4.0~5.7m。斜拉索共设36对，倾角12.9°~32.7°。

　　桥梁主塔外伸向上的造型象征宁波在改革大潮中锐意进取、勇往直前。塔柱横梁形成"未来之窗"的造型，寓意宁波作为对外开放的窗口，面向世界，面向未来。

　　受航空限高、水上施工和轨道交通等因素制约，主桥上部结构采用了"浮式起重机吊装+边跨滑移+主塔竖转+中跨悬拼"的组合施工工艺，在"上下夹缝"中实现了主桥的精准架设。

Ningbo Zhongxing Bridge is a grand bridge crossing the Yong River in Ningbo City, with a total length of 1.7km. The main bridge crosses the river in one span and is the world's largest extradosed cable-stayed bridge with a main span of 400m by 2022.

The span arrangement of the main bridge is 64m+86m+400m+86m+64m, and its width is 29m. The main girder for 468m-long section of the mid-span and some of the side spans is a steel box girder, and a steel-concrete composite box girder for the rest of the section. The girder height at the center of the middle span is 4.5m and 10.5m for the bearing point. The deck has two layers, with the upper level used as a two-way six-lane motorway, the lower level used as the cantilevered pedestrian and non-motorized lanes cantilevered on the lower edge of the main girder. The lower level has a width of 5.5m on one side, solving the problem of communication between the slow-moving systems on both sides of the Yong River. The main pylon is limited by the aviation height restriction of the airport, so it adopts a steel V-shaped pylon with a section width of 3.6m in the transverse direction and 4.0-5.7m in the longitudinal direction. 36 pairs of stayed cables are installed with an inclination angle from 12.9° to 32.7°.

The main pylon extends upwards to symbolize Ningbo's enterprise and courage to move forward in the reform and opening-up. The pylon's crossbeam forms a shape of "window to the future", symbolizing Ningbo's openness to the world and to the future.

Considering the construction constraints such as aviation height restrictions, over-water construction and rail traffic, the superstructure of the main bridge is installed using a combination of "floating crane lifting + sliding for the side span + vertical rotation for the main pylon + cantilever assembling for the mid-span", achieving a precise erection.

# 宁波三官堂大桥
## Ningbo Sanguantang Bridge

宁波三官堂大桥位于宁波市东部，是连接鄞州区院士路与镇海区明海大道的主要过江通道，南起高新区已建的江南路，上跨甬江水道和四条规划河道，北接镇海区中官西路。大桥线路全长3.3km，桥梁全长2.203km，按城市主干道设计，设计速度为60km/h。

主桥为三跨连续钢桁梁桥，一跨过江，跨径布置为160m+465m+160m，桥面为双向八车道，标准宽度为45.9m。受航空限高及通航净高要求的影响，主桥采用低高跨比（1/11.1）、低边中跨比（0.34）的变高度连续钢桁梁，整体造型呈起伏弧线构架，形似蝙蝠，寓意宁波"福桥"。上部结构采用双榀主桁，两榀钢桁中心距为33.7m，桁式为N形桁，变高度桁梁跨中桁高14.5m，边墩顶桁高15.0m，主墩墩顶附近桁高42.0m。桁架标准节间距离为15.0m，在主墩墩顶附近为18.75m，主墩处桥面下设置V形撑。弦杆采用矩形断面，宽2.2m，高1.8~2.8m。桥面系采用正交异性钢桥面板，板桁结合，结构采用全焊接连接方式。主墩采用整体式哑铃形承台，边墩采用门式墩，桩基为ϕ2.0m钻孔灌注桩。主桥施工采用在主墩墩顶区域散拼、在中跨大节段悬臂拼装的方案。

Ningbo Sanguantang Bridge is located in the east of the Ningbo City, and is the main river-crossing passageway connecting Yuanshi Road in Yinzhou District and Minghai Avenue in Zhenhai District. It starts from south at Jiangnan Road in Gaoxin District, then crosses the watercourse of Yong River and other four planned river ways, and ends finally at the West Zhongguan Road in Zhenhai District in the north. The whole length of the bridge and the south and north connecting lines is 3.3km. The overall length of the bridge part is 2.203km. The bridge and its connecting lines are designed as an urban main road with a design speed of 60km/h.

The main bridge is a three-span continuous steel truss beam bridge and crosses the river by one span. Its span arrangement is 160m+465m+160m. The bridge deck is of 8 driving lanes in dual directions, and the width of its standard cross section is 45.9m. Subjected to the height limit for aviation and the clear height requirement for navigation, the main bridge adopts a height-varying continuous steel truss beam with a low height-to-span ratio of 1/11.1 and a low side-central span ratio of 0.34, and exhibits an overall shape of undulate arc framework, similar in form to a bat, thus carrying a meaning of a "Lucky Bridge" of Ningbo, based on their same Chinese pronunciations. The superstructure, namely the truss beam, contains twin N-shaped main trusses with a transverse central distance of 33.7m. The truss height is 14.5m at the mid-span, 15.0m at the tops of two abutment piers and 42.0m at the locations near the main pier tops. The truss internode distance is 15.0m for the standard segments and becomes 18.75m for the segments near the main pier tops. A V-shaped support is set beneath the bridge deck at each main pier. The truss chords adopt a rectangular cross section, 2.2m in width and 1.8-2.8m in height. The bridge deck is made of orthotropic steel bridge plates, which are combined with the truss. The whole truss beam is assembled with all welded mode. Integrated dumbbell-shape bearing platforms are used for the main piers. The abutment piers are of portal type. The pile foundations use cast-in-situ bored piles with a diameter of 2.0m. The main bridge is constructed by assembling piece-by-piece for the zone near the main pier tops, and by cantilevered assembling of large segments for the main span.

| | |
|---|---|
| 桥　　名： 宁波三官堂大桥 | **Name:** Ningbo Sanguantang Bridge |
| 桥　　型： 连续钢桁梁桥 | **Type:** Continuous steel truss beam bridge |
| 主跨跨径： 465m | **Main Span:** 465m |
| 桥　　址： 浙江省宁波市 | **Location:** Ningbo City, Zhejiang Province |
| 建成时间： 2020年9月 | **Completion:** September, 2020 |
| 建设单位： 宁波市市政工程前期办公室 | **Owner(s):** Ningbo Municipal Engineering Office for Earlier Stage |
| 设计单位： 上海市政工程设计研究总院（集团）有限公司 | **Designer(s):** Shanghai Municipal Engineering Design Institute (Group) Co., Ltd. |
| 施工单位： 四川公路桥梁建设集团有限公司 | **Contractor(s):** Sichuan Road and Bridge (Group) Co., Ltd. |

# 广州海心桥
Guangzhou Haixin Bridge

广州海心桥位于广州市新中轴线西侧,是连接珠江南北两岸的首座人行桥。主桥为中承式曲梁斜拱桥,桥面设置了东、西两条步道,二者在平面上均呈圆弧形布置,东侧步道总长500.961m,西侧步道总长273.149m;东、西两侧步道在边跨部分平面呈分叉分幅布置,在中跨又合并成一整幅桥。该桥是截至2022年世界上跨度最大、桥面最宽的曲梁斜拱人行桥。

主桥采用拱梁固结的推力拱受力体系,拱轴线为二次抛物线,拱肋平面向东倾斜10°,拱跨198.152m,矢高57.95m,矢跨比为1/3.4。拱肋采用等高变宽圆端形单箱三室钢箱结构,高2.6m,宽4.2~6.5m。主梁采用单箱三室钢箱梁断面,宽度为15m,其轴线在平面上呈圆弧曲线,圆弧半径为139.11m,通过23根间距6m的吊杆悬挂于拱肋上。主梁通过西侧箱室梁高的变化来实现横向高低错层设计,西侧梁高2.0~3.5m,东侧梁高2.0m,在两个拱梁结合处分肢,东、西箱室各分出东、西侧边跨,与边跨的慢行坡道及快行梯道相接。箱梁内部设置28套总重25.6t的TMD,以抑制人致振动。施工中采用了大节段整体吊装的快速化施工技术。

广州海心桥造型概念来自"琴鸣绢舞·岭南花舟",结合了粤曲水袖、水上花市、岭南古琴等具有浓厚岭南文化气息的代表元素。凭借其复合的功能、飘逸的造型,成为珠江上的新景观。

| | |
|---|---|
| 桥　　名： | 广州海心桥 |
| 桥　　型： | 中承式曲梁斜拱组合体系拱桥 |
| 主跨跨径： | 198.152m |
| 桥　　址： | 广东省广州市 |
| 建成时间： | 2021年6月 |
| 建设单位： | 广州市建设投资发展有限公司 |
| 设计单位： | 广州市市政工程设计研究总院有限公司、华南理工大学建筑设计研究院有限公司 |
| 施工单位： | 中铁广州工程局集团有限公司 |

**Name:** Guangzhou Haixin Bridge
**Type:** Half-through curved-beam inclined-arch combination bridge
**Main Span:** 198.152m
**Location:** Guangzhou City, Guangdong Province
**Completion:** June, 2021
**Owner(s):** Guangzhou Construction Investment Development Co., Ltd.
**Designer(s):** Guangzhou Municipal Engineering Design & Research Institute Co., Ltd. and Architectural Design & Research Institute of SCUT Co., Ltd.
**Contractor(s):** China Railway Guangzhou Engineering Group Co., Ltd.

Guangzhou Haixin Bridge is located on the west of the new central axis of Guangzhou City, and is the first foot bridge connecting the south and north sides of the Pearl River. The main bridge is a half-through curved-beam inclined-arch combination bridge. It has an east footpath and a west footpath, and both of them are of circular arc on the horizontal plane. The overall length of the east footpath is 500.961m while that of the west one is 273.149m. The east and west footpaths are arranged on two furcate girders in the side spans, and on an integrated girder in the central span. This bridge has the longest main span and the widest deck in the world by 2022 among the same-type foot bridges.

The main bridge adopts a mechanical system of thrust arch with fixed connection between arch and beam. The arch axis is of quadratic parabola. The arch plane tilts 10° to east. The arch span is 198.152m and the arch rise is 57.95m, leading to a rise-span ratio of 1/3.4. The arch rib is of a steel box structure with a single three-chamber box round-ended cross section, which has a constant height of 2.6m and a varying width from 4.2m to 6.5m. The main girder also has a steel single three-chamber box cross section with a width of 15m, and its axis is of a circular arc curve on the horizontal plane, with a radius of 139.11m. The main girder is suspended to the arch rib through 23 suspenders with a constant interval of 6m. The main girder is designed to be of split-level in transverse direction and fulfilled by changing the height of the west chamber of the box. Therefore, the heights of the girders on the west side are between 2.0m and 3.5m, whilst the height of the girder on the east side is 2.0m. The girder furcates at the two junctures of the arch and beam into the east side spans and the west side spans, respectively from the east box chamber and the west box chamber of the integrated box girder, and connected to the slow-walking ramps and the fast-walking stairways. In all, 28 TMDs with a total mass of 25.6t are installed inside the steel girder box to depress pedestrian-induced vibration. The rapid construction technology of large segment integral lifting is adopted in the construction.

The shaping concept of Guangzhou Haixin Bridge comes from "Silk Dance and Zither Sound · Lingnan Flower Boat", and combines the typical elements, which is characteristic of rich Lingnan culture, such as Long Sleeves in Cantonese Opera, Water Flower Fair and Lingnan Zither, etc. Guangzhou Haixin Bridge has become a new scenery over the Pearl River by virtue of its multiple functionality and elegant shape.

# 乌兰木伦河 3 号桥
## Third Bridge over Ulan Moron River

桥　　名：乌兰木伦河 3 号桥
桥　　型：双飞翼中承式拱桥
主跨跨径：200m
桥　　址：内蒙古自治区鄂尔多斯市
建成时间：2021 年 6 月
建设单位：鄂尔多斯市城市建设投资集团有限公司
设计单位：林同棪国际工程咨询（中国）有限公司
施工单位：广西路桥工程集团有限公司

乌兰木伦河 3 号桥是连接鄂尔多斯市的康巴什区和伊金霍洛旗的重要通道，坐落于乌兰木伦湖核心景区，两岸是全国知名艺术家创作的内蒙古民族特色文化壁画，风景独特。

桥梁采用双飞翼中承式拱桥结构形式，全长 348m，主跨 200m，桥面标准宽度 42m，最大宽度 65m。主拱跨度 192m，为外倾式钢箱拱，偏离道路中心面外倾 17°，截面高 4.0m，宽 3.0m。副拱为内倾式钢箱拱，向道路中心面内倾 45°，截面标准段高和宽均为 2.0m，变截面段高和宽均在 2.0～3.0m 之间渐变。主梁为三跨连续结构，跨径布置为 74m+200m+74m，采用扁平双主箱钢箱梁，梁高 3.5m，标准梁宽 42m（含两侧各 4m 宽下沉式悬挑人行道），中跨两侧设下沉式悬挑弧线边缘观景平台，跨中处最大宽度为 15.5m。

桥梁采用钢-STC+高黏高弹 SMA 轻型组合桥面技术，解决高温差及高寒地区钢桥铺装易受损及焊缝疲劳开裂问题。

充分结合当地环境景观及草原文化，取"鲲鹏展翅、草原雄鹰"之形意，设置飘带般的副拱，使得主拱的结构尺寸相应减小，从而平衡了主拱的厚重感，提升视觉效果，巧妙彰显了力与美。

Third Bridge over Ulan Moron River is an important passageway connecting Kangbashi District and Ejin Horo Banner in Ordos City, and is located in the core scenic spot of Ulan Moron Lake. This bridge together with the murals on both riverbanks, created by nationally renowned artists and reflecting distinctive ethnic culture of Inner Mongolia, forms a unique landscape.

The bridge is a double-wing half-through arch bridge, with a total length of 348m and a main span of 200m. The standard width of the bridge deck is 42m while the maximum one is 65m. Two main arches span 192m and adopt a structure of steel box rib and incline outward from the central plane of the road by 17°. The cross-section height and width of the main arch ribs are 4.0m and 3.0m, respectively. Two auxiliary arches are of steel box structure and incline inward to the central plane of the road by 45°. Both the cross-section heights and widths of the auxiliary arch ribs are 2.0m for the standard sections and vary from 2.0m to 3.0m for the variable sections. The main girder is of three-span continuous structure, and its span arrangement is 74m+200m+74m. The main girder has a configuration of double flat steel boxes. Its height is 3.5m and its standard width is 42m (including two 4m-wide sunken-type cantilever sidewalks). A sunken-type cantilever viewing platform with an arc edge is arranged at each side of the bridge deck in the middle span, with its width reaches to a maximal value of 15.5m at the mid-span.

The bridge adopts a lightweight deck composed of steel-STC+high-viscosity and high-elasticity SMA to solve the problems that steel deck pavement is prone to damage and fatigue-induced cracking of weld seam in high temperature difference and alpine regions. Blending sufficiently the local environmental landscape and grassland culture, this bridge exhibits the form and meaning of "Kunpeng spreading its wings, eagle flying over grass land". The setting of the ribbon-like auxiliary arches reduces the structural dimensions well as the visual size of the main arches, thus balances out the heaviness of the main arches, and subtly highlights the strength and beauty of the bridge.

**Name:** Third Bridge over Ulan Moron River
**Type:** Double-wing half-through arch bridge
**Main Span:** 200m
**Location:** Ordos City, Inner Mongolia Autonomous Region
**Completion:** June, 2021
**Owner(s):** Ordos Urban Construction Investment Group Co., Ltd.
**Designer(s):** T.Y.Lin International Engineering Consulting (China) Co., Ltd.
**Contractor(s):** Guangxi Road and Bridge Engineering Group Co., Ltd.

# 东莞滨海湾大桥
## Dongguan Binhai Bay Bridge

| | |
|---|---|
| 桥　　名：东莞滨海湾大桥 | **Name:** Dongguan Binhai Bay Bridge |
| 桥　　型：独柱塔空间扭索面斜拉桥 | **Type:** Single-column pylon cable-stayed bridge with twisted cable planes |
| 主跨跨径：2×200m | **Main Span:** 2×200m |
| 桥　　址：广东省东莞市 | **Location:** Dongguan City, Guangdong Province |
| 建成时间：2022年6月 | **Completion:** June, 2022 |
| 建设单位：东莞滨海湾新区工程建设中心 | **Owner(s):** Dongguan Binhai Bay New Area Construction Center |
| 设计单位：广东省交通规划设计研究院集团股份有限公司 | **Designer(s):** Guangdong Communication Planning & Design Institute Group Co., Ltd. |
| 施工单位：中铁大桥局集团有限公司 | **Contractor(s):** China Railway Major Bridge Engineering Group Co., Ltd. |

　　东莞滨海湾大桥地处珠江入海口东岸，是跨越东莞市滨海湾新区磨碟河的沿海城市主干道特大桥，与深中通道伶仃洋大桥隔海相望。

　　主桥为独柱塔空间扭索面斜拉桥，跨径布置为60m+200m+200m+60m，桥宽60m，布置双向八车道和人行道及非机动车道。主梁采用中央开口10m并设置抑涡板的分体式钢箱梁，梁高3.5m。桥塔采用世界首创的钢-钢壳混凝土独柱混合塔，总高度149.8m。斜拉索采用平行钢丝索，梁上索距9m，塔上索距2.5m。全桥为塔墩梁固结体系，桥塔两侧各设置一个辅助墩以提高结构整体刚度。

　　主塔结合东莞市花和珠江口航标灯塔地域文化，用装配式双层薄壁钢壳的纤腰塔柱结构演绎出"玉兰花开、丝路明灯"的结构艺术品。玉兰花含苞欲放，素雅高洁，象征朝气与实干精神；而当夜幕低垂，其又化作丝路明灯指引航路，守护港湾。

　　大桥建造通过开展异型钢结构BIM（建筑信息模型）正向设计计算、智能化制造、装配化架设等系列创新工作，推动了桥塔结构创新和工业化建造技术的发展。

Dongguan Binhai Bay Bridge is located on the east bank of the Pearl River estuary, which is a grand bridge in the coastal city main road across Modie River in Dongguan Binhai Bay New Area. This bridge and the Lingdingyang Bridge of Shenzhen-Zhongshan Link are located across the sea.

The main bridge is a single-column pylon cable-stayed bridge with twisted cable planes, and its span arrangement is 60m+200m+200m+60m and its width is 60m. The bridge is arranged with two-way eight lanes as well as pedestrians and non-motorized traffic lanes. The main girder is a central-slotted steel box girder with a central opening of 10m and vortex suppression countermeasures, with a girder height of 3.5m. The single-column pylon is the world's first composite pylon which combines steel and steel shell concrete, with a total height of 149.8m. The stayed cables adopt parallel steel wire cables, with a cable spacing of 9m on the girder and 2.5m on the tower. The whole bridge is a pylon-pier-girder rigid system, with an auxiliary pier on each side span to improve the overall stiffness of the structure.

The main pylon takes the city flower of Dongguan City and the regional culture of the beacon lighthouse at the mouth of the Pearl River as the aesthetic imagery, and uses a slim-waisted pylon column made of assembled double-layer thin-walled steel shell to interpret the structural artwork of "blossoming magnolia, lighthouse on the silk road". The magnolia is budding, elegant and noble, symbolizing vitality and practicality; and when the night falls, it becomes a "lighthouse on the silk road" to guide the navigation and guard the harbor.

The design and construction of this bridge include a series of innovative work such as BIM forward design calculations for shaped steel structures, intelligent manufacturing and assembly erection, which promotes the development of structural innovation of the pylon and industrialized construction techniques.

# 香港将军澳跨湾大桥
## Hong Kong Tseung Kwan O Cross Bay Bridge

香港将军澳跨湾通道全长约1.8km，其中1km为海上高架桥，即香港将军澳跨湾大桥，横跨将军澳湾，双向四车道，并设有自行车道和人行道。该通道连接兴建中的将军澳-蓝田隧道及将军澳第86区的环保大道，疏解现有将军澳隧道、将军澳市中心以及环保大道一带的交通压力。

香港将军澳跨湾大桥主桥为主跨200m的外倾式蝶形钢拱桥，桥宽35.8m，建筑高度超40m，为全香港跨度最大和单体最重的钢拱桥。主桥的外观设计以"活力无限"为主题，以两扇蝴蝶羽翼状向外倾斜的主拱，与逐渐收窄的V形桥墩构成相连环状，呈现出代表"无限"的数学符号，象征跨湾通道能带来无限活力，大大提升市民对将军澳新市镇的观感。

相较于传统大型钢结构桥梁在工厂制造小节段、桥位逐段架设施工的工艺，香港将军澳跨湾大桥主跨为一体成型预制钢结构，即主桥模拟桥位施工状况在工厂完成钢箱梁和钢拱的拼装，将桥位现场架设的大部分工序前移至工厂完成，并整体发运至桥位现场安装，其主桥整体发运（含工装）达到1.3万t。

| | |
|---|---|
| 桥　　名： | 香港将军澳跨湾大桥 |
| 桥　　型： | 外倾式蝶形钢拱桥 |
| 主跨跨径： | 200m |
| 桥　　址： | 香港特别行政区 |
| 建成时间： | 2022年12月 |
| 建设单位： | 香港特别行政区土木工程拓展署 |
| 设计单位： | 艾奕康有限公司 |
| 施工单位： | 中国路桥工程有限责任公司 |

**Name:** Hong Kong Tseung Kwan O Cross Bay Bridge
**Type:** Outwardly inclined butterfly-shaped arch bridge
**Main Span:** 200m
**Location:** Hong Kong Special Administrative Region
**Completion:** December, 2022
**Owner(s):** Civil Engineering and Development Department
**Designer(s):** AECOM Asia Company Limited
**Contractor(s):** China Road & Bridge Corporation

The Cross Bay Link (CBL), Tseung Kwan O is a dual two-lane carriageway of approximately 1.8km long with a cycle track and a footpath, including a 1km long marine viaduct across Junk Bay (Tseung Kwan O Cross Bay Bridge) connecting Tseung Kwan O – Lam Tin Tunnel under construction and Wan Po Road in Area 86 of Tseung Kwan O, with an aim to relieve the traffic pressure of the existing Tseung Kwan O Tunnel, the town centre of Tseung Kwan O town centre and Wan Po Road.

The main bridge of Hong Kong Tseung Kwan O Bridge is an outwardly inclined butterfly-shaped arch bridge with 200m main span, a width of 35.8m and a construction height of over 40m. It is the longest and the heaviest steel arch bridge in Hong Kong. The design theme founds on the concept of the "Eternity Vitality". Two outwardly leaning main arches and the gradually narrowing V-shaped piers form an inter-connected ring which represents the mathematical symbol of "infinity". This symbol not only is a well-known expression of eternity for vibrancy brought by the CBL, but also improves citizen's impressions of Tseung Kwan O new town.

Compared to traditional large steel bridges whose small sections are fabricated in a factory and erected section by section at the bridge site, the construction process of the main span of the Hong Kong Tseung Kwan O Cross Bay Bridge is based on a factory-assembled monolithic construction concept. The steel box girders and steel arches of the main bridge are assembled in the factory to simulate the construction conditions of the bridge. Most of the processes of the bridge site erection are moved forward to the factory for completion and shipped to the bridge site for installation. The mass of the main bridge when full assembly completed is 13000t.

中国桥梁　BRIDGES IN CHINA　2013—2023

# Appendix

附录

# 中国参建的国外桥梁

Overseas Bridges Built by China

# 引言

中国建造国外桥梁的历史可以追溯到中华人民共和国成立初期的20世纪50年代。1954年，中国组织专家团队赴越南参与修复因战争损毁的桥梁。60年代到70年代，中国陆续在缅甸、越南等国完成10余项援外工程，特别是1970—1975年由中国政府援建的1860km长的坦赞铁路中的大量桥梁，这些工程成为中国与许多国家友谊的见证。改革开放初期，由于以美国、日本、欧洲为代表的发达国家或地区掌握着桥梁建设的关键技术、核心工艺和管理经验，中国参与国外桥梁建设，主要表现为以中国路桥为代表的外经公司组织的劳务输出形式，并集中在中东地区，例如在科威特布比延桥的建造过程中，积累了大量的施工经验。到了90年代，得益于改革开放政策和大规模基础设施建设，中国高速公路、提速铁路建设水平不断提升，中国桥梁施工和管理技术突飞猛进，以中国路桥、中国港湾、中国土木、中国建筑、中国成套等为代表的大型企业，大规模踏入国际工程承包市场，建成了伊拉克摩苏尔四桥和五桥等精品之作。

进入21世纪后，随着中国高速公路和高速铁路建设水平跻身世界先进行列，中国桥梁设计、施工、装备、管理成套技术日臻完善，一批国有大型企业不甘于只承担国际工程施工承包，而是抢滩施工上游的规划和设计，参与国际设计竞标或设计和施工总承包，例如，印度尼西亚第一座跨海大桥——泗水—马都拉大桥，"中国桥梁"走出国门的速度随之加快。2010年以来，随着国家"一带一路"倡议的提出和亚洲基础设施投资银行的成立，改革开放向纵深发展，中国完成了由资本输入大国向资本输出大国的转变，中国企业利用在桥梁建设高速发展中获得的先进技术与管理经验，成功推动中国桥梁技术、装备、工艺和标准"走出去"，并逐渐走向世界桥梁建设舞台的中央，"中国方案"和"中国故事"在世界桥梁界吸引力倍增，"中国标准+中国资本"正在海外催生更多的"中国桥梁"新地标、新品牌和新名片。

近10年来，中国参与建设了几十座国外桥梁，本画册选择了10座国外桥梁，包括2座梁式桥、3座斜拉桥、3座悬索桥和2座多塔索辅梁桥。对于这些国外桥梁，中国参与建设的方式有设计和施工总承包、中国标准桥梁设计、桥梁施工承包、桥梁构件（主缆、钢主梁、桩基等）制造等。中国国外桥梁建设输出了中国技术、中国规范，促进中国桥梁建设水平与国际接轨，打破了国外工程界对我们的质疑。这些横跨世界江河湖海的中国参与建设的国外桥梁，是中国优质基础设施建设的代表作，它们勾连起世界经济文化交流，成为中国走向世界、世界认识中国的通道，是中国桥梁的又一重要代表渠道和全球经济一体化的缩影。

# INTRODUCTION

The history of Chinese bridge building overseas can be traced back to the initial post-liberation years of the 1950s. In 1954, China organized an expert team to take part in the repair of bridges damaged by war in Vietnam. In the 1960s and 1970s, China completed more than 10 foreign aid projects in succession, in Myanmar, Vietnam, and other countries. Noteworthy among these projects is a large number of bridges along the 1860km-long Tanzania-Zambia Railway built by the Chinese government from 1970 to 1975. These projects bear witness to the friendship between China and many overseas countries. At the beginning of reform and opening-up policy, because the key technologies, core industrial skills, and management experience in the bridge construction were possessed by developed countries including the United States, Japan, and European countries, Chinese participation in overseas bridges was mainly limited to labor service export organized by the China Road & Bridge Corporation and mostly in the Middle East. For instance, valuable experience was accumulated in the construction of Bubiyan Bridge in Kuwait. In the 1990s, due to the reform and opening-up policy and the massive infrastructure construction underway domestically, China has been able to improve the construction of expressways and railways together with bridge construction and management technologies. Chinese large enterprises such as China Road & Bridge Corporation (CRBC), China Harbor Engineering Company (CHEC), China Civil Engineering Construction Corporation (CCECC), China State Construction Engineering Corporation (CSCEC) and China National Complete Engineering Corporation (CCEC), strode into the international market, and completed several high-profile works, of which the Fourth and Fifth Bridges in Mosul, Iraq is but one example.

After entering in the 21st century, as Chinese highway and high-speed railway technologies reached up to the international advanced level, Chinese bridge design, construction, equipment, and management technologies were greatly improved. A number of large state-owned enterprises not only undertook the construction of overseas projects, but also started to participate in the international design tender and engineering procurement construction (EPC). For instance, the Surabaya-Madura Bridge, Indonesia's first sea-crossing bridge, is a milestone in the acceleration of "Chinese Bridges" going abroad. Since 2010, as the announcement of "the Belt and Road" Initiative and the founding of Asian Infrastructure Investment Bank (AIIB), together with the deep and broad development of reform and opening-up policy, China has completed the transformation from a big capital importer to a big capital exporter. Chinese companies have successfully pushed out to other countries Chinese bridge technologies, equipment, industrial skill, and standards owing to the advanced technology and management experience accumulated rapidly in a large number of bridge projects. China is gradually moving to the center of the international stage of bridge construction. "Chinese solution" and "Chinese story" are attracting more and more attention in the bridge industry world widely. "Chinese standard plus chinese capital" is associated with more and more new landmarks, new brands, and new business cards of "Chinese bridges" overseas.

In the past ten years, China has taken part in building more than twenty overseas bridges, ten of which are included in this album, including two girder bridges, three cable-stayed bridges, three suspension bridges, and two extradosed girder bridges. The participation forms of Chinese enterprises in these bridges include EPC, bridge design according to Chinese standards, construction contracting, and manufacturing of bridge components (including main cables, steel girders, and pile foundations, etc.). Chinese overseas bridge construction has exported Chinese technology and Chinese specifications, which have promoted the level of Chinese bridges in line with international standards and have broken the doubt of foreign engineers and ended any remaining isolation of Chinese engineers from their peers worldwide. These overseas bridges crossing rivers, lakes and seas are excellent representatives of the high quality of Chinese infrastructure construction. They connect the world's economy and cultures, and become a channel for China to go global and for the world to know China. They are also another important representative of Chinese bridges beside domestic bridges and an epitome of global economic integration.

# 旧金山—奥克兰新海湾东桥
## San Francisco-Oakland Bay Bridge New East Span

旧金山—奥克兰新海湾东桥位于美国加利福尼亚州，用于替换旧海湾大桥在地震中受损严重的东跨部分。主桥是一座标志性的独塔非对称自锚式悬索桥，设计时是世界上首座独塔空间缆索自锚式悬索桥，主跨 385m，边跨 180m，塔高 160m。

该桥主梁全宽 78.74m，采用分体双箱梁，悬吊在两个倾斜的缆索系统上。空间主缆固定在箱梁的东墩，穿过塔顶后在西墩的梁端鞍座处绕回。主缆为预制平行钢丝索股，采用优化的对称八角形布局以减少空间索面引起的钢丝扭转，并通过 S 形缠丝和除湿系统来进行防腐。该桥位于两个地震断层之间的强震区，主塔被设计为四肢塔柱，并由可熔断的剪力连接梁相互连接。该结构可为桥塔提供所需的刚度，并吸收地震能量，在地震期间防止塔柱被破坏。

上海振华重工（集团）股份有限公司承担了该桥钢塔和主梁全部 4.5 万 t 钢结构的制造和运输，上海浦江缆索股份有限公司承担了该桥全长 1730m 主缆的制造并提供安装指导。

**桥　　名：** 旧金山—奥克兰新海湾东桥
**桥　　型：** 独塔自锚式悬索桥
**主跨跨径：** 385m
**桥　　址：** 美国加利福尼亚州旧金山、奥克兰
**建成时间：** 2013 年 9 月

**Name:** San Francisco-Oakland Bay Bridge New East Span
**Type:** Single-tower self-anchored suspension bridge
**Main Span:** 385m
**Location:** San Francisco and Oakland, California State, USA
**Completion:** September, 2013

The San Francisco-Oakland Bay Bridge New East Span, located in California State, USA, is built to replace the east span of the old Bay Bridge, which was badly damaged in an earthquake. The main bridge is an iconic single-tower asymmetric self-anchored suspension bridge, designed as the world's first single-tower spatial cable self-anchored suspension bridge, with a 385m-long main span and a 180m-long side span. The height of the tower is 160m.

The main girder is a steel separated twin box girder with a 78.74m full width, and it is suspended by the cable system with two inclined cable planes. The main cable retraces continuously around the saddles at the girder near the west abutment pier, then goes through the tower top. Its two ends are finally anchored within the deck at the east pier. The main cable is comprised of prefabricated parallel wire strands (PPWS) with an optimized symmetrical octagonal layout to reduce the wire torsion caused by the spatial configuration. S-wiring wrapping and dehumidification system are adopted for the anti-corrosion of the cable. The bridge is located in a strong seismic zone between two geological faults. Four tower columns are connected with fusible shear links to absorb the seismic energy to prevent from severe earthquake damage to the tower, and to ensure the tower stiffness at the same time.

Shanghai Zhenhua Heavy Industries Co., Ltd. completed the manufacture and transportation of all the 45000t. of steel tower and main girder. Shanghai Pujiang Cable Co., Ltd. manufactured the 1730m-long main cable and guided the main cable installation.

# 槟城第二跨海大桥
## Second Penang Bridge

槟城第二跨海大桥位于马来西亚槟岛海峡南部水域，连接槟岛东南部的巴都茅和威斯利省的巴都加湾。该桥全长24km，跨海桥长16.9km，设双向四车道加双向摩托车道，设计使用寿命为120年。主桥采用固结体系双塔三跨预应力混凝土梁斜拉桥，跨径布置为117.5m+240m+117.5m，塔高103.28m。主梁采用π形梁，两侧肋板宽2.6m，梁高2.8m，桥面梁宽35.0m，采用⌀2.0~2.3m变直径钻孔灌注桩群桩基础。非通航孔桥为跨径55m的节段架设预制连续箱梁，基础为打入桩、钻孔桩基础。

该桥设计和施工严格按照英国规范和马来西亚规范执行，结构耐久性和抗风险等级采用欧洲最高标准。设计中对海啸、地震、船撞和航行安全等进行了专门研究，并采用了防撞套箱措施。拉索体系采用分丝管式索鞍，克服了传统双重管索鞍中各根钢绞线受力不均的不足。引桥采用高阻尼橡胶支座，减小了地震对主梁的破坏作用。该桥主梁施工采用反吊三角托架挂篮，主桥钻孔桩基础施工平台利用桩基钢护筒作为承重桩，平台面层结构同时作为防撞套箱底板。

该桥为中国交通建设股份有限公司在国外较为发达地区，按设计-施工总承包模式承建的大型海外土建项目。中交公路规划设计院有限公司承担了该桥的勘察设计工作，中国港湾工程有限责任公司承担了该桥海中桥的主桥、引桥及辅助设施建设工作。

| | |
|---|---|
| 桥 名： | 槟城第二跨海大桥 |
| 桥 型： | 双塔混凝土梁斜拉桥 |
| 主桥跨径： | 240m |
| 桥 址： | 马来西亚槟城 |
| 建成时间： | 2014年3月 |

**Name:** Second Penang Bridge
**Type:** Double-tower concrete girder cable-stayed bridge
**Main Span:** 240m
**Location:** Penang, Malaysia
**Completion:** March, 2014

Second Penang Bridge is located in the southern waters of the Penang Straits, Malaysia, and connecting Batu Maung in southeastern Penang Island and Batu Kawan in Wellesley Province. The total length of the bridge is 24km, including a 16.9km-long sea-crossing part. It has four automobile lanes and two motorcycle lanes in dual directions. The designed service life is 120 years. The main bridge is a prestressed concrete cable-stayed bridge with two towers and a three-span girder, which are consolidated to each other. The bridge span arrangement is 117.5m+240m+117.5m, and the height of the tower is 103.28m. The main girder has a π-shaped configuration with two 2.6m wide side ribs. Its overall height and width are 2.8m and 35.0m, respectively. The adopted pile group foundations consist of bored piles with variable diameters from $\phi$ 2.0m to 2.3m. The non-navigable bridges are of prefabricated continuous box girder with a span of 55m constructed by segmental erection, and their foundations are comprised of driven or bored piles.

The bridge design and construction are carried out in strict accordance with the British and Malaysian specifications, and the structural durability and risk resistance grade adopted the highest one in European standards. In the design, tsunami, earthquake, ship collision and navigational safety are specially investigated, and anti-collision sleeve measures are adopted. Split-tube type cable saddles are used in the cable system, which can overcome the shortcoming of uneven force among different strands when using traditional double-tube type cable saddles. High damping rubber bearings are employed in the approach bridges to reduce the earthquake effect on the girder. The main girder is constructed by using inverted triangular bracket hanging baskets. The construction platform for bored pile foundation uses steel guard cylinders as its bearing pile, and the surface structure of the platform is also used as the bottom plate of the anti-collision sleeve box.

The bridge is a large-scale offshore civil engineering project with EPC mode, which is completed by China Communications Construction Company(CCCC) Ltd. in a relatively developed area abroad. CCCC Highway Consultants Co., Ltd. undertakes the survey and design work of the bridge, while China Harbor Engineering Co., Ltd. takes on the construction work of the main bridge, approach bridges and auxiliary facilities.

# 穆罕默德六世大桥
## Mohammed VI Bridge

穆罕默德六世大桥是摩洛哥王国乃至非洲开工建设的第一座现代化斜拉桥。全桥横跨布里格里格河谷，全长950m，主桥为183m+376m+183m组合梁斜拉桥，桥面总宽30.4m。

该桥造型具有典型的阿拉伯建筑特点，主塔设计灵感源自摩洛哥传统的拱形大门，采用钻石结构外形，由底部向上呈弧形逐渐打开，在中部渐分为四肢，至塔顶又合为一体，其造型具有"胜利之门""理想之门"的寓意，被当地人称为"梦想之桥"。主塔的四个肢柱在空间上均呈曲线，既有效增加了桥塔的纵向及横向刚度，也与周围环境协调统一。塔柱设计中创新性地采用了竖向分节的拉板式钢锚箱，传力途径明确，有效缩短了工期。主梁采用混凝土边主梁、钢横梁和混凝土桥面板相结合的组合梁形式，有效减轻了桥梁上部结构的自重，充分发挥了混凝土、钢两种材料的特性，经济合理。该桥施工中建立了全桥监控模型，解决了温差大、主梁柔、节段异步施工条件下主梁线形及应力控制的技术难题。

该桥由中铁大桥勘测设计院集团有限公司参与设计，中铁大桥局集团有限公司和中国海外工程有限责任公司主要承建，中铁大桥局集团第六工程有限公司参建。中铁山桥集团有限公司承担了该桥的索塔钢锚箱及桥面钢横梁制造。

桥　　名：穆罕默德六世大桥
桥　　型：双塔组合梁斜拉桥
主跨跨径：376m
桥　　址：摩洛哥拉巴特
建成时间：2016年7月

**Name:** Mohammed VI Bridge
**Type:** Double-tower composite girder cable-stayed bridge
**Main Span:** 376m
**Location:** Rabat, Morocco
**Completion:** July, 2016

The Mohammed VI Bridge is the first modern cable-stayed bridge in the Kingdom of Morocco and even in Africa. The bridge crosses the Bouregreg Valley, with a total length of 950m. The main bridge is a cable-stayed bridge with three spans of 183m+376m+183m and a 30.4m wide composite girder.

The bridge has a typical Arab architectural feature. The tower design is inspired by the Moroccan traditional arched gate. With a diamond shape, the tower column integrated together at the bottom opens gradually upward in an arc way, and becomes four separated columns in the middle zone, which finally merge again into a single whole at the tower top. The tower modelling embodies a moral of "victory gate" or "the door of ideal", and the bridge is called as "the bridge of dreams" by the local residents. The four curved tower columns not only effectively increase the longitudinal and lateral stiffness, but also harmonize with the surroundings. Pull-plate type steel anchor boxes segmented vertically are innovatively adopted in the design of the tower columns to simplify the transmission of anchor forces and shorten the construction period. The main girder adopts a composite structure consists of concrete side beams, steel cross beam and concrete deck plates, which can effectively reduce the self-weight of the superstructure and make full use of the material advantages of concrete and steel, attaining to economy and rationality. In the construction, a monitoring model of the whole bridge is established to solve the technical problems in the alignment and stress control for the main girder under the conditions of large temperature difference, low structural stiffness of main girder and asynchronous installation of main girder segments.

The bridge is designed by China Railway Major Bridge Reconnaissance & Design Institute Co., Ltd., constructed mainly by China Railway Major Bridge Engineering Group Co., Ltd. and China Overseas Engineering Group Co., Ltd.. The 6th Engineering Co., Ltd. of China Railway Major Bridge Engineering Group also participates in the construction. China Railway Shanhaiguan Bridge Group Co., Ltd. prefabricates the steel anchor boxes in the towers and steel cross beam in the deck.

# 中马友谊大桥
## China-Maldives Friendship Bridge

中马友谊大桥位于马尔代夫北马累环礁，连接首都马累和机场岛，是马尔代夫最重要的岛屿连接工程。项目路线全长2km，其中跨海桥梁长1.39km，桥面标准宽度21m。主桥为100m+2×180m+140m+100m+60m 六跨组合梁V形墩刚构桥。

该桥采用"混凝土V形刚构+组合梁"的连续刚构桥体系，解决了长联大跨混凝土刚构桥基础和主梁在收缩徐变作用下难以协调受力的难题。由于该桥建造在珊瑚礁上，因此在设计和施工中探索了在远洋深海无遮掩环境下和珊瑚礁地层上建造特大型桥梁的技术。通过揭示珊瑚礁地质特性，研发了珊瑚礁灰岩地层下大直径桩基础设计与施工关键技术。针对所在区域高温、高湿、高盐的环境特点，采用高镍耐候钢作为桥梁主体结构用钢，建立了混凝土综合防腐体系，形成了热带海洋环境下组合梁桥耐久性关键技术。同时，还研发了长周期涌浪条件下大型工程船舶运动特性及适应性、大节段钢箱梁安装等关键技术。

该桥建设全面采用中国标准、中国规范、中国技术和中国管理。中交公路规划设计院有限公司、中铁大桥勘测设计院集团有限公司共同完成了项目设计，工程总承包单位为中交第二航务工程局有限公司。

The China-Maldives Friendship Bridge, located in the North Male Atoll, Maldives, connects the capital Male to Airport Island, making it the most important island connection project in Maldives. The total project length is 2km, in which the sea-crossing bridge is 1.39km long, and the standard girder width is 21m. The main bridge is a six-span continuous rigid frame bridge with a composite girder and integral V-shaped piers. Its span arrangement is 100m+2×180m+140m+100m+60m.

The bridge adopts the continuous rigid frame bridge system with "concrete V-frame+composite girder", which solves the problem of coordinating forces between the foundation and the girder of long-span concrete rigid frame bridge under the action of shrinkage and creep. Because the bridge is built on a coral reef, technologies of constructing large scale bridges on the coral reef strata under the environment of deep sea and open ocean are explored in the design and construction of the bridge. By revealing the geological characteristics of coral reef, key technologies are developed for the design and construction of large diameter pile foundation in limestone strata of coral reef. In view of the local environmental characteristics of high temperature, high humidity and high salinity, high nickel weathering steel is used for the main structure and a comprehensive concrete anti-corrosion system is developed, forming the key technology of durability for composite girder bridges in tropical marine environment. Key technologies such as the motion characteristics and adaptability of large engineering ships under long period surge, and the installation of large steel box girder segments are also developed at the same time.

Chinese standards, specifications, technologies and management are fully adopted in the bridge construction. CCCC Highway Consultants Co., Ltd. and China Railway Major Bridge Reconnaissance & Design Institute Co., Ltd. jointly completed the design. The prime contractor was CCCC Second Harbor Engineering Co., Ltd..

桥　　名：中马友谊大桥
桥　　型：六跨组合梁 V 形墩刚构桥
主跨跨径：2×180m
桥　　址：马尔代夫马累
建成时间：2018 年 8 月

**Name:** China-Maldives Friendship Bridge
**Type:** Six-span composite girder continuous rigid frame bridge with integral V-shaped piers
**Main Span:** 2×180m
**Location:** Male, Maldives
**Completion:** August, 2018

# 卡腾贝大桥
## Katembe Bridge

| | | | |
|---|---|---|---|
| 桥　名： | 卡腾贝大桥 | Name: | Katembe Bridge |
| 桥　型： | 单跨钢箱梁悬索桥 | Type: | Single-span steel box girder suspension bridge |
| 主跨跨径： | 680m | Main Span: | 680m |
| 桥　址： | 莫桑比克马普托 | Location: | Maputo, Mozambique |
| 建成时间： | 2018年11月 | Completion: | November, 2018 |

　　卡腾贝大桥位于莫桑比克南部马普托湾入海口，是"一带一路"倡议在南非区域落地的工程，是"中非基础设施合作计划"的标志性项目。该桥全长3.071km，主桥为单跨680m悬索桥，截至2022年是非洲最大跨度的悬索桥。主缆跨径布置为260m+680m+284m，中跨主缆垂跨比为1/10。加劲梁采用正交异性流线型扁平钢箱梁，梁高3.0m，宽（含风嘴）25.6m，在索塔位置设置竖向支座、横向抗风支座以及纵向阻尼器。桥塔采用门型塔。锚碇采用重力式锚碇、地下连续墙基础。

　　该桥融合中国标准、欧洲标准及南非标准，系统地形成了涵盖设计、施工、材料、制造、验收的莫桑比克大桥建设标准体系，填补了当地大桥建造标准体系的空白。该桥建立了地域性材料用于大桥混凝土工程的技术指标体系，解决了地域性材料质量不合格的难题。同时，该桥建设者还建立了资源匮乏地区钢桥面铺装技术体系，解决了非洲地区材料和施工机械设备匮乏的问题。

　　该桥由中国路桥工程有限责任公司总承包，中交第二公路勘察设计研究院有限公司、中国公路工程咨询集团有限公司、中交公路规划设计院有限公司、中交路桥建设有限公司、中交第二公路工程局有限公司、中交第四航务工程局有限公司、上海振华重工（集团）股份有限公司等单位参与设计与施工。

The Katembe Bridge, located at the mouth of Maputo Bay in southern Mozambique, is a landmark project both of the Belt and Road Initiative in South Africa and the China-Africa Infrastructure Cooperation Plan. With a total length of 3.071km, the main bridge is a 680m-long single-span suspension bridge, and is the largest suspension bridge in Africa up to 2022. The span arrangement of the main cables is 260m+680m+284m, and the sag-span ratio of the middle span cables is 1/10. The stiffening girder is an orthotropic streamlined flat steel box girder with a height of 3.0m and a width of 25.6m (including the wind fairings). The girder is supported on the portal towers with vertical bearings, transverse wind resistant bearings and longitudinal dampers. The anchorages are of gravity type with underground diaphragm walls as foundations.

The bridge integrated Chinese, European and South African standards, forming systematically a Mozambican bridge standard system covering design, construction, materials, manufacturing and acceptance check, which filled the gap in the local bridge construction standard system. The technical index system for the use of regional materials in bridge concrete engineering has been established, which solved the problem of unqualified regional materials. The bridge builders also established the technical system of steel bridge deck pavement in resource-deficient areas, which solved the shortage of materials and construction machinery in Africa.

The prime contractor was China Road & Bridge Corporation. Several other cooperates also involved in the design and construction, including CCCC Second Highway Consultants Co., Ltd., China Highway Engineering Consulting Corporation, CCCC Highway Consultants Co., Ltd., Road & Bridge International Co., Ltd., CCCC Second Highway Engineering Co., Ltd., CCCC Fourth Harbor Engineering Co., Ltd., Shanghai Zhenhua Heavy Industries Co., Ltd., etc.

# 哈罗格兰德大桥
Halogaland Bridge

哈罗格兰德大桥位于挪威北方港口城市纳尔维克，跨越挪威北部奥福特峡湾，截至 2022 年，是北极圈内跨径最大的跨海悬索桥，同时也是挪威第二大跨径桥梁。该桥全长 1.533km，主桥为单跨 1145m 悬索桥。加劲梁采用扁平钢箱梁，梁宽 18.6m。两岸均为 A 形混凝土主塔，塔高分别为 172m、175m。主跨主缆直径为 475mm，单根主缆由 40 根通长索股和背索组成，钢丝抗拉强度为 1770MPa。主缆采用空间线形，主缆在塔顶处间距 3m，在跨中处间距 15.646m。吊索为带高密度聚乙烯（HDPE）护套的密封钢绳结构。该桥索鞍与索夹均采用焊接结构。索塔海中基础采用沉井结构，两岸锚碇均采用预应力岩锚结构。

该桥主缆采用了在欧洲应用较少的预制平行索股（PPWS）法架设，更好地适应了当地严酷的自然环境。为在成桥后形成空间索面，主缆架设时先按照平行索面架设主缆并紧缆，其后拆除猫道间约束和抗风系统，由主桥跨中向索塔方向逐道分阶段顶推主缆，每一道支撑的顶推分多次循环进行。

该桥严格按照挪威规范及欧洲规范进行设计和施工，桥梁防腐工艺要求极高。该桥采用了先进的智能机器人焊接，突破了薄板钢箱梁制造变形控制，解决了涂装前清洁度、盐分控制、锌层拉拔力、大节段成品防护等技术难题。

该桥由四川路桥建设集团股份有限公司承建，并与中交公路规划设计院有限公司、西南交通大学及国内各知名钢结构加工厂合作，提出了柔性带抗风体系整体式猫道、主缆横向顶推系统、大节段钢箱梁浮式起重机整体拼装等关键工艺、工法等。

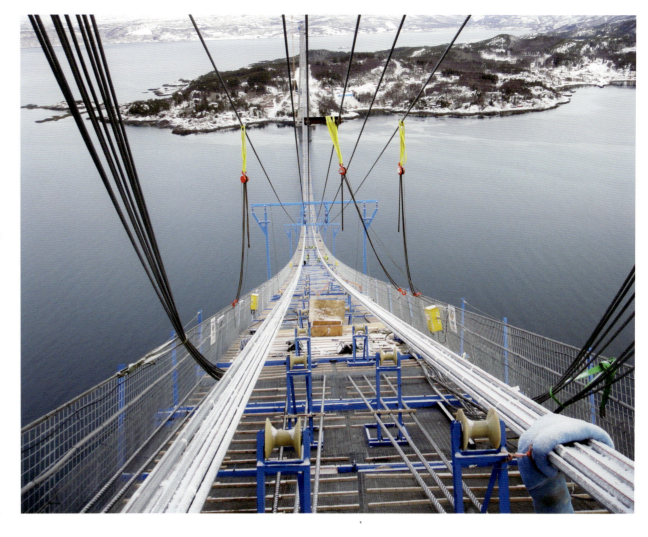

The Halogaland Bridge, located in the port city of Narvik and spanning the Ofotfjorden in northern Norway, is the largest sea-crossing suspension bridge inside the Arctic Circle and the second largest bridge in Norway up to 2022. The total bridge length is 1.533km and the main bridge is a 1145m-long single-span suspension bridge. The stiffening girder is a flat steel box girder with a total width of 18.6m. The bridge towers are A-shaped concrete towers with heights of 172m and 175m. The diameter of each main cable in the main span is 475mm. Each main cable is composed of 40 continuous cable strands and additional back cables in side spans, and the tensile strength of the steel wire is 1770MPa. The main cables are in spatial planes, with a 3m distance at the tower top and a 15.646m one at the span center. The hangers are sealed steel ropes with high density polyethylene (HDPE) sheathes. The saddles and cable clamps are all welded structures. Caissons and prestressed rock anchor structures are used as the submerged tower foundations and anchorage foundations, respectively.

The main cables are erected with the precast parallel wire strand (PPWS) method, unusual in Europe, to better adapt to the local harsh natural environment. In order to reach the final spatial alignment, the main cables are firstly erected and tightened in vertical planes. After the catwalk constraints and wind resistant system being removed, the main cables are pushed laterally outside, the span center first and to towers gradually, and the pushing procedure is performed in multiple cycles for each bracing.

The project is designed and constructed in strict accordance with Norwegian and European specifications, in which the anti-corrosion techniques is strictly requested. Advanced intelligent robot welding is adopted to ensure the flatness of thin steel girder plates, and to solve the technical problems such as cleanliness before painting, salinity control, zinc layer adhesive force, and protection of large prefabricated segments.

The project was constructed by Sichuan Road and Bridge Group Co., Ltd., with the cooperation of CCCC Highway Consultants Co., Ltd., Southwest Jiaotong University, and domestic well-known steel structure manufacturers. Several key technologies and construction methods are developed, including the flexible monolithic catwalks with wind resistant system, lateral pushing system for the main cables, large girder segments installation by floating cranes, etc.

# 巴拿马运河三桥
## Third Bridge over Panama Canal

Since Panama is located in the seismically active region of South America, the structural-pile-soil seismic interaction is thoroughly studied, and the seismic isolation design is introduced to solve the structural system and seismic design problems in the high intensity earthquake zone. The vehicle load and structural control parameters are compared between Chinese highway specification and AASHTO one. Through CFD numerical simulation and previous wind tunnel test results, the original design with π-shaped girder recommended by the owner is optimized to separated twin box girder to satisfy the requirements of durability, cost and wind resistance. Due to the highly corrosive environment, the stay cables adopt a new type of thick coated anticorrosive steel strands and are anchored by a type of special device with replaceable key components.

CCCC Highway Consultants Co., Ltd. and Louis Berger Group, Inc. of United States formed a joint venture in the design technical construction services and supervision. The bridge is a large project won by Chinese survey and design enterprises through international open tender.

巴拿马运河三桥跨越位于巴拿马共和国中部的巴拿马运河，是该运河大西洋侧的第一座大桥。该桥全长2667m，采用双向四车道"干线公路"标准设计，桥梁标准宽度为20.8m，设计速度为90km/h。主桥为79m+181m+530m+181m+79m五跨连续混凝土梁斜拉桥。采用独柱式下塔柱和倒V形桥塔，桥塔高度为212.5m。

由于巴拿马位于南美地震活跃区域，该桥设计中深入研究了地震作用下斜拉桥的结构-桩-土相互作用，确定了减、隔震设计实施方案，解决了高烈度地震区混凝土梁斜拉桥的结构体系及抗震设计问题。总体计算中对比了中国公路荷载与美国高速公路与运输协会（AASHTO）车道荷载和结构控制参数。通过计算流体力学（CFD）数值模拟和以往抗风试验结果，将原业主推荐的π形梁断面优化为分离式双箱梁，兼顾了耐久性、经济性和抗风要求。由于桥位环境的强腐蚀性，斜拉索采用新型厚防腐涂层钢绞线，并采用可更换关键构件的特殊装置进行锚固。

中交公路规划设计院有限公司与美国路易斯·伯杰集团公司组成的竞标联合体承担了设计工作和施工阶段技术服务及施工监理工作。巴拿马运河三桥项目是我国勘察设计企业通过参加国际公开竞标中标的大型桥梁工程项目。

The Third Bridge over Panama Canal is located in the central part of the Republic of Panama, and is the first bridge on the Atlantic side of the canal. The bridge has a total length of 2667m, with a 4-lane dual carriage way "arterial highway" standard design. The total width is 20.8m, and the design speed is 90km/h. The main bridge is a 79m+181m+530m+181m+79m five-span continuous concrete girder cable-stayed bridge. The inverted V-shaped bridge tower with lower pylon column is adopted, and the bridge tower height is 212.5m.

| | |
|---|---|
| 桥　名： | 巴拿马运河三桥 |
| 桥　型： | 双塔混凝土梁斜拉桥 |
| 主跨跨径： | 530m |
| 桥　址： | 巴拿马科隆 |
| 建成时间： | 2019年8月 |

**Name:** Third Bridge over Panama Canal
**Type:** Double-tower concrete girder cable-stayed bridge
**Main Span:** 530m
**Location:** Colón, Panama
**Completion:** August, 2019

# 坦桑蓝跨海大桥
## New Selander Bridge

坦桑蓝跨海大桥位于坦桑尼亚达累斯萨拉姆市中心，跨越长约1000m的浅海区域。该桥全长1.03km，其中主桥长0.67km，为85m+4×125m+85m双索面五塔预应力混凝土梁索辅梁桥，桥面宽20.5m，双向四车道布置。主塔造型取自坦桑尼亚国徽，中塔顶为火炬装饰，边塔为双手托举造型，象征自由与和平。

该桥塔柱结构新颖、造型独特，变截面大曲率塔柱施工难度大。上塔柱标准直线节段采用爬架法施工；下塔柱变截面曲线节段摒弃常规钢管支架法，采用托架法施工。全桥5座桥塔以中塔为轴呈对称布置，每座桥塔对称布置有6对斜拉索。斜拉索施工包含挂索前准备工作、钢绞线穿束、钢绞线张拉调索、附件安装及防腐处理4个步骤。挂索前采用3D空间模拟软件计算施工期间索鞍和索导管的空间相对位置，以此作为施工控制的依据，有效地保证了矮塔斜拉索的受力体系达到设计要求。斜拉索采用"等值张拉法"张拉，保证同一束钢绞线的每根钢绞线受力均匀。

中铁大桥局集团有限公司为桥梁结构分包商，柳州欧维姆机械股份有限公司提供了斜拉索系统、锚具及体外索等多种产品，中联重科股份有限公司为两台塔机做了本地化研制设计。

| | |
|---|---|
| 桥　　名： | 坦桑蓝跨海大桥 |
| 桥　　型： | 五塔预应力混凝土梁索辅梁桥 |
| 主跨跨径： | 4×125m |
| 桥　　址： | 坦桑尼亚达累斯萨拉姆 |
| 建成时间： | 2022年2月 |

**Name:** New Selander Bridge
**Type:** Five-tower prestressed concrete extradosed girder bridge
**Main Span:** 4 × 125 m
**Location:** Dar es Salaam, Tanzania
**Completion:** February, 2022

The New Selander Bridge is located in the center of Dar es Salaam, Tanzania. It spans a shallow water area approximately 1000m long. The total bridge length is 1.03km, among which the main bridge is 0.67km long. It is an 85m+4×125m+85m double-cable plane five-tower prestressed concrete extradosed girder bridge, with a 20.5m wide deck and a 4-lane dual carriage way arrangement. The tower shape is in imitation of the national emblem of Tanzania. The top of the middle tower is decorated with a torch, and the side towers are shaped with two hands lifting, symbolizing freedom and peace.

Since the towers adopt novel structure and unique shape, it is difficult to construct them due to the variable section and large curvature. The straight upper tower columns with a uniform section are constructed by climbing frame method. The curved lower tower columns with variable sections are constructed by bracket method instead of conventional steel tube bracing method. The five towers are arranged symmetrically about the middle one, and each tower is arranged symmetrically with six pairs of stay cables. The installation of the stay cables includes several steps: preparation before cable hanging, strand wire threading, strand wire tension and adjustment, accessory installation and anti-corrosion treatment. 3D spatial simulation software is used to calculate the spatial position of cable saddles and cable conduits during the construction, which is used as the basis for construction control to effectively ensure the required cable force distribution. Equivalent tensioning method is employed to ensure uniformly distributed strand forces in the same stay cable.

China Railway Major Bridge Engineering Group Co., Ltd. was the subcontractor in construction. Liuzhou OVM Machinery Co., Ltd. provided variety of products including the stay cable system, anchorage devices and external cables. Zoomlion Heavy Industry Science and Technology Co., Ltd. completed the research and design for the localization of two tower cranes.

# 帕德玛大桥
## Padma Bridge

帕德玛大桥位于孟加拉国南部，是连接中国与东南亚的泛亚铁路的重要通道之一，主桥为6.15km公铁两用桥，上层是双向四车道公路，下层为单线铁路。该桥由7联41跨钢桁梁组成，单孔跨径为150m、重3200t，是孟加拉国历史上最大的基建工程项目。

帕德玛河施工环境是世界上最恶劣的施工环境之一，在这里建桥需要克服各种最具有挑战性的技术和施工难题。为此，建设单位发明了"多层套管静探技术"，创造了水上超深静探孔的新纪录；工程下部结构采用了长125m、入土深度120m的斜钢桩基础；上部结构采用了单跨跨径长、质量大的整体钢梁结构；900m长的公路桥面板整联预制、胶拼。

该桥是中企海外中标金额较大的单体桥梁工程，由中铁二院工程集团有限责任公司参与地质勘查，中铁大桥勘测设计院集团有限公司参与下部结构施工图设计，中铁大桥局集团有限公司承建，中铁山桥集团有限公司、中铁九桥工程有限公司等参建。其中，中铁山桥集团有限公司承担了全部13.15万t桥梁钢结构生产制造任务。

The Padma Bridge, located in the south of Bangladesh, is one of the important passageways in Trans-Asian Railways connecting China and Southeast Asia. The main bridge is a 6.15km-long highway and railway bridge. The upper deck is a 4-lane dual carriage way, and the lower deck is a single-track railway. The bridge is made up of seven steel truss bridges totaling 41 spans, and each span is 150m in length and 3200t in weight. It is the largest infrastructure project in Bangladeshi history.

Located in one of the most severe environments in the world, the bridge construction over the Padma River has to overcome the most challenging technical and construction problems. Therefore, the contractor invented new geotechnical investigation techniques and created a new depth record for off-shore ultra-deep static cone penetration holes. Inclined steel piles with a length of 125m and a buried depth of 120m are used in the foundation. The superstructure is a monolithic steel girder with long single span and large mass. The concrete bridge deck with a total length of 900m is prefabricated and assembled with epoxy resin joints.

The bridge is among those overseas bridge projects with high tender price won by Chinese enterprises. China Railway Eryuan Engineering Group Co., Ltd. participated in the geological investigation. China Railway Major Bridge Reconnaissance & Design Institute Co., Ltd. participated in the construction drawing design for substructures. China Railway Major Bridge Engineering Group Co., Ltd. constructed. China Railway Shanhaiguan Bridge Group Co., Ltd. (CRSBG), China Railway Jiujiang Bridge Engineering Co., Ltd. and etc., participated in the construction. Among them, CRSBG prefabricated all the 131500t of bridge's steel structure.

桥　名：帕德玛大桥
桥　型：公铁两用钢桁梁连续梁桥
主跨跨径：41×150m
桥　址：孟加拉国达卡
建成时间：2022年6月

**Name:** Padma Bridge
**Type:** Continuous steel truss highway and railway girder bridge
**Main Span:** 41×150m
**Location:** Dhaka, Bangladesh
**Completion:** June, 2022

# 佩列沙茨大桥
Peljesac Bridge

佩列沙茨大桥位于克罗地亚达尔马提亚地区的杜布罗夫尼克-内雷特瓦县，横跨克罗地亚南部亚得里亚海的小斯通湾，用于连接克罗地亚大陆与佩列沙茨半岛。该桥全长3.94km，其中主桥长2.44km，宽22.5m，为六塔中央单索面钢箱梁索辅梁桥，包含五个跨径285m、通航净宽200m的中央通航孔。

该桥首次在欧盟海洋保护区进行超长钢管桩整根打设的施工，最大打入桩达130.6m。钢管桩打设中采用气泡幕降噪措施，降低打桩施工对海洋生物的影响。索塔施工大规模应用C85自密实混凝土，基于当地原材料条件并结合欧洲规范对新型混凝土的配合比、制造工艺、质量控制措施等进行了系统研究，保证了索塔施工质量。钢箱梁制造和装配中，通过提升机械化水平，采用相控阵超声检测来配合传统的无损检测方法，加强了焊缝质量控制，最终满足了欧洲标准EN 1090-2：2008中的最高等级EXC4钢箱梁制造标准。钢主梁悬臂拼装时采用海上大节段钢箱梁无支架悬吊安装施工技术，通过1000t浮式起重机进行52m或56m大节段梁的吊装作业，减少了施工临时结构，保护了海洋环境。

由中国路桥工程有限责任公司牵头，中交第二公路工程局有限公司、中交公路规划设计院有限公司组成的联营体承建了该桥项目。中铁宝桥集团有限公司承制81个梁段共计1.8万t的钢结构。

Peljesac Bridge, located in Dubrovnik-Neretva County, Dalmatia, Croatia, crosses the Mali Ston Bay in the Adriatic Sea in southern Croatia, connecting Croatian mainland with Peljesac Peninsula. The total bridge length is 3.94km, in which the main bridge is 2.44km long and 22.5m wide. The steel-box-girder extradosed bridge has six towers with a single central cable plane. It has five 285m-long spans with a 200m wide net navigational channel each.

Being the first project with ultra-long steel pipe piles in the European Union Marine Reserve, the deepest driven piles are 130.6m long. Bubble curtain is deployed to reduce the piping noise and the impact to marine organism. Based on local material conditions and the Eurocode, the composition, manufacturing process and quality control measures of the novel C85 self-compact concrete in towers are systematically investigated. The steel box girder segments are prefabricated and assembled by improving the mechanization level, combining the phased array ultrasonic testing method with the traditional nondestructive methods, and improving the welding quality control. Thus the steel box girders finally meet the highest criterion requirement as EXC4 in the Eurocode EN 1090-2: 2008. The non-support suspension construction technology for offshore large segments is utilized in the cantilever assembly of the steel girders. The 52m or 56m long large girder segments are hoisted by a 1000t floating crane, by which temporary facilities are reduced and the ocean environment is protected.

China Road & Bridge Corporation led the bridge construction by a joint venture cooperating with CCCC Second Highway Engineering Co., Ltd. and CCCC Highway Consultants Co., Ltd. China Railway Baoji Bridge Group Co., Ltd. prefabricated the 81 steel girder segments with a total mass of 18000t.

| 桥　名： | 佩列沙茨大桥 | **Name:** Peljesac Bridge |
| --- | --- | --- |
| 桥　型： | 六塔钢箱梁索辅梁桥 | **Type:** Six-tower steel-box-girder extradosed bridge |
| 主跨跨径： | 5×285m | **Main Span:** 5 × 285m |
| 桥　址： | 克罗地亚达尔马提亚 | **Location:** Dalmatia, Croatia |
| 建成时间： | 2022年7月 | **Completion:** July, 2022 |

## 出版后记

经过编辑委员会、编写组和出版社三方的共同努力，这本精美的中国桥梁画册终于同读者们见面了。

本画册的编写工作始于 2022 年 7 月。8 月，编辑委员会投票遴选出了 103 座桥梁。9 月，结合 2013 年至 2022 年曾获詹天佑奖的桥梁项目，编写组经过集体商议增加补充了 5 座获詹天佑奖的桥梁和 2 座其他桥梁（包括 1 座台湾的桥梁），共 110 座桥梁入选本画册，以纪念李国豪校长 110 周年诞辰。

编写组于 7 月召开了筹备会议，开始工作，就桥型、内容、篇幅、分工和进度等问题进行了讨论。8 月，编写组召开了两次会议，除了明确桥型和内容之外，还写出了每一种桥型的中文样稿，并讨论确定了统一形式。10 月，编写组连续召开了两次会议，分别完成和修改了中文稿和英文稿，并精心配置了照片和图片。11 月，编写组经过相互审核，完成了全书 110 座桥梁的中英文介绍和照片或图片书稿，提交人民交通出版社。编写组用高效、辛勤的工作来表达对李国豪校长的怀念和敬意。

《桥梁》杂志社和桥梁建设单位热情支持编写组的工作，提供了珍贵的桥梁照片和背景材料，方便了编纂工作。人民交通出版社的工作人员在很短的时间里完成了繁重的编辑、排版和印刷任务，使我们能在李校长 110 周年诞辰之际献上收录 110 座桥梁的画册作为纪念礼物。在此对他们的贡献表示衷心感谢！

我们希望这本画册的出版发行，能成为中国改革开放 40 多年特别是近 10 年桥梁建设事业发展的珍贵记录，让国际桥梁界同行更加了解中国的桥梁建设，并促进中国从桥梁大国走向桥梁强国。

葛耀君

2023 年 4 月

# AFTERWORD

The publication of this beautiful album of Chinese bridges is the result of the joint efforts of the Editorial Committee, the Compilation Board, and the publishing house.

The work began with the establishment of the Compilation Board and Editorial Committee in July 2022. In August, the Editorial Committee voted for 103 bridges. In September, in consideration of the bridge projects that won the Zhan Tianyou Prize from 2013 to 2022, collective discussion within the Compilation Board resulted in the addition of five Zhan Tianyou Prize winning bridges and two other bridges (including one bridge in Taiwan). Altogether, 110 bridges were selected for this album to commemorate the 110th anniversary of the birth of Professor Guohao Li.

The Compilation Board held a preparatory meeting in July to start the work and discussed the bridge type, content, length, division of labor, and progress. In August, the Compilation Board held two meetings to clarify the bridge type and content. The Compilation Board members wrote Chinese sample drafts of each bridge type, and discussed and determined the unified form. In October, the Compilation Board held two meetings, completed and revised the Chinese version and the English version, and carefully arranged photos of the birdges and other images. In November, the Compilation Board members completed the introductory texts for the 110 bridges in both Chinese and English, as well as the captions of photos and other images after mutual review, and submitted them to the China Communications Press. The Compilation Board members expressed their remembrance and respect for Professor Guohao Li with their efficient and hard work.

Both *Bridge* Magazine and the bridge construction industry enthusiastically supported the work of the Compilation Board, providing precious bridge photos and background materials, which greatly facilitated the compilation work. The staff of the China Communications Press completed the arduous task of editing, typesetting and printing in a very short time, enabling us to present the commemorative gift of 110 bridges' album on the 110th anniversary of Professor Li's birthday. I would like to express my heartfelt gratitude to their great contributions!

We hope that the publication of this album will become a precious record of the development of bridge construction in China over the past 40 years of reform and opening-up, especially in the past 10 years, so that international bridge industry peers can better understand China's bridge construction and celebrate China's transition to a true bridge power.

*Yaojun Ge*
April 2023

图书在版编目（CIP）数据

中国桥梁：2013-2023 / 项海帆等主编. — 北京：人民交通出版社股份有限公司，2023.4
ISBN 978-7-114-18656-1

Ⅰ.①中… Ⅱ.①项… Ⅲ.①桥—中国—画册 Ⅳ.①U448-64

中国国家版本馆CIP数据核字(2023)第039925号

本书由人民交通出版社股份有限公司独家出版发行。未经著作权人书面许可，本书图片及文字任何部分，不得以任何方式和手段进行复制、转载或刊登。版权所有，侵权必究。

Copyright © 2023

All rights reserved. No part of this publication may be reproduced, stored in a retrieval system, or transmitted in any form or by any means, electronic, mechanical, photocopying, recording or otherwise, without the prior written permission of the copyright holder. Printed in China.

| | |
|---|---|
| 书　　名： | 中国桥梁　2013—2023 |
| 著 作 者： | 项海帆　葛耀君　肖汝诚　孙利民　杨志刚 |
| 责任编辑： | 卢俊丽　李　晴　李　瑞　陈虹宇 |
| 责任校对： | 孙国靖　宋佳时 |
| 责任印制： | 刘高彤 |
| 出版发行： | 人民交通出版社股份有限公司 |
| 地　　址： | （100011）北京市朝阳区安定门外外馆斜街3号 |
| 网　　址： | http://www.ccpcl.com.cn |
| 销售电话： | （010）59757973 |
| 总 经 销： | 人民交通出版社股份有限公司发行部 |
| 经　　销： | 各地新华书店 |
| 印　　刷： | 北京雅昌艺术印刷有限公司 |
| 开　　本： | 965×635　1/8 |
| 印　　张： | 38.75 |
| 字　　数： | 720千 |
| 版　　次： | 2023年4月　第1版 |
| 印　　次： | 2023年4月　第1次印刷 |
| 书　　号： | ISBN 978-7-114-18656-1 |
| 定　　价： | 580.00元 |

（有印刷、装订质量问题的图书，由本公司负责调换）